Honolulu & O'ahu
Including Waikīkī

A Great Destination

Honolulu & O'ahu
Including Waikīkī
A Great Destination

Stacy Pope
with photographs by the author

The Countryman Press ✳ Woodstock, Vermont

SECOND EDITION

Honolulu & O'ahu: A Great Destination

ISBN 978-1-58157-122-6

Interior photos by the author unless otherwise specified
Book design by Bodenweber Design
Page composition by PerfecType, Nashville, TN
Maps by Mapping Specialists, Ltd., Madison, WI, and Erin Greb Cartography,
© The Countryman Press

Published by The Countryman Press, P.O. Box 748, Woodstock, Vermont 05091

Distributed by W. W. Norton & Company, Inc., 500 Fifth Ave., New York, NY 10110

Printed in the United States of America

10 9 8 7 6 5 4 3 2 1

Ua mau ke ea o ka ʻāina i ka pono.
The life of the land is perpetuated in righteousness.

EXPLORE WITH US!

This *Explorer's Guide* offers a wide variety of information about Oʻahu, from local foods to the best beaches to political issues. Use it as a directory for the exact information you need, or read it from start to finish for a more comprehensive experience.

In the beginning of the book you'll find "What's Where on Oʻahu," an alphabetical listing of highlights and important information that you may want to reference quickly. It's followed by comprehensive descriptions of Oʻahu's history, culture, and recreational opportunities, plus a guide to traveling to and from Oʻahu.

The next six chapters zero in on specific island regions: Waikīkī, Greater Honolulu, Windward Oʻahu, the North Shore, Central Oʻahu, and Leeward Oʻahu. Area-specific options for sightseeing, recreation, lodging, dining, and more are listed. The last chapter, "Information," includes exactly that: supermarkets, recommended reading, banks, marriage license information, and so on.

Throughout this book and your travels in Hawaiʻi you'll encounter the Hawaiian language, which is written using five vowels (*a, e, i, o, u*) and seven consonants (*h, k, 1, m, n, p, w*). The letter *w* is sometimes pronounced like a *v*, and the second-to-last syllables of words are generally most stressed. The ʻokina, or glottal stop (ʻ), indicates a throat pause in speaking, such as English speakers make in the middle of "uh-oh." The kahakō, or macron (¯), indicates a slight lengthening of the vowel sound it hovers above. These subtle sound differences can change the meaning of a word entirely—for example, *ʻāina* means "land," *ʻaina* means "meal," and *aina* means "sexual intercourse"! You'll find a glossary of Hawaiian and other common Hawaiʻi words in the "Information" chapter, along with a list of food terms in "Culture."

No dogged fact checking can keep up with Hawaiʻi's constant changes, especially after a book has gone to press and hit the shelves. And with the economic rise and fall of late, plenty has indeed changed almost overnight (it's even changing as we write this sentence!). We've done our best to present information accurately and to confirm details as close to the publication date as possible. Be sure to call your destination before heading out to prevent any surprises or disappointments.

LODGING PRICES

Accommodation prices skyrocketed several years ago in the wake of massive renovations and a boom economy, giving us the highest per-night rates in the nation. With the recession, we've seen astonishing price drops in hotel rack rates, as well as in condo and house rental fees. Value-added services and other special offers have helped keep occupancies stable.

We're giving you ranges on "modest-sized room" rack rates with a bit shaved off the top, since rack rates are usually not what you end up paying. As the economy improves and prices inch up, our calculations may be a little low.

Book as early as you can and employ the art of negotiation. Visit hotel Web sites directly for deals, as well as Hotels.com, Expedia.com, Kayak.com, and other online travel businesses. Most hotels also offer special AARP and AAA rates in addition to corporate, military, kama'āina, and government rates. Hawai'i's high season runs from about late November to early April and from June through August; during this time, as well as holidays, rates go up and availability goes down.

Hawai'i transient accommodations must charge a 13.962 percent state tax, and even most unlicensed lodgings will add this to your bill.

Inexpensive: Up to $125
Moderate: $125–250
Expensive: $250–400
Very expensive: More than $400

DINING PRICES

We've targeted a price range for each establishment that includes appetizer, entrée, and dessert for the average person, but not drinks, taxes, or tips. In pricing, we've allowed breakfast and lunch service to temper higher dinner costs. Tipping is the usual 15 percent or more.

Inexpensive: Up to $20
Moderate: $20–35
Expensive: $35–55
Very expensive: $55 or more

KEY TO SYMBOLS

☙ **Special Value**. The blue ribbon symbol appears next to selected lodging and restaurants that combine quality and moderate prices.

✎ **Child-friendly**. The crayon symbol appears next to lodging, restaurants, activities, and shops of special interest or appeal to youngsters.

✪ **Authors' favorites**. These are the places we think have the best to offer in each region, whether that means great value, exceptional food, outstanding rooms, beautiful scenery, or overall appeal.

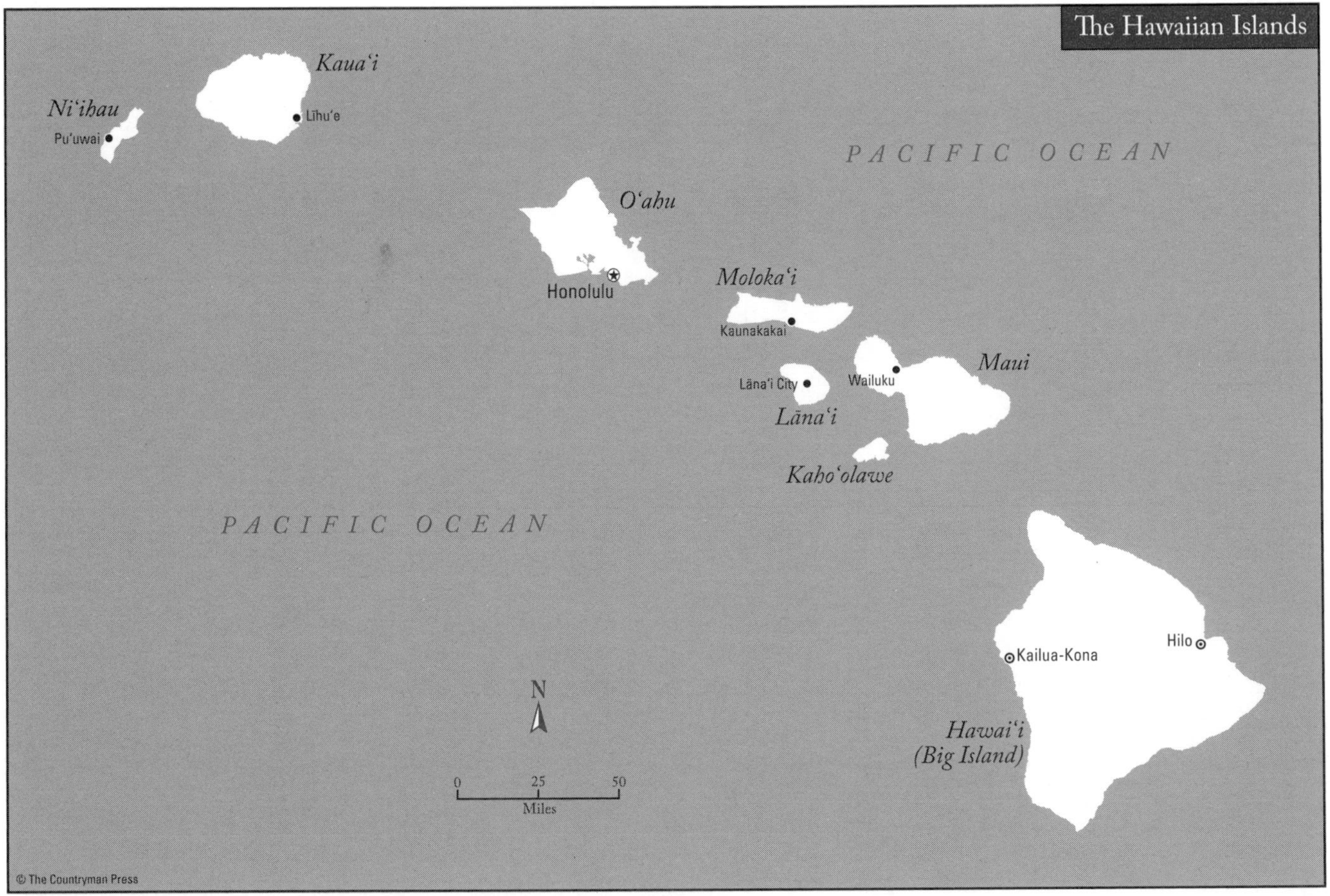

The Hawaiian Islands

PACIFIC OCEAN

Ni'ihau
Pu'uwai •

Kaua'i
• Līhu'e

O'ahu
Honolulu ✪

Moloka'i
Kaunakakai •

Maui
Wailuku •

Lāna'i
Lāna'i City •

Kaho'olawe

Hawai'i
(Big Island)
• Kailua-Kona

Hilo ◉

PACIFIC OCEAN

N

0   25   50
Miles

© The Countryman Press

CONTENTS

MAPS

ACKNOWLEDGMENTS

Mahalo to the many individuals and organizations, including the folks at Countryman Press, for your support of this guidebook. I hope your expectations will be met.

A special thanks to friends and family for joining me in adventuring—and sometimes misadventuring—across Oʻahu in the spirit of building a personal, comprehensive collection of information. I hope you enjoyed it as much as I did!

Stacy Pope
Honolulu, Hawaiʻi

INTRODUCTION

For me its balmy airs are always blowing, its summer seas flashing in the sun; the pulsing of its surfbeat is in my ear; I can see its garlanded crags, its leaping cascades, its plumy palms drowsing by the shore, its remote summits floating like islands above the cloud wrack; I can feel the spirit of its woodland solitudes, I can hear the splash of its brooks; in my nostrils still lives the breath of flowers that perished twenty years ago.

—Mark Twain

How does one introduce what are perhaps the most renowned and enchanting isles in the world? For more than two centuries tales of the distant Hawaiian Islands have stirred imaginations. The call of Hawai'i is so profound that it has almost become encoded in our collective DNA—and millions of people answer each year with pilgrimages across the Pacific toward the promise of paradise.

Surrounded by thousands of miles of open sea and sky, Hawai'i did indeed develop as a sort of paradise. When plants and animals found their way to its shores, they were free to reinvent themselves and had little to fear, resulting in a Darwinian landscape filled with unique species and unbridled wilderness.

By the first millennium, Polynesian

DIAMOND HEAD, THE CROWN OF WAIKĪKĪ

voyagers had settled the Hawaiian Islands in epic migrations that are still only vaguely understood. "Modern Hawai'i" officially begins in 1778 with the first known encounters between European explorers and Hawaiians. History accelerates from there, with a remarkable transformation over two centuries from grass huts to glass towers, and from King Kamehameha to President Barack Obama.

Perhaps the best way to experience Hawai'i's story is by visiting the island of O'ahu, home to the capital city of Honolulu and the majority of Hawai'i's 1.3 million people. Honolulu's a vast city of tall buildings, tropical gardens, shopping centers, and suburban homes meandering for miles between green foothills and surfer-studded, turquoise waves. Life here is original and colorful, and at the same time passionately traditional—and that's exactly how we like it. Rustic plantation houses, Japanese temples, art deco government buildings, and skyscrapers intertwine. Men wear floral aloha shirts in the financial district. We eat salad with chopsticks. More than after-school ballet and soccer, kids hula and outrigger-canoe paddle.

LIFE ON O'AHU IS CONNECTED TO THE SEA

Honolulu's most illustrious neighborhood, Waikīkī, is wrapping up an unprecedented face-lift that has definitely infused it with a new cool factor. While it hasn't been able to shake away every ounce of kitsch, entire blocks of the neighborhood have been literally blown up and replaced by upscale shops, hip hotels, and new cafés.

Outside metropolitan Honolulu you'll find that much of O'ahu is remarkably rural and peaceful, with chickens clucking along the side of the road and kids jumping from bridges into streams. Many travelers don't realize that our island possesses some of the best beaches and surfing in Hawai'i, as well as some of its most timelessly beautiful scenery. Miss the rest of O'ahu, and you miss much of the heart and soul of Hawai'i.

Best of all, Hawai'i's multicultural residents radiate heartfelt warmth fueled by modesty, quiet passion, humor, love of the land, and soulful joie de vivre. Here, everyone's our "uncle" or "auntie." We rarely push, honk, yell, or let a door close on someone. We always bring homemade food to a party. We try to remember that we live in a very special place and show it respect.

O'ahu rolls out the welcome mat to five million visitors every year—that's five visitors to each resident—so your aloha really makes a difference. Here are a few simple ways you can help preserve our unique culture and environment, keeping it more wonderful for everyone.

- Honor local ways of life. Remove shoes before entering a home, avoid using the car horn, wait your turn, and exhibit patience and graciousness when interacting with others.
- Allow natural areas and cultural sites to remain as you found them, including plants, reefs, animal habitats, trails, archaeological or historical elements, and shrines. Resist the temptation to import pets, plants, and foods; and before you arrive in Hawai'i, clean your shoes to remove any traces of non-native seeds or insects.
- Consider choosing more personal, low-key, ecologically friendly activities, such as historic walks or nature club hikes, instead of large "packaged" coach tours and activities.
- Respect residents' personal space so they can continue to feel at home. This is especially important at very "local" hole-in-the-wall food establishments, surf spots, secluded beaches, campsites, and rural parks outside Honolulu, where extensive tourism can permanently alter the character of special places.

Hawai'i is so much more than snorkeling, mai tais, and burgers! In fact, we don't think of it that way at all. Reach beyond the clichés during your stay. Let this *Explorer's Guide* help you discover the "real O'ahu" and grow to cherish it as

RURAL O'AHU

much as we do. We've worked hard to provide honest, personal, sophisticated, and conscientious content that takes you from hip urban bars and earthy family cafés to the most heart-wrenchingly beautiful natural sites—hopefully without sacrificing the integrity of the local community or turning you into a tourist instead of a traveler.

Our goal is to help you enjoy O'ahu to the fullest and leave with both wonderful memories and a deeper appreciation of Hawai'i. We hope this book is dog-eared, marked up, and worn down by the time you return home. Then it will have done its job.

Your guide is an Island-born-and-raised writer whose family has lived in Honolulu since 1935, and who still thinks O'ahu is nō ka 'oi—the best! Whether this is your first visit to Hawai'i or your hundred-and-first, we welcome you. Let go and immerse yourself in O'ahu's tropical foliage, pounding surf, local-style grinds, night rains, "slippers-rule" attitude, flower lei, trade winds, and eternal and intoxicating spirit of aloha.

EXPLORE MORE ONLINE! Visit explorersguideoahu.com for updates and fun extras from your O'ahu guidebook author.

WHAT'S WHERE ON OʻAHU

AREA CODE The entire state of Hawaiʻi falls under the area code 808, so you do not need to use it when calling on-island. When calling island-to-island, however, you do need to dial the area code before the seven-digit number.

ANTIQUES & COLLECTIBLES Honolulu's not much of a quaint antiques-shop town, but we have a few unique vintage, collectibles, and antiques stores, many of which emphasize Asiatic and Hawaiʻi artifacts. The **Hawaiʻi All-Collectors Show** and **Wiki Wiki One-Day Collectibles & Hawaiiana Show** (941-9754; ukulele.com) take place once a year and several times a year, respectively, each a treasure trove of goodies. Check out their Web site for dates as well as links to other antiques and collectibles information.

ARCHAEOLOGICAL AND SACRED SITES Hawaiʻi's archaeological and sacred sites include the remains of heiau, or places of worship, as well as fishponds, stones, agricultural terraces, home foundations, petroglyphs, artifacts, grave sites, walls, and more. When visiting, please do not touch or in any other way disrupt the integrity of the sites. The practice of placing tī-leaf-wrapped stones, candy, lei, and other items as offerings, or stacking stones, is neither traditional nor welcome, although frequently done. In addition to showing respect for cultural traditions and historic preservation, you'll also save yourself fines up to $25,000 that come with disturbing Hawaiian relics on state land.

Even into the 1800s heiau were a dominant feature of Hawaiʻi's landscape. Waikīkī had at least seven, several of which hosted human sacrifices. Today the few that remain on Oʻahu

Courtesy HTA/Kirk Lee Aeder

17

may appear as nothing more than a simple wall or pile of lichen-crusted rocks. In their prime they were stone foundations or boundaries that would have supported grass structures such as drum houses and oracle towers, guarded by enormous akua ki'i (tiki gods). They still hold powerful mana, or spiritual energy, for many residents today.

Coastal and inland fishponds (loko 'ia) were one of the ways in which Hawaiians supported a large population. Several ancient Hawai'i fishponds are still operational, and many across the state are undergoing restoration. O'ahu once had more than any other island; today only a handful remain.

Visiting O'ahu's significant remaining archaeological and sacred sites can help you better understand Hawai'i and its people. We've listed several sites in their respective chapters under *To See*.

BEACHES Whether you wish to drift upon shallow swells with a cocktail, beachcomb a windswept coastline, see thrashing wave action, or build the perfect high-school-reunion tan, your beach is here. We have about 130 beaches on O'ahu alone, each with a unique personality. Except for one or two that the military has blocked access to, every one of them is public. Be sure to also use public access routes to reach them. Outside Waikīkī, weekdays make the best beach days—you'll find easier parking and fewer people.

Topless and nude sunbathing are rarely seen on O'ahu, except in remote and well-hidden pockets. Discretion and a bit of caution are advised for those who go bare. To prevent automobile break-ins, especially in secluded areas, be sure to remove all valuables and other belongings from your vehicle.

Hawai'i's sea turtles are federally protected animals, and it's against the law to crowd, touch, or feed them. Although you may witness some beachgoers approaching turtles in the water or on beaches, these sensitive creatures prefer their personal space. Should you be so lucky as to spot an endangered Hawaiian monk seal sunning on the beach, keep your distance. For the animal's safety, report the location immediately to the **National Marine Fisheries Service** (888-256-9840). Although tempting, swimming out to dolphin pods can be dangerous.

We've listed some of the best beaches on the island in their respective regional chapters along with more information on enjoying them to the fullest.

BICYCLING With fast-paced highways, winding coastal roads, and a lack of good bike lanes, O'ahu could be better for the serious street bicyclist. Still, the Diamond Head side of Waikīkī, and especially small-town Kailua, are fairly beach-cruiser-friendly. On the North Shore an offroad bike and pedestrian lane winds the entire coastline from Sunset Beach to Waimea Bay; you'll also find a few good mountain trails. TheBus system features bike racks on the front of every bus so you can haul your bike where you like. Contact the **Hawai'i Bicycling League** (735-5756; hbl.org) if you need more information, bike route maps, or to find out about its weekend rides. For guided bicycle adventures, especially trail rides, in exotic settings around the island, call **Bike Hawai'i** (734-4214; 877-682-7433; bikehawaii.com).

For more options, see the listings under *To Do* in each chapter.

BIRDING Although many of O'ahu's feathered friends are introduced species, we still have a number of native seabirds and other birds found nowhere else in the world. Pick up *Hawai'i's Birds*, by the Hawai'i Audobon Society, then visit Kapi'olani Park, Lyon Arboretum, the James Campbell National Wildlife Refuge, or any coastal or densely forested area to explore our bird life.

BOATING EXCURSIONS We can think of many reasons to pop a ginger pill and head out on the briny blue. Snorkeling trips, whale-watching, sunset sails, big-game fishing, kayaking, and other adventures await along our coastlines. Browse entries in this section for ideas, then look up the how-to both in the dedicated "Recreation" chapter and under *To Do* within each regional chapter.

BODYBOARDING, STAND-UP PADDLING, & SURFING These sports are just plain good fun in the sun for almost every age, and—let's be honest—surfing's cool! It's a truly Hawai'i-made export, enjoyed by Hawaiian royalty and the regular folk for centuries. Waikīkī's a great place to try bodyboarding, stand-up paddling, and surfing, as well as rent equipment. To learn more, plus get recommendations on lessons, see the "Recreation" chapter as well as *To Do* in regional chapters.

BOOKSTORES In addition to the bookshops listed under *Selective Shopping* in each chapter, local museum shops are a good source for books and CDs, especially relating to Hawai'i. **The Academy Shop** (532-8703; honoluluacademy.org) in Makiki specializes in art books. The **Mission Houses Museum Store** (531-0481; missionhouses.org) downtown carries Hawai'i-related books, as does **Shop Pacifica** (848-4158; bishopmuseum .org)—part of the Bishop Museum— which carries Bishop Museum Press books. See the "Information" chapter for recommended reading.

BOUTIQUES Honolulu's boutiques are either sweet and petite or cool and "street." The largest gathering of locally owned gems is at Ward Centers, where shops such as Cupcake, Mamo Howell, and The Wedding Café have found a home. In Waikīkī, Pineapple County is one of several pop-trend shops appearing between big and small surf shops and boutique houses such as Chanel and Fendi. Check the listings under *Selective Shopping* in each chapter.

CAMPING on O'ahu's beaches is common among extended local families, highly coveted, and to some degree a modern-day manifestation of traditional Island village living. We've focused on describing the most safe and welcoming-to-tourists camping sites on O'ahu—which happen to be some of the most beautiful, too. If you're up for the experience, it could very well turn out to be the most wonderful aspect of your visit.

Each camping location has different fees, regulations, and requirements;

be sure to call as far in advance as possible for information on how you can arrange your stay. Bring all your own equipment! At the time of writing (as well as for some time prior), nobody offers rental camping gear on O'ahu.

Contact the **Department of Land and Natural Resources** (587-0300; hawaiistateparks.org) regarding camping at state parks. County parks across the island are under the jurisdiction of the **City and County of Honolulu** (768-3003; honolulu.gov/parks). Some permits can now be arranged online.

There's more information on camping in the "Recreation" chapter. Specific campgrounds are listed in each chapter under *To Do*.

CANOEING & KAYAKING Canoeing isn't just a sport—it's been a way of life for thousands of years in the Pacific. The only canoe form historically used in Hawai'i is the outrigger canoe, which features a balancing arm connected to the boat by two beams, keeping it upright even against strong waves. Knowing how to paddle an outrigger canoe well is a quick way to earn respect in the Islands, and many kids and adults are members of paddling teams. **Waikīkī Beach Services** (waikikibeachservices.com) and **Hawaiian Oceans Waikīkī** both offer outrigger canoe rides; see the Waikīkī chapter for details.

Kayaking has also become popular here in recent years. Kayaks are stable, relatively lightweight, and manageable for anyone with moderate upper-body strength and a touch of determination. O'ahu doesn't have any significant rivers to comb, so kayakers usually paddle the Kailua or Hale'iwa coastal areas.

CHILD CARE Ready to experience the romantic side of Hawai'i, or at least get some much-needed rest while you're here? Time to call a babysitter. Check with your hotel for services, or visit our "Information" chapter for more options.

CINEMA O'ahu's movie houses mainly feature large-scale, first-run blockbusters, but we have two venues that host classics, documentaries, foreign productions, and other "alternative" films on a regular basis.

Waikīkī was once filled with movie theaters, but now has none. **Sunset on the Beach** (923-1094; http://waikiki improvement.com/eventspage.html) is in its sunset phase as well—you'll see the giant outdoor movie screen on the beach near the zoo, but the free film nights are increasingly rare. Check the schedule in case something's on.

The **Louis Vuitton Hawai'i International Film Festival** (697-2463; hiff.org) in fall features approximately 150 selections from Asia, the Pacific, and North America. It's considered by some to be one of the best film festivals in the country. There's also a spring showcase.

Other movie houses are listed in each chapter under *Entertainment*. For more information and for advance tickets (except for the Lā'ie Palms Cinemas and Movie Museum), contact **Fandango** (800-326-3264; fandango.com).

COMMERCIAL ART GALLERIES Artists have always been attracted to the natural beauty of Hawai'i. And like countless scenic and heavily visited regions of the world, Hawaiʻi has galleries swollen with paintings of doe-eyed maidens and abandoned coastlines, as well as glass sculptures of leaping dolphins—especially in Waikīkī and Haleʻiwa. Wyland Galleries Hawaiʻi, Galerie Lassen, and Tabora Gallery, all found along Waikīkī's main drags, specialize in these themes. For more progressive art by local artists, the Chinatown-area galleries are your best bet.

Local art guild shows are a great opportunity to meet artists and purchase their unique crafts. Try the **Hawaiʻi Watercolor Society** (hawaii watercolorsociety.com), **Honolulu Printmakers** (536-5507; honolulu printmakers.com), or **Hawaiʻi Potters Guild** (941-8108; hawaiipotters guild.org). We've seen very high-quality works at the shows. To mingle with artists and art lovers, take part in **First Friday** (739-9797; firstfriday hawaii.com) and **ARTafterDARK** (532-6099; artafterdark.org). Both events are described in the Greater Honolulu chapter.

For more art options see *Selective Shopping* in each chapter.

CUISINE Hawaiʻi's cuisine is one of a kind. And although folks like to make fun of how much Spam we eat, Spam doesn't characterize local cuisine much more than trail mix does Californian gastronomy. Hawaiʻi cooking is as diverse and colorful as our culture, a true success story of togetherness and harmony. In fact, the classic "plate lunch" meal—a paper plate piled high with local-style meat, two scoops of "sticky" white rice, and macaroni salad—is said to be a descendant of plantation days, when workers from different ethnic camps would share foods at the break whistle.

Food is a central theme of the local lifestyle. Newly arrived residents discover this the first time they're invited to a work-related luncheon and try to get right down to business. We don't want to hear it—we eat and socialize first, do business later. At the office we've seen rice cookers bubbling away on desks, mountains of homegrown mangoes and starfruit—and we expect to see a hibachi before long.

So what are we eating? Chinese crack seed; Hawaiian raw squid poke; Korean kim chee; Portuguese malasadas; Japanese saimin noodles with fish cake. Yes, and Spam musubi. Breakfast in an Island diner might include fresh fish, soba noodles, hamburger patty, eggs, Portuguese sausage, fried rice, and taro bread, and it might be eaten with chopsticks.

Many of these are "local" foods at their most basic and hearty. But Hawaiʻi also has gourmet cuisine born from these elements and raised by classically trained Hawaiʻi chefs. The Hawaiʻi Regional Cuisine movement emphasizes fresh local ingredients and a creative, healthful, upscale approach to Island comfort dishes. Regional chefs such as Sam Choy, George Mavrothalassitis, Peter Merriman, Philippe Padovani, Alan Wong, Roy Yamaguchi, Russell Siu, Hiroshi Fukui, Bev Gannon, Wayne Hirabayashi, and D. K. Kodama have reached local, national, and in some cases international acclaim for their contributions to the culinary arts, and they still preside over some of Hawaiʻi's best kitchens. You'll find Hawaiʻi Regional Cuisine, Pacific

HTA/Joe Solem

Rim, fusion, mom-and-pop-style local dishes, and Hawai'i takes on American and Japanese classics everywhere you go on O'ahu.

Let's not forget traditional Hawaiian food. The best known are taro (which makes poi), kālua pork, laulau, haupia, poke, and the post-contact pipikaula and lomilomi salmon, all typical at a modern lū'au. Early Native Hawaiian diets also included bananas, fish, sweet potato, kūlolo, breadfruit, sugarcane, freshwater shrimp, limpets, seaweed, pork, and even dog meat.

A Hawaiian feast was originally referred to as an 'aha'aina; the word lū'au appeared in its place around 1850, taken from one of the dishes often served. Today's commercial lū'au, however, is almost a burlesque of the old days. Some are better than others, but for the most part they still offer mediocre food and coconut-shell-bra Polynesian revues, complete with the drunk guy dragged up to shake it with the ladies. We urge you to bypass this tourist-hazing ritual and head for several authentic Hawaiian-food cafés to taste the good stuff.

Because we're on a very remote island, most of our food must be flown in. The few crops we grow on O'ahu are generally small-scale and often organic. Combine these with astronomical restaurant square-footage prices, and you've got a high meal tab coming. Waikīkī can be particularly brutal, with few good eats under $20 per person unless you're willing to go to IHOP, Denny's, or Burger King. We hope you won't—so we've offered you as many of the "little guys" as we can. (See *Where to Eat* in each chapter, and check out *Restaurants* below.)

Our island is rich with humble drive-ins, roadside shrimp trucks, holes-in-the-wall, burger quickies, noodle shops, plate-lunch take-outs, delicatessens, and other homey, affordable, quick and not-so-quick stops. This is how most residents eat day-to-day. Some, you'll fall in love with and keep returning to. Others may tide you over on the way home from the beach. Most are inexpensive. We hope you'll enjoy!

Don't plan to lose weight while in Hawai'i, because we have local-specialty sweet treats that you simply must try. The most famous of these are malasadas (a hole-free doughnut rolled in sugar), manapua (a pork-filled bun), Portuguese sweet bread (fluffy, sweet-tasting bread), and shave ice (snow cone).

DOLPHINS Four species of dolphins are typically found in Hawai'i: Pacific bottlenose; rough-toothed; spotted; and spinner. None is considered threatened or endangered, but they've been gradually changing their habits in response to encroaching human activity. The National Marine Fisheries Service (NMFS) advises people to keep at a distance of 150 feet or so from wild dolphins. This does not mean, however, that the dolphins cannot come to you—and they sometimes do, curious creatures that they are.

To experience dolphins in the wild, join in a responsible, small-scale adventure like **Wild Side Specialty Tours** (306-7273; sailhawaii.com), on the leeward side. To interact with non-native, non-wild Atlantic bottlenoses with no harm done to them or you, try **Dolphin Quest O'ahu** (739-8918; 800-248-3316; kahala resort.com).

FAMILY FUN With more than 130 beaches and plenty of hiking, O'ahu is undoubtedly a paradise for families. Be sure to visit natural sites that are safest for your keiki; we've noted them throughout the book with a wee crayon ✐ symbol. We've also noted a few extra-kid-friendly dining options.

The most popular family adventure parks on the island include the Honolulu Zoo, the Waikīkī Aquarium, Wet 'n' Wild, Sea Life Park, Dole Plantation, the Polynesian Cultural Center, and Kualoa Ranch. Many of our museums also offer fun activities for kids.

FARMERS' MARKETS are growing in popularity in Hawai'i. Among the finest are the upscale and festive **KCC Farmers' Market** (391-3804; hfbf .org), Saturday in Greater Honolulu; the petite-chic **Kailua Farmers' Market** (391-3804; hfbf.org), held Thurs-

day on the Windward Coast; and the country-style **Hale'iwa Farmers' Market** (388-9696; haleiwafarmers market.com) in Hale'iwa Town, North Shore, every Sunday. See the regional chapters for more details.

FISHING Choose from big-game fishing all the way to bamboo-pole fishing. The time of year and your fishing location will dictate what you might catch, of course. Most sportfishing outfits may also claim your prize for you after the requisite souvenir photos have been snapped.

You don't need a permit in Hawai'i for basic rod-and-reel angling or to spend the day fishing from a licensed vessel. Wade or boat fishing for smaller game fish is a great way to get to know the local folks and local lifestyle.

See *To Do* in each chapter for details; also check out our "Recreation" chapter.

GARDENS & PARKS O'ahu is filled with wonderful parks and gardens of all types, ranging from dog parks to mysterious deep-valley preserves. The parks we've listed in each chapter (under *To Do*) are "multifunctional," designed for play. The best of these include Ala Moana Regional Park and Kapi'olani Park. The gardens listed offer serene exploration. Our favorites include Ho'omaluhia Botanical Garden, Lyon Arboretum, Foster Botanical Garden, and Waimea Valley.

GOLF has been played in Hawai'i since the late 1890s and we have more than 80 courses. Because of the space they require, most of O'ahu's best public links are found outside Honolulu. Each chapter in this book includes golf courses, listed under *To Do*; also see the "Recreation" chapter.

If you're here in January, get tickets for the famous **Sony Open** (sonyopen inhawaii.com), a PGA event running for about 40 years at the prestigious (and private) Wai'alae Country Club golf course. To pick up a set of clubs or even an individual club at a good price, here's a local secret for used and new equipment both: **Roots & Relics** (538-3311), found downtown.

HAWAIIANA & OTHER HAWAI'I-MADE CRAFTS Many of our best stores carry a beautiful selection of koa-wood bowls and jewelry boxes, hand-sewn Hawaiian quilts, Ni'ihau shell necklaces, lauhala hats, 'ukulele, and other Hawaiiana. Items such as these are highly prized crafts and require monetary investment, but you'll keep them the rest of your life.

If they're beyond your reach, don't fret—all shapes and sizes of more affordable locally made treasures abound. Specialties include koa bracelets, hand mirrors, and cribbage boards; hula implements such as 'uli'uli; Tahitian-style pareo and bags; quilted pillowcases; and bone fish-hook necklaces. Other Hawai'i-made crafts include soaps, lotions, honeys, jams, bookmarks, jewelry, picture frames, ceramics, prints, and textiles.

Craft shops are listed in each chapter under *Selective Shopping*. Tune in for around-town craft fair events such as the excellent **Mission Houses Museum Holiday Craft Fair** (531-0481; missionhouses.org), downtown, held the last week in November. Here you'll find quality, authentic Hawaiiana sold by the artists themselves. The **Pacific Handcrafters Guild**

(254-6788; pacifichandcraftersguild .com), which periodically holds public shows and sales, is a great opportunity to meet the artists and purchase crafts wholesale.

Local calendar listings can steer you toward additional craft venues.

HAWAIIAN CULTURE Hawai'i may be a multicultural rainbow today, but Hawaiians laid first claim on these Islands, establishing themselves here more than 1,500 years ago. Hawaiian cultural traditions and language permeate modern Hawai'i, despite two centuries of Western influence, shaping Islanders of every ethnicity. Learn more about both the past and the present in the "History" and "Culture" chapters.

HIKING O'ahu has amazing hikes of all kinds. Because Honolulu is so urban, it's easy to forget that most of the island is rural and mountainous. Even our most popular trails introduce you to bamboo thickets, giant ferns, forest birds, trickling waterfalls, sand dunes, sensual aromas of wild ginger and guava, and sweeping valley or coastal views. The trails and trail systems we've suggested in this book

Courtesy HTA/Tor Johnson

(see *To Do* in each chapter, as well as the dedicated "Recreation" chapter) are all family-friendly, relatively easy, and generally safe. We also point you to opportunities for more serious hiking adventures.

Maps and trail descriptions are available online through **Hawai'i's Division of Forestry and Wildlife** (587-0166; hawaii.gov/dlnr/dofaw). Information on selected trails is also available online at **Nā Ala Hele** (hawaiitrails.ehawaii.gov), the state of Hawai'i's trails and access system.

HISTORIC SITES O'ahu has approximately 170 sites on the National Register of Historic Places, most of which are in the metropolitan Honolulu area. They include buildings, homes, archaeological remains, and historic areas like the Hawai'i Capital Historic District, the Merchant Street Historic District, and the Chinatown Historic District.

Several of Pearl Harbor's sites are actually National Historic Landmarks, including the USS *Bowfin* submarine and the USS *Arizona* Memorial. Pearl Harbor is a fascinating experience for both kids and adults and deserves a full day of exploration.

Most of the historic sites we describe in this book (listed under *To See* in each chapter) are open to the public. Some are museums or offer tours. Also see *Museums* later in this chapter.

HISTORIC WALKING TOURS Nothing beats the personal experience of walking a historic area, especially with a knowledgeable guide. We offer you a basic self-guide to Honolulu's **Chinatown Historic District**,

Hawai'i Capital Historic District, and **Merchant Street Historic District**, under *Neighborhoods* in "Greater Honolulu." You'll also find a few walking tour group recommendations under the heading *Historic Walking Tours* in that same chapter—and see *Where to Eat* there for food-oriented walking tours.

In Waikīkī keep an eye out for surfboard-shaped markers, which feature well-presented historic information on the area. Free tours of the historic Royal Hawaiian and Moana hotels are also available.

HOLIDAYS & EVENTS Although we observe Mainland holidays, we also have a few "offices closed" holidays of our own, such as King Kamehameha Day. Check out our "Information" chapter for the "411." Not coincidentally, some of these special holidays are celebrated with exciting, Hawai'i-style events. We don't need much excuse to hold a craft fair, parade through Waikīkī, or surf meet, either, so be sure to see a starter kit of gems in our "Culture" chapter. Local newspaper calendar listings, as well as online resources such as the Hawai'i Visitors and Convention Bureau (gohawaii.com) Web site, can reveal the breadth of activities before or after your arrival.

LODGING Welcoming visitors with open arms has always been a trademark of Hawai'i's aloha spirit. Back in the old days travelers on the road were invited—and even expected—to stop and stay in the *hale* (house) of villagers who lived along the way. With more than five million people now visiting O'ahu each year, the entire island has become one great overflowing hale, and about 95 percent of its accommodations are hotel rooms and condos in Waikīkī. We've presented a diversity of recommended hotels in Waikīkī, plus several others islandwide. (Also see *Camping*, above, for more options.)

Waikīkī is wrapping up an unprecedented face-lift that has definitely infused it with a new cool factor. Many of its larger hotels now offer full spas, wedding planning, vow renewal ceremonies, activity desks, and cultural learning opportunities, and even the smaller ones are embracing fully nonsmoking facilities, free WiFi, plasma televisions, seated check-in, trendy Balinese-inspired decor, and spa touches.

If you're looking to "go country" for your stay, you're not alone. More and more travelers to Hawai'i these days are renting homes or staying in B&Bs outside Waikīkī. For either a B&B or home rental, Kailua and the North Shore top the list of availability and popularity; Web sites such as vrbo .com are your best friends for finding them. While you'll certainly find more tranquility and authenticity out of town, be aware that the recent astronomical explosion of tourist presence in otherwise quiet neighborhoods and at secluded beaches has pushed some residents to the limit of tolerance.

Additional caveats. O'ahu has more than 1,000 homes listed on the Internet as "B&Bs," but the vast majority neither are licensed to operate nor perhaps offer the traditional experience you're expecting. They tend to be typical suburban homes with an extra room or two to be rented out for extra cash; and because of strict food service laws in Hawai'i, you might be offered a kitchenette to make your own fixin's instead of breakfast service. At the time of writing, the Hon-

olulu City Council had killed yet another bill to grandfather in all the illegally operating B&Bs and to permit new ones. We'll see what happens down the road. If you do contact a B&B, ask whether they're licensed and what kinds of services they offer before you commit.

Renting a private home can be an outstanding Hawai'i experience. Prices for a beach house can range from $300 a night to $30,000 per month or more depending on quality, size, and region. Again, a large number are operating outside the law, which requires an owner to either have a hard-to-obtain "nonconforming use" certificate, or rent out the unit for a minimum of 30 days.

A property claiming to be "beachfront" should actually have a shoreline directly in front of it. "Beachside" doesn't necessarily mean "beachfront." When it comes to hotel room views, "oceanview" can mean "partial ocean view," "full ocean view," or "oceanfront view." And no matter what anyone tells you their property offers—there are no private beaches in Hawai'i!

Each hotel offers something different; some only have 600-square-foot studios with kitchens, and others only 200-square-foot city-view rooms. Some are right on the beach, some are right on the alleyway. So before making up your mind on value, read beyond the price range category and get the details.

Hotel names, reservation phone numbers, and Web site addresses have been turned upside down by the countless hotel management and ownership changes these days. We've updated them as close to book printing as possible to help you out.

MUSEUMS Honolulu lacks the colossal museums that some other cities our size can boast, but we make up for it with impressive, well-presented, unique collections. Our two most notable and sizable are **Bishop Museum** and the **Honolulu Academy of Arts**. Our smaller museums are original gems worth your time. Several are even free. On O'ahu many of them also happen to be housed in historic structures, providing a double dose of visiting pleasure. Most close on state and federal holidays, as well as selected days of the week. Be sure to call in advance. Check out specific museum listings under *To See* in each chapter.

NIGHTLIFE O'ahu has a pretty mellow night scene, but it still offers good diversity within the city limits. From surf bars to late-night shopping, your poison is here.

A staple of Hawai'i's sunset hour is what we call pau hana, or "finished-with-work-time." Like the happy hour of the Mainland, most bars serve discounted drinks along with affordable edibles ranging from from light pūpū (appetizers) to a full menu. This can be a great substitute for an expensive and bloating Waikīkī dinner, and a great way to meet other people—even residents. All happy campers end up at the bar.

Speaking of bars, the drinking age in Hawai'i is 21, and driving with a 0.08 percent or greater blood alcohol level is illegal. Smoking is not allowed inside bars and nightclubs, or within 20 feet of entryways. While many places have no dress codes, wearing slippers and shorts—or at least shorts—at anywhere but a casual Waikīkī bar like **Duke's Waikīkī** is a fashion faux pas. On the other extreme, sophisticated spots like the Halekūlani's **Lewers Lounge** will expect you to comply with the tone. Nightspots are listed in each chapter under *Entertainment*.

For a more wholesome evening, Waikīkī still comes through. You'll notice that after dark Kalākaua Avenue seems to get even busier, with families and friends wandering up and down just for the fun of it. Many of the shops stay open until 11 PM, and of course there's never a bad moment for ice cream or a decaf. Try **Lappert's Ice Cream** at the Hilton Hawaiian Village, or the "secret" **Starbucks** patio oasis hidden in the back of DFS Galleria. Browse the books at **Borders Express**, Royal Hawaiian Center, or people-watch from **Honolulu Coffee Co.** at the Moana Surfrider. Nestle on the beach or even night swim (sober, please) in front of the Moana and Royal Hawaiian hotels. After about 10 PM Kūhiō Avenue can get slightly "hookerish"—you might want to steer the kids clear.

PERFORMING ARTS Visitors often don't think of Hawai'i as the place for opera or community theater. While we're certainly no Manhattan, you might take a night off from aimlessly roaming Kalākaua Avenue to see, let's say, international opera stars in *La Traviata*, local stars in *Doubt*, or the San Francisco Ballet in *The Nutcracker*. How's about a nationally touring Broadway show, like *The Lion King*, or a band like U2? We thought you'd take notice. Tickets can be tough to get, though, so check on our upcoming events in advance of your visit.

We also have a full-time municipal band, the **Royal Hawaiian Band** (922-5331; honolulu.gov/rhb). Founded in 1836, one of its most famous bandmasters, a Prussian who arrived in the Islands in 1872, so popularized European music in Honolulu that it was said Hawaiians whistled grand opera airs while pounding poi. Catch a free performance every Friday at noon at 'Iolani Palace and selected Sundays at 2 PM at Waikīkī's Kapi'olani Park Bandstand.

In our annual calendar (see the "Culture" chapter) we highlight several events that celebrate Hawaiian and Hawai'i-style music. We cannot recommend more enthusiastically that you attend an authentic Island music concert during your visit. In fact, choose a show outside of Waikīkī and you might be the only visitor in the house. It's easy to see some of our biggest names in the industry today—performers who've produced countless classic albums, won Grammys—playing right at the local bar. Why? Because Hawaiian music (and for that matter, hula) is still an integral part of daily local life, and Honolulu, in fact, is really a small town with a lot of tall buildings.

By the way, *Hawaiian music* is a fairly generic term. It could be interpreted as hapa-haole (part Caucasian), traditional, chant, "Jawaiian," contemporary, slack-key guitar, 'ukulele, falsetto singing, and so on, in Hawaiian or English. Traditional Hawaiian musicians around these days include the Mākaha Sons, Maunalua, Amy Hānaiali'i Gilliom, Nā Palapalai, and Raiatea Helm. If you're staying at a hotel, ask your concierge for the secret scoops on quality upcoming shows.

Courtesy OVB

RESTAURANTS Under *Where to Eat* in each chapter we've listed our favorites from among several thousand establishments islandwide. Check out *Eating Out* for casual (and mostly inexpensive) stops—shrimp trucks, holes-in-the-wall, sandwich and burger counters, delicatessens, noodle shops, and so on. These are neighborhood nooks you'll fall in love with, or that are perfect for take-out.

Under *Dining Out* we've mingled "big-name," high-priced destinations (meaning, comb your hair and prepare for a substantial dining experience) with midpriced favorites and even a few low-priced full-dining Island landmarks. A brief index in the back of the book allows you to search by price or cuisine type.

Resort attire is acceptable for most restaurants, but at dinnertime save the shorts for casual eateries only. Smoking is no longer permitted in any eating establishments. Tipping is the usual 15 percent or more.

Please take our dish descriptions as ballpark samples only, since menus constantly change. As always, call in advance to make sure your destination is open, especially on holidays, and consider making reservations. For a list of supermarkets, visit the "Information" chapter.

SCUBA DIVING & SNORKELING
About 2 percent of the world's oceans contain coral reefs, which house a diversity of life second only to tropical rain forests. Coral is made from the calcareous skeletons of thousands of tiny, stinging critters called polyps. Extremely fragile, they require certain conditions to thrive.

More than 500 different kinds of fish—plus turtles, rays, sea urchins,

The twin powerhouse venues **Neal S. Blaisdell Center** and the **Waikīkī Shell** (591-2211; blaisdellcenter.com) usually host Honolulu's biggest performance events, like operas or rock concerts. For smaller-scale events, check with the companies and venues listed in each chapter under *Entertainment*.

PETS, TRAVELING WITH Bringing your dog or other pet with you to Hawai'i is tricky business. Hawai'i's absence of rabies means the state will quarantine incoming animals for up to 120 days to ensure they're healthy. The only way around it is by arranging for lab tests and paperwork in advance and paying considerable fees. For more details, contact the Hawai'i Department of Agriculture (HDA) **Animal Quarantine Station** (837-8092; http://hawaii.gov/hdoa/ai/aqs/info). Guide or service dogs will also require advance paperwork preparation.

dolphins, whales, seals, sea cucumbers, anemones, hermit crabs, eels, lobsters, snails, octopus and sea stars—thrive in and around Hawai'i's coral reefs. Don't miss the opportunity to see them in their own habitats via snorkeling or scuba diving. You can rent or purchase a snorkel, mask, and fins or book a snorkel trip, which includes all the equipment you'll need. The latter is best if you're uncomfortable in the ocean or new to snorkeling. See the "Recreation" chapter for details.

SHARKS Hawai'i has about 40 different species of sharks, from the 8-inch pygmy shark to the 50-foot whale shark. Eight can be aggressive to humans and are occasionally seen close to shore. But it's the massive tiger shark that perpetrates Hawai'i's extremely rare attacks (out of many millions of dips taken in Hawaiian waters each year, only a few folks get nibbled).

Several well-meaning tour companies have been offering North Shore "shark encounters." Their point of view is that it's educational, which is most certainly true. The opposing point of view, shared by many surfers, area residents, and ocean organizations, is that these outfits are illegally feeding the sharks, disrespecting the animals, and creating a potential problem that will end with increased attacks. These are good points, too.

See the North Shore chapter for information about shark tours.

SHOPPING Louis Vuitton handbag. Shark-tooth necklace. Antique kimono. Hawai'i-themed Hello Kitty wallet. Whatever your souvenir wish list may include, you can get it in Honolulu. We love to shop, and so do our five million annual visitors. Because Honolulu is so spread out, we don't really have a central shopping district. Thank goodness all roads lead to **Ala Moana Center**, one of the largest outdoor shopping malls in the world and our unofficial "town square." Everyone shops at Ala Moana, from visiting celebrities cruising Harry Winston to local homies strumming 'ukulele and playing cards next to Longs Drugs.

Thanks to our many shoppers from Japan, Waikīkī grows more upscale every year. In 2007 it made a major leap with the new **Waikīkī Beach Walk**, the largest development project in Waikīkī's history, and an $84 million upgrade to **Royal Hawaiian Center**. Then **DFS Galleria** (dfs galleria.com/en/hawaii) reinvented itself, transforming from trinketville to designerville, and **Waikīkī Shopping Plaza** (waikikishoppingplaza .com) expanded.

The incredible variety of visitors Waikīkī attracts explains how Gucci can live on the same block as the gumball-machine-quality Waikīkī Discount Mart. It also explains how **International Market Place** (inter nationalmarketplacewaikiki.com)—a surreal, 1950s bazaar overflowing with suspect tourist trinkets—persists in popularity (although we must admit that we scored a few interesting tiki gifts there last year).

On the edge of town nearer the airport, the 700-vendor **Aloha Stadium Swap Meet** (486-6704; aloha stadiumswapmeet.net) at Aloha Stadium is another popular destination, although we feel that 90 percent of it is the same trinkety junk sold at International Market Place. If you go, home in on the few unusual booths selling dried octopus snacks and other true local treasures and tidbits. Even farther afield, **Waikele Premium Outlets** (676-5656) offers deep discounts on mid-range designer wear.

In this book we've focused on unique vendors and the "best places" to score particular items. Check out the listings under *Selective Shopping* in each chapter; also see *Antiques & Collectibles, Bookstores, Boutiques, Commercial Art Galleries, Farmers' Markets, Hawaiiana & Other Hawai'i-Made Crafts*, and *Swimwear* here in "What's Where."

SWIMWEAR Gals, we know that finding the right bathing suit can be an intimidating task. In Hawai'i, the hottest bikinis and one-pieces are toned-down floral prints and solids with very few embellishments. Skip the thong. Guys, most surf shops can hook you up with the coolest board shorts. Go long on length and mellow in either floral print or solid colors. Look under *Selective Shopping* in each chapter.

Rash guards for men, women, and children are available at most surf-clothing shops. These snug, water-

friendly shirts not only protect bellies from chafing on bodyboards, but also can keep the sun from scorching you into a coma while you swim. Some even have sun protection built in.

TENNIS O'ahu has nearly 200 public courts at which you may play—most are outdoor, and many are lit for night games. To use the courts, simply wait your turn in person; play is limited to 45 minutes when someone else is waiting. See the listings under *To Do* in each chapter.

WEATHER When our Euro in-laws came to visit one summer, they were mystified by Hawai'i's soft trade winds, moderate heat, and valley rainbows. They'd been expecting blazingly clear skies, searing temperatures near 100 degrees, and enough mugginess to slay a senior. Mercifully, Hawai'i's weather is milder than in the South Pacific—or, for that matter, Florida—with just enough heat year-round for a perfect tan and just enough cool year-round for comfort. Learn more about our climate in both "History" and "Information."

WEDDINGS Who hasn't been married in Hawai'i, or wished to be? They come by the tens of thousands, kicking off shoes, oozing onto the beach for sunset ceremonies, and staying put for the honeymoons. If you're interested in taking the plunge or renewing your vows, see *Marriage in Hawai'i* in our "Information" chapter.

WHALE-WATCHING From November through March or early April, more than 5,000 humpback whales loll about in Hawaiian waters. They swim several thousand miles from Alaska, bask in the warmth of the lower latitude, mate, and give birth before trekking all the way back with babies in tow. The 1,400-square-mile **Hawaiian Islands Humpback Whale National Marine Sanctuary** helps to protect these still-endangered, 45-foot-long creatures. Although the gargantuan humpbacks are local stars, Hawai'i also has sperm whales, Hawaiian pilot whales, and Hawaiian melonhead whales in its waters.

Maui has some of the best whale-watching in the state, but you can often see whales off O'ahu from Diamond Head, Turtle Bay Resort, and Makapu'u Point, as well as on a whale-watching boat excursion. We've even seen them spouting in Waikīkī just off the Hilton Hawaiian Village. The law requires you to stay at least 300 feet from humpbacks for your safety as well as theirs.

HISTORY

The Hawaiian Islands is made up of more than 130 reefs, islands, islets, and shoals stretching 1,500 miles across the Pacific Ocean. From Honolulu you'd have to swim more than 2,000 miles to reach a continental coastline or other major island groups, no matter which direction you headed.

This is the most remote inhabited place in the entire world, a reality made clearer en route to Hawai'i. After a half day or longer of flying over open sea, the sight of Honolulu's glass-tower metropolis and bright green peaks rising from the water seems a preposterous mirage. Approach in the evening, and hours of pitch darkness are suddenly broken by fiery rivulets of light winding downhill like slow-moving streams of lava. Hawai'i's extreme isolation is in fact the cornerstone of its unique and fragile environment and even perhaps fundamental to its allure.

About 1.3 million people live here, and we occupy only seven islands: Maui, Kaua'i, Hawai'i, Moloka'i, Lāna'i, Ni'ihau, and O'ahu. Together these main islands add up to about 99 percent of Hawai'i's total landmass.

Hawai'i's cultural history is as emotionally compelling as its breathtaking beauty. We have been an American state for only about 50 years—so many residents consider themselves "people of Hawai'i" first and foremost, taking pride in perpetuating traditions distinctly different from Mainland communities. Nowhere else is Hawai'i's storied past more evident than on the island of O'ahu, which is the state's political, cultural, and economic heartbeat.

NATURAL HISTORY

A LAND APART Hawai'i is barely visible on world maps, appearing as no more than a spray of dots along the Pacific Ocean's Tropic of Cancer, north of the equator. In actuality, these dots are the above-water peaks of some of the largest mountains on the planet, built up over many millions of years by volcanic eruptions that originate from the bottom of the ocean. When measured from its undersea base, Mauna Kea on the island of Hawai'i stands 6.2 miles high—taller than Mount Everest. The volcanic process is still under way there, as well as at its little-known southerly neighbor, Lō'ihi Seamount, which is expected to erupt through the waves in about 10,000 years.

The island of O'ahu began to take shape more than three million years ago. Once rising at least 10,000 feet above sea level, its two massive shield volcanoes have eroded into 600 square miles of wide plains, steep shorelines, and magnificently rippled mountain ranges now less than half their original heights. The ancient volcanoes that created the Wai'anae and Ko'olau Ranges are long extinct, as are the rare and more recently developed tuff cones that pock the island, such as Hanauma Bay, Punchbowl Crater, and Waikīkī's world-famous landmark, Diamond Head Crater.

While our tiny islands are known for evenly warm weather all year, they also feature as many different climate zones as exist from coastal Alaska to coastal Costa Rica. Kaua'i's Mount Wai'ale'ale is one of the wettest spots on earth, with an annual rainfall exceeding 35 feet; the Island of Hawai'i's Ka'ū Desert is a hot, barren, rocky landscape reminiscent of Mars. In the distance the snow-dusted, active volcano Mauna Loa steams and curdles molten lava.

O'ahu's climate zones are less dramatic. Along Windward O'ahu, east of the Ko'olau Range, the weather can be significantly more temperamental than elsewhere on the island. It's often overcast, and in the valleys it can rain more than 200 inches in a year. On Leeward O'ahu, or the lands south and west of the Wai'anae Range, the climate is generally very dry and hot, with an annual rainfall closer to 20 inches. On the North Shore, relative dryness and moderate sun prevail. Waikīkī, on the southeast shore, basks in a near-perfect harmony of cheery sun softened by puff clouds and soothing tropical breezes. Wherever you are on the island, valleys and mountains tend to be cooler and rainier than near the beaches.

We recognize two seasons in Hawai'i: summer and winter, distinguishable by several subtle trademarks. On O'ahu the summer months of May through September tend to be hotter, with relatively light precipitation and refreshing trade breezes. Days are often bright and sunny, with temperatures between 85 and 90 degrees Fahrenheit. Evenings reach the high 70s. The winter months of October through April bring slightly cooler days, more frequent rain, variable winds, and intermittent storms. Day temperatures laze between 75 and 82 degrees, and evenings are perfect for a light sweater at 65 to 75.

A BANYAN TREE PLANTED DURING THE MONARCHY YEARS STILL STANDS AT 'IOLANI PALACE.

THE ARID LEEWARD COAST

Rainbows, even double rainbows, abound. On occasion, so-called kona winds prevail from the south, bringing muggy weather that can carry volcanic ash fallout (called "vog") from eruptions on the Big Island. Volcanic activity has heightened in the last several years; it has increased our vog and sometimes casts an eerie, smog-like pall over Honolulu. Volcanoes aside, Hawai'i has some of the cleanest air in the world.

Under the influence of the North Equatorial Current, Hawai'i receives relatively cool waters with sea surface temperatures ranging between about 72 and 81 degrees Fahrenheit year-round. The spectacular high surf for which we're world famous originates from distant storms in the Northern and Southern Hemispheres. During winter months, northern storms spawn wind-driven waves that travel unimpeded, sometimes hitting Hawai'i's northern and western shores at heights of 25 feet or more. In summer, North Shore waters fall flat and southern storms kick up moderately high surf on the southern and eastern shores of the Islands. Although tidal range is small, tidal rip currents and waves can be powerful enough to subdue even the strongest swimmers.

WHERE THE WILD THINGS ARE Hawai'i has a colorful landscape of flora and fauna, but many of its most vivid creatures are hidden below the ocean's surface. We're surrounded by 40 different types of corals, more than 500 species of fish, and 40 species of sharks, as well as whales, seals, eels, rays, dolphins, turtles, urchins, and other unusual sea life, some of which exist only in Hawai'i.

The Galapagos Islands may be famous for specialized species, but Hawai'i is an even more important site for evolutionary studies because of its lengthy history of development and isolation. At one time each of our islands was no more

HAWAI'I'S "HIDDEN" ISLANDS

Visitors often think Hawai'i is a total of six islands: O'ahu, Kaua'i, Maui, Moloka'i, Lāna'i, and Hawai'i (also called "the Big Island"). In fact, Hawai'i has eight main islands and more than 100 islets and shoals, all stretching across 1,500 miles of open sea toward Japan.

Uninhabited Kaho'olawe is the seventh of Hawai'i's eight main islands. It's a dry, windswept landscape ravaged by goats and extensive military bombing exercises; few people aside from archaeologists and activists know its terrain today. Officially transferred back to the State of Hawai'i from the US Navy in 2003, it's currently managed by the Kaho'olawe Island Reserve Commission and generally off-limits to the public.

Tiny Ni'ihau, our eighth main island, is also known as "the Forbidden Isle." Privately purchased from the Kingdom of Hawai'i in 1864, it's home to about 150 Hawaiian-speaking Native Hawaiians. The island is off-limits to all outsiders, unless expressly invited, for the protection of Ni'ihauans and their more traditional ways of life.

Beyond Ni'ihau, the numerous Northwestern Hawaiian Islands form the largest marine sanctuary in the world and a World Heritage Site: the Papahānaumokuākea Marine National Monument. The sanctuary includes Nihoa, Mokumanamana, Maro Reef, Laysan Island, and Midway, where the renowned Battle of Midway took place. This 138,000-square-mile natural environment is home to more than 7,000 marine species, a quarter of which exist nowhere else on Earth. Cultural remains include Hawaiian archaeological sites, shipwrecks, and World War II artifacts. The preserve is closed to the general public.

Most of O'ahu's offshore islets are official sanctuaries for seabirds and native coastal vegetation. Several are open to the public by day. We do not recommend you walk to any at low tide, despite this suggestion in other guidebooks—coral can be destroyed underfoot, and people have drowned in strong currents. The safest and most ecofriendly way to visit an offshore islet is via a guided kayak tour to the Mokulua Islands, near Kailua.

than a rocky basalt and coral landscape. Over millions of years plant spores, insects, seeds, and larvae borne on the wind, tucked in the feathers of migrating seabirds, or drifting on bits of wood slowly found their way to each new island. On average, only one species per 70,000 years managed to establish itself. Other creatures became seasonal visitors to Hawai'i, such as the kōlea (golden plover) and humpback whale, both of which travel approximately 6,000 miles round-trip from Alaska every year.

With few plants and animals to compete with, newly arrived species gradually responded to and flourished in Hawai'i's unusual surroundings, evolving into a remarkable breadth of new wildlife found nowhere else on earth. Hawai'i was once home to 1,100 native species and subspecies of flowering plants, of which 89 percent were unique to the Islands. It also had nearly 400 different types of native ferns, a variety of at least 10,000 insects, nearly 100 singular bird species, and an array of more than 1,000 snails. In the Galapagos, Darwin observed the specialization of finches; in Hawai'i we have, for example, the Hawaiian honeycreeper, which evolved into more than 50 unique species—each with a distinctive bill adapted for its circumstances.

ENDANGERED ENDEMIC MOORHEN

HTJ

Hawai'i's delicate natural environment has been taxed to the limit by habitat destruction, human encroachment, pollution, and the continual introduction of alien species, leading to predation on native wildlife, ecosystem damage, competition for resources, and widespread diseases against which native flora and fauna have limited immunity.

Each year new invasive species are purposefully or accidentally introduced in the Islands and disrupt the balance further. Most plant and animal life you'll encounter during your stay—from mangoes, pineapples, and orchids to myna birds, cockroaches, ants, and mosquitoes—have been introduced by humans in the last two centuries. It's estimated that more than 4,500 invasive alien species have taken hold here. Our daily impact on the environment of Hawai'i cannot be overstated; in fact, Hawai'i now suffers the highest rate of species extinction anywhere in the United States and one of the highest in the entire world.

ENDANGERED ENDEMIC SILVERSWORD

HTJ

SOCIAL HISTORY

THE FIRST HAWAIIANS How the isolated Hawaiian Islands came to be inhabited by people is a story still tentatively told. The majority of books begin Hawai'i's history with the arrival of Western explorers, as if anything prior is insignificant. Of pre-contact times, it's true that knowledge is comparably scant, a conflicting and incomplete series of accounts cobbled together from reports by early Westerners, archaeological and linguistic research, ethnobotany, and Hawaiian oral genealogy and legend.

That Hawai'i was first populated by Polynesians is well accepted. The earliest people probably arrived sometime in the first millennium, perhaps as early as AD 500, from the Marquesas. They were followed several hundred years later by waves of voyagers from the Society Islands. Overwhelming evidence—right down to place-names such as Kealaikahiki, the name of a sea channel between two of Hawai'i's main islands that translates to "the way to Tahiti"—indicates strong cultural and migratory connections between Tahiti (or a similar distant island homeland) and Hawai'i throughout several centuries. This seems to end abruptly by about AD 1200. We have no definitive answers as to why the earliest peoples migrated here, or how they could have known that Hawai'i existed.

The first Islanders seemed to have led peaceful, agrarian lives, making the most of native birds, fish, and plants. Some accounts suggest that these first people were the so-called Menehune, whom Hawaiians credit with building Hawai'i's oldest fishponds and other structures. Menehune have long been described as dwarf-like and possessed of supernatural powers; today they're considered mythical and appear mostly as cartoonish mascots in local advertising. Interestingly, an 1820 census taken on Kaua'i revealed that more than 60 individuals living in one of its remote valleys claimed to be of Menehune stock. What happened to these first Hawai'i dwellers when Tahitians arrived here is unknown. The two populations could have intermixed, although socially it seems clear that the Tahitian culture became dominant.

The Tahitians brought more than 35 plants and animals to Hawai'i, including dogs, small pigs, a Polynesian strain of chicken, taro, a variety of bananas, and coconuts. They also brought the South Pacific gods Kū, Kāne, Lono, and Kanaloa as well as the kapu system—a code of laws and societal caste system.

The people that became the Hawaiian race established permanent settlements on O'ahu, the Big Island, Maui, Kaua'i, Moloka'i, Lāna'i, and Ni'ihau and frequented the smaller islands of Kaho'olawe, Nihoa, and Mokumanamana. On O'ahu the lush Windward communities of Kailua, Waimānalo, and Kāne'ohe appear to have been the nuclei of their earliest settlements. Honolulu was probably populated by AD 1,000 and Waikīkī before AD 1400, and the latter eventually served as the capital of the island. By the late 1700s the Hawaiian Islands were home to at least 300,000 people and possibly as many as a million.

Hawaiians had no written language, no natural metals to work with, and no pottery. Homes were indeed thatched huts, and tools often stone or bone. Yet life here was complex, orderly, and advanced. It hinged heavily on the viewpoint that all animate as well as inanimate creations were alive, even in death, and fully intertwined with one another in time and space. Genealogy chants related the development of the earth and heavens, the Hawaiian Islands, its people, and specific family histories. Genealogies were essential for societal order and extremely sacred, for understanding the cosmology of the world and Hawaiians' place in it was the ultimate grounding force. This was especially true for ali'i, or chiefs and chiefesses, who traced their lineages to divine ancestors and intermarried as closely as possible to preserve their mana, or spiritual power.

In the old days the Islands were partitioned into moku, and each in turn was divided into smaller slices called ahupua'a. On O'ahu many of these ancient boundaries are still the basis for our modern naming and mapping system.

ARRIVAL OF "THE LONG NECKS" By the late 1700s Hawaiians had been flourishing for centuries out of contact with Tahiti and other cultures. Westerners seemed to have had no knowledge of Hawai'i. It certainly wasn't on any map belonging to the Englishman Captain James Cook, one of the world's greatest explorers. In early 1778 Cook was in command of two ships sailing northward from the Society Islands when his crew sighted the peaks of O'ahu. The ensuing encounter between Cook and the Hawaiian people marks the beginning of what is called modern Hawaiian history.

The *Resolution* and *Discovery* made first landfall on southern Kaua'i. Hawaiians spotted the massive vessels long before Cook anchored offshore, and canoes quickly launched to meet them. Onshore, the Hawaiians reportedly fell to their knees. Had Cook been mistaken for the pale-faced god Lono, who was to return one day on a vast ship during the celebration of Makahiki?

Although Cook learned he had arrived in "Owyhee," in his own records he renamed Hawai'i the Sandwich Islands after England's Earl of Sandwich. He

THE OLD FISHING VILLAGE OF KOU, NOW DOWNTOWN HONOLULU, DEPICTED BY LOUIS CHORIS IN 1816

Courtesy Hawai'i State Archives

noted the similarity between the Tahitian and Hawaiian languages, that Hawaiians were physically beautiful and extremely friendly, and that they appeared to already know of the existence of iron, although they had none. His ships stayed at Waimea Bay for several weeks for trading, restocking, and research, then continued their journey to find the Northwest Passage along the Americas.

A year later Cook returned to Hawai'i for a winter break—this time, at Kealakekua Bay, on the island of Hawai'i. It was immediately clear that news of Cook's earlier visit to Kaua'i had spread throughout the Islands (along with venereal disease from his crew). He had again arrived during Makahiki, a season of rest as well as of tribute to Lono. The men were warmly welcomed and for weeks lived in the utmost luxury Hawaiians had to offer.

After a grand farewell from Hawai'i in early February, the two ships battled an open-sea storm, breaking a mast. They decided that their best course of action was an anticlimactic return to Kealakekua to make repairs. Instead of the usual fanfare as they pulled into the bay, there was silence. A kapu, or "taboo," was in effect, rendering the villagers mute. Perhaps, too, there was the underlying sense of guests long overstayed, of guests who seemed less like gods and more like men—vulnerable, needy, unpredictable. Something wasn't right.

As the days rolled by, scuffles between Hawaiians and the English began to develop. Small items were snatched from the ships. And then a larger item: a cutter, spirited away in the night. Cook and his men went ashore with a plan to kidnap one of the chiefs and hold him hostage. Meanwhile the ships' men fired into a crowd, killing another chief. Suddenly Cook was surrounded—and with a feeble shot from his pistol, he disappeared into the shallow water under a flurry of Hawaiian bodies and clubs.

The fighting continued for two days before a truce was established. Captain Charles Clerk, now in command, would not leave Hawai'i until Cook's remains were retrieved. These turned out to be several pounds of sliced flesh, charred bone fragments, and hands preserved in salt, which he submitted for Western burial rites. The *Resolution* and *Discovery* limped away from Kealakekua Bay, never to return, and without their legendary leader.

As for Hawaiians, a new chapter of foreign visitations, ravaging diseases, and other challenges to their way of life was just beginning.

KAMEHAMEHA, KING OF HAWAI'I Of the many Hawaiian chiefs Cook had met while in Hawai'i, one was to become its greatest leader in its history: Kamehameha, said to be born under a blazing star. An enormous man of impossible strength, courage, and determination, by his mid-20s Kamehameha was already in a leading position of power among the nobles of Hawai'i Island.

Several years after Cook's death at Kealakekua Bay, Kamehameha instigated a series of civil wars that ravished the Islands for more than a decade. In 1795 he summoned an army of 16,000 men to conquer the island of O'ahu. With troops stretched for miles along Waikīkī's shores and beyond, he drove hundreds, perhaps even thousands, of defenders into the mountains and finally off Nu'uanu Pali, a steep precipice 1,000 feet high. It marked the final subjugation of O'ahu. In time Kaua'i and little Ni'ihau would concede to Kamehameha without a struggle, and by 1810 the "slayer of chiefs" commanded the Hawaiian Islands. For the first time, Hawai'i would be ruled as one kingdom.

Once king of Hawai'i, Kamehameha proved a compassionate, wise, and reasonable leader. Despite many deaths brought by the wars, he grew to be deeply loved by the Hawaiian people, and the unification ushered in an era of peace and stability to the Islands that had long been absent.

But there was no way for him to undo or halt the cultural transformations that Western contact had begun. Nine years after Cook's ships had returned West to report on Hawai'i, foreign ships from all over the world began to arrive; with them came both desirable and destructive new ways of life. In 1810 Kamehameha moved his court from Waikīkī to the downtown Honolulu harbor front, marking the beginning of its role as the center of Hawai'i's government. Kamehameha tried to maintain tradition despite increasing Western influences in the Islands. But by the time of his death in 1819, Hawai'i was straddling two worlds and losing foothold on the past.

Courtesy Hawai'i State Archives

KING KAMEHAMEHA

"MISSIONARY-STYLE" The arrival of Congregational missionaries in Hawai'i was to have a profound impact on the Hawaiian way of life. Inspired by a Christianized Hawaiian student then living in New England, as well as upsetting traveler accounts of a "heathen" Pacific people, in 1819 the American Board of Commissioners for Foreign Missions gathered up several well-educated, newly married men and women and shipped them from Boston Harbor to "save" the people of the Sandwich Islands. This was the first of many missionary companies sent to Hawai'i over four decades, puritan in spirit and committed to the greatest challenge of their young lives. Surnames such as Judd, Baldwin, Dillingham, Alexander, Cooke, Dole, Castle, Rice, and others still resonate with both prestige and controversy in Hawai'i today.

As the missionaries' brig approached the Islands five months later, they were relieved to learn that King Kamehameha, who would have challenged their intentions, had just died. Moreover, his death had set into motion a reaction against traditional cornerstones of Hawaiian life, including religious practices and the kapu system. A gap had opened among the people, wedged apart by 40 years of exposure to Western lifestyles. 'Iolani Liholiho, Kamehameha's youthful son, had now ascended to power and, in partnership with Kamehameha's favorite wife, Ka'ahumanu, had ended the strictest of taboos. The missionaries immediately set about filling the cracks with Christianity.

Conveying the nuances of a Christian life across cultural boundaries proved challenging, to say the least. Hawaiians remained cheery during sermons that were meant to stir in them the fear of hell; they shuddered at forgoing the well-loved practice of adultery; they might don a top hat in public, but go without any pants. One devout Hawaiian couple brought their infant to be baptized, requesting the child be given the biblical name "Beelzebub." When told this was unacceptable, they compromised by naming the baby "Mikalakeke," or "Mr. Richards," after the baptizing minister. And although the missionaries worked hard to suppress "un-Christian" activities such as hula, many traditional Hawaiian practices continued alongside the encroaching Western lifestyle, growing gnarled together like tree roots. It took nearly two decades of effort, but by 1840 more than 20,000 Hawaiians were officially converted.

The missionaries felt that it was important for Hawaiians to be able to read the Bible. Since the Hawaiian language was an oral language, they took it upon themselves to translate it into written form, assigning 12 Latin-based letters to represent all the sounds they discerned. They also opened Hawai'i's first Western-style schools. From a little printing press imported from New England, the missionaries began to produce millions of pages of hymnals, Bibles, and other Christian literature.

When they first introduced the palapala, or "written word," to the people, it was received with some suspicion. King Liholiho, after reviewing letters on paper that were said to spell his name, replied, "It looks neither like myself, nor like any other man." Within 10 years, however, the missionaries had enrolled 50,000 children and adults in schools that taught reading and writing in Hawaiian. Hawai'i soon became the most literate society in the world for its era, and by the late 1800s it had more than 100 Hawaiian-language newspapers in circulation.

The missionaries also attempted to care for the sick and dying. The population of Hawaiians had been decreasing at an alarming rate since Captain Cook's first visit in 1778. Diseases such as measles, influenza, smallpox, and whooping cough were sweeping across Hawai'i, and venereal illnesses were causing a decline in births. As it was said among Hawaiians themselves, *Nā kānaka 'ōku'u wale aku no i kau 'uhane,"* or "the people dismissed freely their souls and died." The prestige of native institutions and the cultural elements that gave life meaning were waning away, and many people were inconsolable.

By 1831 Native Hawaiians numbered closer to 130,000 than the 300,000 or more Captain Cook had estimated in 1778. By 1853 only 73,000 were left. In 1872 the census counted 52,000. And in 1900 a pathetic 40,000 people of pure- and part-Hawaiian ancestry remained.

As their numbers waned, others readily took their place: The 1900 census also counted a total of 110,000 people from America, Europe, Asia, and elsewhere living in Hawai'i. In 1853 Native Hawaiians made up 97 percent of the population. By 1923 Hawaiians—including part Hawaiians—made up only 16 percent of Hawai'i's population.

A PACIFIC KINGDOM After the death of Kamehameha I, a succession of the Kamehameha bloodline ascended the throne: 'Iolani Liholiho, Kauikeaouli, Alexander Liholiho, and Lot Kapuāiwa. Kamehameha I's dowager, Queen Ka'ahumanu, remained powerful and instrumental in the rule of the land alongside Liholiho and Kauikeaouli. They were followed in turn by William Lunalilo and David Kalākaua, elected rulers from other noble lineages. Kalākaua's sister, Lili'uokalani, would be the last ruler of Hawai'i. In many ways, these years of the monarchy resembled life in Hawai'i today more than they did the reign of Kamehameha I and the centuries before him.

Only five years after taking the throne, Kamehameha I's son 'Iolani Liholiho contracted measles during a visit to England and died. Having left no heirs, Liholiho's 10-year-old brother, Kauikeaouli, was crowned King Kamehameha III.

Kauikeaouli reigned for 30 years, and during that time would face increasing pressure from foreign and naturalized residents who wanted Western freedoms and rights. He was presented with challenges that included reforming ancient systems into Westernized political and social structures; managing international relations and a growing foreign population; and helping his people cope with introduced diseases, industries, and land divisions. He would also combat unsanctioned coups by both a British naval captain and a French admiral.

A sandalwood trade with China, developed during the era of Kamehameha I, had temporarily brought unprecedented riches to the kingdom. By the mid-1820s foreign whaling vessels had begun combing the Pacific from Peru to Japan and the Arctic. As both a mid-Pacific location and whale breeding ground, Hawai'i was the perfect place for crews to restock, repair, and hunt. In 1846 alone, nearly 600 whaling ships docked in Lahaina and Honolulu, and there seemed no way to control their arrival. Their presence had an enormous impact on town life: Thousands of rowdy foreign seamen filled ports, demanding liquor, prostitutes, and the right to kick up some dirt. Some deserted in Hawai'i, or were dumped by their ships. Hawaiians, needing to feed armies of foreigners who disliked local foods, began planting Western crops and establishing cattle ranches. Hawaiian men enlisted on whalers in droves. Many never returned home, either dying aboard ship or disappearing into crowded ports of call. The heat of the whaling era lasted more than two decades; meanwhile, missionaries' attempts to counteract the mayhem created a widening breach between the pious and the unrepentant.

In 1848 Western-minded businessmen convinced Kauikeaouli to enact the "Great Mahele"—a division of land that completely contradicted Hawaiian ways of thought. While it

THE HAWAIIAN FLAG

seems natural to us today to assume that land should be owned, this was an entirely foreign, and even horrific, concept to Hawaiians. Land was seen as a birthright everyone shared and took responsibility to care for, as you would your family. It did not "belong" to anyone.

In many ways the Great Mahele was a scandalous disaster for Hawaiians, essentially destroying the ancient ahupua'a system of mountain-to-sea and the entire framework of life. Instead of sharing land, land was now to be hoarded for oneself. Accessing a breadth of resources now meant trespassing on someone else's property. The group- and family-oriented Hawaiians were now fragmented, instead of working together. Disoriented by the meaning and rules of the Mahele, most Hawaiian commoners made no effort to formally claim the ground they dwelled on. Naturalized citizens of Hawai'i as well as foreign nationals, fully schooled in the concept and benefits of Western landownership, leapt to purchase every square mile they could get their hands on. By 1890 about 75 percent of Hawai'i's lands would be owned by foreign businessmen. What Kauikeaouli had thought would save his people added to their destruction.

Six years after the Mahele began, Kauikeaouli passed away, and King Kamehameha IV, Alexander Liholiho, succeeded the throne. To regain footing for the Hawaiian kingdom and reestablish "Hawai'i for Hawaiians," he attempted to swing away from the growing American presence, allying himself more firmly with European powers. Local government representatives, such as one missionary-turned-official who had hoped to sell Hawai'i to an American businessman for $5 million, consistently thwarted his progress in an effort to strengthen America's hold on the Islands.

Alexander died unexpectedly in 1863, and the last of the Kamehameha dynasty, his brother Lot Kamehameha, continued Alexander's fight to maintain control of the kingdom. But the Caucasian and Hawaiian legislative team was becoming increasingly disenfranchised, and rumors of an American coup were growing. When Lot passed away in 1872 with no named heir, the first elected king of Hawai'i, Lunalilo, stepped up to the throne. He contracted pulmonary tuberculosis after only a year and soon joined his many ancestors in the grave.

Although initially the selection of Lunalilo's royal-blooded successor David Kalākaua stirred public outrage, in time he became a favorite of the people. The "Merrie Monarch's" controversial and high-profile reign from 1874 until 1891 included relinquishing Pearl Harbor to the United States in exchange for tax-free sugar importation, reviving Hawaiian cultural practices such as hula, building a luxurious palace in Honolulu, touring the world, and hosting foreign dignitaries and other public figures in magnificent style.

The most critical incident of his career in office was what became known as "the Bayonet Constitution" of 1887. Backed by militiamen, the pro-American legislative team forced Kalākaua to relinquish most of his executive power under threat of removal from the throne. Included in the new constitution's amendments were expansive voting reforms based on property ownership, which greatly limited the voting power of Hawai'i's Native Hawaiians and Asians. Further amendments would eventually grant full voting rights to wealthier Europeans and Americans.

A TASTE FOR SUGAR In the midst of the whaling boom, small-scale sugar, coffee, and rice plantations also began to quietly take shape. Since the 1840s, and especially once Western businessmen could claim ownership of Hawai'i land, the sugar industry had been building steam. The Gold Rush had created sharp demand for sugar, followed by skyrocketing prices once the South was embroiled in the American Civil War and the Reciprocity Treaty of 1875. By the late years of Kauikeaouli's reign, several missionaries-turned-businessmen had entered the sugar trade, developing large tracts of land granted in earlier years to their families by the kingdom. They imported from southern China the first official group of laborers, who were offered five-year contracts with all essentials to be provided by the plantation—a paternalistic arrangement that continued in various forms through the 1940s.

Entities known as the "Big Five," primarily run by Island-established Caucasian businessmen, began to emerge as the sugar industry grew: American Factors, Theo H. Davies & Co., Alexander & Baldwin, C. Brewer & Co., and Castle & Cooke. Started mainly as factoring agencies, these five powerhouses evolved into corporate fiefdoms that became the core of Hawai'i's business and political world. Executives from the Big Five joined the same clubs, sent their children to the same schools, attended the same churches, married one another's relatives, and amassed constantly expanding wealth and control in sugar and other profitable businesses.

Interestingly, sugar plantation operations would forever change the demographics of Hawai'i as much as its politics. Plantations required enormous numbers of workers, a need that could not be met in the Islands. Between 1850 and 1930, plantation owners imported nearly 50,000 Chinese, primarily from the Canton region; more than 200,000 Japanese (by the turn of the century, nearly 40 percent of Hawai'i's total population was Japanese); 8,000 Koreans; 130,000 Filipinos; 20,000 Portuguese, mainly from the islands of Madeira and the Azores; and a smaller number of workers from Kiribati, Norway, Russia, India, Germany, and other countries.

Plantations typically kept ethnic groups separated in worker camps, and each group was treated and paid differently. The work was difficult and dirty. As contracts expired, some workers left Hawai'i, but the majority stayed, spreading out to start life anew with humble business operations and intermarrying with Hawaiians or other immigrants. A large percentage of Hawai'i's residents today descend from, or were themselves, plantation workers who arrived during the years of agricultural domination. Even as late as 1959, when Hawai'i became a state, 1 in every 12 residents worked for the sugar industry.

ALOHA 'OE By the time of his death in San Francisco in 1891, Kalākaua was more of a figurehead, having been stripped of significant power through the Bayonet Constitution. His sister, Lili'uokalani, now became queen, and her desire was to restore power to the Hawaiian monarchy and Hawaiian people. The sugar industry was suffering from an economic downturn caused by the new McKinley Tariff Act, and a brooding knot of pro-American businessmen known as the Annexation Club—many of whom were descendants of the missionaries and in control of finance, land, and labor in Hawai'i—intended to prevent the queen from taking any such step.

In January 1893, when Lili'uokalani announced she would be introducing a new constitution to do just that, the annexationists called it an act of treason. Upon witnessing their extreme reaction, Lili'uokalani publicly withdrew her statement—but it was too late. Annexationists and armed American supporters rallied in the streets, accompanied by sailors and marines from the USS *Boston*, who marched through town. Acting entirely without official backing from the United States, they stormed the government building, declared a takeover of the nation of Hawai'i in the name of the US, and read a proclamation that announced their own provisional government to be in effect. Hoping to avoid bloodshed and believing that the US could not possibly back the overthrow (the third by "representatives" of a foreign nation in several decades), Lili'uokalani and her party withheld immediate action.

Meanwhile, the annexationists assembled their provisional government and began preparing for the process of annexation to the United States. The Hawai-

EXCERPTS FROM THE QUEEN'S APPEAL

I, Lili'uokalani of Hawai'i . . . do hereby protest against the ratification of a certain treaty . . . I declare such a treaty to be an act of wrong toward the native and part-native people of Hawai'i, an invasion of the rights of ruling chiefs, in violation of international rights both toward my people and toward friendly nations with whom they have made treaties, the perpetuation of the fraud whereby the constitutional government was overthrown, and, finally, an act of gross injustice to me. . . .

Perhaps there is a kind of right, depending on the precedents of all ages, and known as the 'Right of Conquest,' under which robbers and marauders may establish themselves in possession of whatsoever they are strong enough to ravish from their fellows. I will not pretend to decide how far civilization and Christian enlightenment have outlawed it. But we have known for many years that our Island monarchy has relied upon the protection always extended to us by the policy and the assured friendship of the great American republic.

If we have nourished in our bosom those who have sought our ruin, it has been because they were of the people whom we believed to be our dearest friends and allies. If we did not by force resist their final outrage, it was because we could not do so without striking at the military force of the United States. . . .

It is enough that I am able to say, and with absolute authority, that the native people of Hawai'i are entirely faithful to their own chiefs, and are deeply attached to their own customs and mode of government; that they either do not understand, or bitterly oppose, the scheme of annexation. . . .

ian national flag, an amalgam of the American flag and the British Union Jack created in an early stroke of goodwill to both nations, was torn down from 'Iolani Palace, and the American flag was raised.

Lili'uokalani and her retinue patiently awaited an overruling of the coup by the American government, and after a three-month on-site review by President Grover Cleveland's commissioner, Cleveland himself declared the incident a "lawless occupation of Honolulu under false pretexts by United States forces."

Six thousand miles away from Washington and surrounded by vast ocean, the annexationists thumbed their noses at orders from the president to restore the Hawaiian monarchy. The American government eventually gave up and moved on to more pressing business. In 1894 (on July 4, no less), the annexationists announced themselves leaders of the so-called Republic of Hawai'i. A year later, when a group of Hawaiians was found to be plotting reclamation of Hawai'i, the deposed queen was implicated without proof and imprisoned in the very palace that was once her home. Soon after, by decree, English-language instruction replaced Hawaiian in every public and private school.

With the arrival of the Spanish-American War in 1898, the United States began to fully recognize the geographically strategic value of mid-Pacific islands. By this time President William McKinley had replaced President Cleveland in office. He agreed to sign a treaty of annexation without the consent or vote of the Hawai'i public, despite a petition demonstrating that 95 percent of the Hawaiian population was against annexation. Although the treaty failed in the Senate, the annexationists managed to get approval through a joint resolution, which required only a simple majority of both Houses of Congress. In 1900 Hawai'i officially became a territory of the US.

Citizens of Hawai'i became citizens of America, governed by the US Constitution and represented by one nonvoting congressman in Washington, DC. American military defense outposts appeared across the landscape, and Hawai'i's governors and judges were to be appointed by the White House, rather than by Hawai'i's people.

Queen Lili'uokalani's son, Prince Jonah Kūhiō, would eventually serve as a Washington delegate and earn respect among the people for championing Hawai'i and rebuilding ethnic pride. His greatest legacy is the Hawaiian Homes Commission Act, intended to redress the Hawaiian people's loss of land for farming.

FROM AMERICAN TO AMERICANIZATION Shortly after the turn of the century, young Mainlander James Dole arrived in the Islands and opened a one-man pineapple operation that was to further stoke American business, power, and wealth in Hawai'i. By 1922 Dole had purchased the entire island of Lāna'i and controlled vast tracts of land on other islands, including O'ahu, where pineapple fields stretched for miles. As the Great Depression hit, however, sales stalled; Castle & Cooke swooped in, eventually making yet another fortune from the acquisition and increasing their empire. Pineapple remained Hawai'i's second biggest industry through the 1940s.

In addition to the explosion of new industries, Hawai'i's social climate was in great flux. World War I had diverted bulk cargo from the Islands, slowed sugar exportation, and sapped the developing tourism industry. However, when the war ended Hawai'i entered what some describe as a golden age of urban expansion, musical proliferation, sophistication, and romance that masked racial divisions in schools, workplaces, and society in general. Once Hawai'i was well established as "America," it became vogue. Visitors and new residents from the Mainland flooded Honolulu. Movie stars lounged on Waikīkī Beach, the internationally broadcast local radio program *Hawai'i Calls* turned Island performers such as Hilo Hattie into household names, and life in the former Hawaiian kingdom assumed the appearance of American life more than ever before.

Along with enthusiasm for an Americanized Hawai'i both on the Mainland and in the Islands themselves, many residents were increasingly asking for statehood, which had been officially sought by Hawai'i legislators since 1903. If this seems like a surprising turnaround, recall that by the early 20th century, the ethnic Hawaiian population was a small minority; immigrants from around the world, many of whom had come to Hawai'i to build more economically advantageous lifestyles, constituted nearly 80 percent of residents. They perceived Hawai'i's American territory status as having numerous disadvantages, such as political and economic instability and "second fiddle" respectability. And few believed Hawai'i could do anything but move forward.

Sentiments on the Mainland, however, reflected concerns that Hawai'i was too lawless, too racially diverse, too non-Caucasian, and, because of growing labor unionization, too communistic to become a state. Several bills were introduced in Congress that would strip Hawai'i of any self-governing capacity at all. One of the key factors in altering Mainland perception of Hawai'i and opening the doors to potential statehood was the bombing of Pearl Harbor during World War II.

SHIRLEY TEMPLE ON WAIKĪKĪ BEACH, 1930S

Courtesy Hawai'i State Archives

JAPAN ATTACKS "Air raid Pearl Harbor. This is not a drill." These words are etched in history, a stark reminder of Japan's successful December 7, 1941, attack on Pearl Harbor and other military bases across O'ahu. That day, Hawai'i was brimming with nearly 50,000 stationed US military men and women (a number that would jump to a quarter million by 1945); at Pearl Harbor nearly 100 American battleships, destroyers, submarines, cruisers, and minesweepers were berthed near countless rows of military aircraft. Although the Pacific arena as a whole was on guard for potential enemy strikes, it came as a complete surprise when more than 300 Japanese attack planes converged in two waves upon on the island, ripping open US ships and damaging or destroying almost all the US planes. In billows of black smoke, the battleship USS *Arizona* alone took 1,177 men to the bottom of the bay, where it remains to this day.

Miles away, near the pineapple fields of O'ahu's central plains, shells dropped from the sky into backyards where children played. Chinatown restaurants and sidewalks blew apart, killing and injuring civilian men, women, and children. Placid beach scenes outside of Honolulu were broken as Japanese midget submarines surfaced. A state of emergency was issued, and by afternoon martial law had been enforced. Approximately 2,400 military personnel were dead and 1,200 wounded; 70 civilians were killed, with many more injured. Later that day the United States declared war upon on Japan in response to the attack.

Hawai'i was rapidly transformed from a beach paradise into a landscape of barbed wire, camouflaged building towers, and blackened windows. Communications censorship and curfews went into effect. Every child had his or her own gas mask, and some schools remained closed for months. Thousands of civilians fled to the Mainland, and Hawai'i's 160,000 Japanese residents faced heightened discrimination. In a poignant demonstration of their loyalty to the United States, hundreds of Japanese Americans from Hawai'i and the Mainland enlisted in the 442nd Regimental Combat Team and 100th Battalion, both of which were among of the most famous and decorated units of the war. Between 1941 and 1945 nearly a million members of the armed forces would be stationed on or pass through O'ahu, which served as the headquarters for the Pacific theater of war.

THE 50TH STAR A small contingency of Republicans within the Big Five had controlled local politics from US annexation through the mid-1950s. By the 1930s, however, plantation workers, mostly of Asian descent but born in Hawai'i, had begun to challenge Big Five authority through massive strikes and unionization. The strongly Republican landscape shifted further as Island-born Asians fought for the United States in World War II, pursued advanced education, and entered politics. The local Democratic Party became representative of all that the Big Five was not and the voice of the working class, which was the majority of Hawai'i's population.

By the mid-1950s Democrats had beaten Republicans for control of the Islands. Delegates appealed to Washington for statehood, which would grant greater autonomy to Hawai'i than the status of territory and offer more opportunity for diversified growth. In 1959 President Eisenhower signed the historic bill.

DOWNTOWN HONOLULU

Jumbo jet service to Honolulu began that same year, and the number of visitors to Hawai'i jumped by 42 percent. Between 1960 and 1990, visitors to Hawai'i increased from 300,000 to nearly 7 million. More than 140 hotels and 42 "mega-resort" complexes opened, and our state population increased by 75 percent.

On O'ahu, low-rise cottages and walk-ups quickly gave way to hotel and business towers, while quiet farming valleys and steep ridges filled with large-scale planned communities. As tourism overtook defense spending and agricultural production as the state's primary income, Big Five corporations transformed themselves into diversified national and international corporations to keep up with the times, closing plantations behind them.

Despite an increase in prosperity after statehood, Native Hawaiians experienced little trickledown, and resentment toward Americanism still smoldered over issues that for many other residents were in the past. The Hawaiian language was in danger of extinction; Native Hawaiians held the lowest life expectancy in the state; the Department of Hawaiian Home Lands was dismally backlogged in implementing Prince Kūhiō's plan of distributing land to Hawaiian-blooded individuals for homesteading. As the economy continued to strengthen, powerful developers from the Mainland and Japan built golf courses and monolithic resorts along Hawai'i's most pristine coastlines, disrupting ancient burial sites, wildlife habitats, and ancestral homelands, despite protest.

These and other indignities helped stoke the fire for what would come to be called the "Hawaiian Renaissance"—a fervor among many Hawai'i people to reclaim traditional practices and rightful heritage, encouraged by civil rights movements then taking place on the Mainland and abroad. They also eventually contributed to a growing battle cry for independence, ranging from "a nation within a nation" to complete secession from the United States.

When the yen skyrocketed in value in the 1980s, Japan's long infatuation with the Islands played out in the Hawai'i real estate arena. Homes, golf courses, and hotels were scooped up like pebbles on a beach at double or triple their values, pricing many longtime residents out of the market. Homes sat empty for years afterward (including this author's family home), their long-distance owners often only dimly interested in the investments. At one point, 90 percent of foreign-owned assets in the state belonged to Japanese investors. Designer stores in Honolulu began catering exclusively to Japanese visitors and alienating many residents who, despite ethnic and historic ties with Japan, began to feel "second class" in their own town.

When the yen crashed in the 1990s, Hawai'i's market bubble burst. It flattened further with the closure of several military bases (although Hawai'i is still the most militarized state in the country). As California's recession worsened, the last of the large-scale plantations closed. The terrorist attacks of 2001 added to Hawai'i's slowdown and drove thousands of residents to the Mainland to find work in the construction and service industries.

In 2003 renewed Mainland prosperity, a low state unemployment rate, and the revitalization of Hawai'i as a destination contributed to another dramatic spike in Hawai'i real estate prices and development. The median price for a basic family home on O'ahu reached a high note of nearly $700,000 a few years later, with countless homes listed at well above a million dollars and some into the tens of millions, mostly purchased by non-Hawai'i residents from the Mainland and Japan. Our homeless population increased, and our credit card debt rose to one of the highest in the nation.

In 2006 Hawai'i's inflation rate jumped 5.9 percent, more than double the national rate. That year, *Forbes* magazine described Honolulu as one of the most challenging places to live in terms of housing affordability, income, and cost of living.

The economic recession that followed the boom increased our unemployment rate from 3 to nearly 8 percent. In 2009 the Council for Community and Economic Research reported that it cost 66.5 percent more to live in Honolulu on average than elsewhere in the United States. We ranked third in cost of living, two steps below Manhattan. Yet while New Yorkers earned a weekly average of $2,149, Hawai'i workers earned only $801. Poor salaries and high cost of living help explain why many Hawai'i adults still live with their parents and work more than one job.

Despite the so-called paradise tax, most of us are persistently passionate about living in Hawai'i. The latest economic surge came with benefits, including the revitalization of older neighborhoods, an overhaul of Waikīkī, and the opportunity for many of Hawai'i's citizens to benefit from higher standards of living than ever before. We continue to battle against unwanted development, and sometimes we're winning. And an increasing number of Native Hawaiians are stepping into leadership roles in our communities, helping to rebirth not only a Hawaiian sense of place, but also a Hawaiian sense of being.

TRANSPORTATION

O'ahu is more than 2,000 miles from the coastline of America and from South Pacific island groups, and more than 3,500 miles from Japan. Although that means we're the most physically isolated population in the world, you'll feel at the center of it all once you're here.

GETTING TO O'AHU

AIR ARRIVAL FROM NORTH AMERICA About 95 percent of all travelers to Hawai'i choose the skyways for transportation, and most major US airlines fly to O'ahu several times daily. They land at Honolulu International Airport (HNL), about 8 miles from Waikīkī. Large domestic and international carriers include:

Air Canada: 888-247-2262; aircanada.com

Air New Zealand: 800-262-1234; airnewzealand.com

Alaska Air: 800-252-7522; alaskaair.com

American Airlines: 800-433-7300; aa.com

Continental Airlines: 800-523-3273; continental.com

Delta Airlines: 800-221-1212; delta.com

Hawaiian Airlines: 800-367-5320; hawaiianair.com

Japan Airlines: 800-525-3663; jal.com

Qantas Airways: 800-227-4500; qantas.com

United Airlines: 800-241-6522; united.com

US Airways: 800-428-4322; usairways.com

Good air deals and packages can sometimes be found through **Pleasant Holidays** (800-742-9244; pleasantholidays.com) and **CheapTickets** (800-755-4333; cheaptickets.com), which originated in Hawai'i. We also recommend **Expedia** (800-397-3342; expedia.com).

From California, nonstop flights take about five hours; from the East Coast, about ten hours. Ticket prices run the gamut—shop around and book early. During the so-called high seasons of mid-November through April and June through August, as well as major holidays, deals can be harder to find.

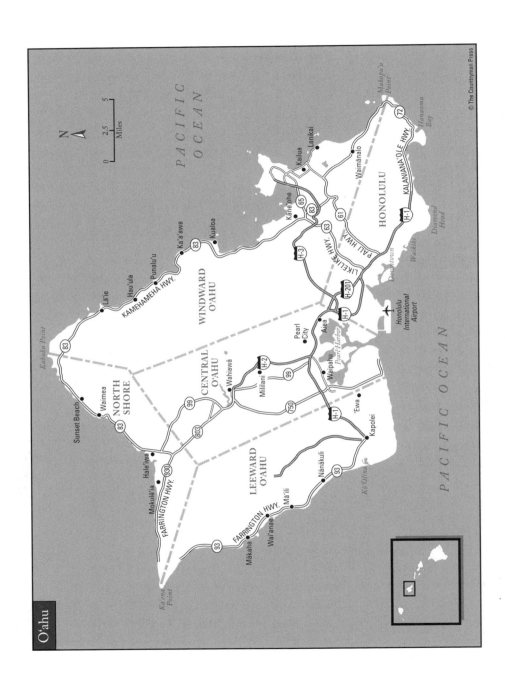

O'ahu

N

0 2.5 5
Miles

PACIFIC
OCEAN

PACIFIC OCEAN

Ka'ena Point

Kahuku Point

Kalaeloa Point

Makapu'u Point

Hanauma Bay

Diamond Head

Waikiki

Downtown

Honolulu International Airport

Pearl Harbor

NORTH SHORE

CENTRAL O'AHU

WINDWARD O'AHU

LEEWARD O'AHU

HONOLULU

Sunset Beach
Waimea
Hale'iwa
Mokulē'ia

Makaha
Wai'anae
Mā'ili
Nānākuli
Kō 'Olina
Kapolei
'Ewa

Lā'ie
Hau'ula
Punalu'u
Ka'a'awa
Kualoa

Kāne'ohe

Kailua
Lanikai
Waimānalo

Wahiawā
Mililani
Pearl City
'Aiea
Waipahu

FARRINGTON HWY.
FARRINGTON HWY.
KAMEHAMEHA HWY.
LIKELIKE HWY.
PALI HWY.
KALANIANA'OLE HWY.

83
83
930
99
803
99
750
93
93
65
63
61
72

H-1
H-2
H-3
H-1
H-1
H-201

Hawai'i's fragile ecosystems mean that bringing agricultural products—even an apple in your bag—is generally not permitted. This protects us from the invasion of foreign microbes, insects, and plants. On the flight over, have a pen handy to complete a form that requests travel data and requires you to report any agricultural products. You'll deal with the latter on your way back as well, when your bags are passed through agricultural inspections at the airport. Returning home with flower lei and pineapples shouldn't be a problem. If in doubt when packing, check with the **HDA Plant Quarantine** (832-0566; http://hawaii.gov/hdoa /Info/doa_importing/traveler).

AIR ARRIVAL FROM NEIGHBOR ISLANDS If you're already in Hawai'i, it's easy to travel to O'ahu or from it. Inter-island flights operate exclusively from Honolulu International Airport at two designated inter-island terminals. The terminal for Hawaiian Airlines flights is connected to the main airport terminal; the terminal for all other inter-island flights is freestanding and located several hundred yards east of the main terminal.

Pricing, destinations, and schedules vary, as do the size of aircraft. You may board a 717 or a tiny prop plane, depending on your destination. Inter-island flight times range from 17 minutes to about an hour. First and last flights of the day and weekend flights can be the most difficult to book, so call in advance. Expect to pay an average of $200 round-trip or more, including taxes and fees.

go! Mokulele: 866-260-7070; mokuleleairlines.com

Hawaiian Airlines: 800-367-5320; hawaiianair.com

Island Air: 800-652-6541; islandair .com

Pacific Wings: 888-575-4546; pacific wings.com

SHIP ARRIVAL FROM NORTH AMERICA Although the days of weekly steamship arrivals in Hawai'i are long past, many cruise lines offer Hawai'i on their itineraries. If you're stopping over for the day in Honolulu you'll be docking at Honolulu Harbor, within walking distance of Honolulu's historic downtown neighborhoods and only a 4-mile taxi ride to Waikīkī. Contact **Holland America** (877-932-4259; holland

america.com), **Princess Cruises** (800-774-6237; princess.com), **Royal Caribbean International** (866-562-7625; royalcaribbean.com), or **Carnival Cruise Lines** (888-227-6482; carnival.com) for information on cruise options.

SHIP ARRIVAL FROM NEIGHBORING ISLANDS Many Hawai'i residents have opposed a large-scale, inter-island ferry system for ecological and other reasons. Thus, we don't have one (those that have tried in the past have failed). **Norwegian Cruise Line** (800-327-7030; ncl.com) offers a seven-day cruise within the Hawaiian Islands aboard its ship *Pride of America*, stopping at O'ahu, Kauai, Maui, and the Big Island. The point of embarkation is Honolulu, however, so you'll still begin your trip here.

GETTING AROUND O'AHU

FROM THE AIRPORT As one of the busiest airports in the United States, Honolulu International features most of the amenities and congestion you'd expect. If you're arriving from the Mainland, shed warm clothing before exiting the plane. At the main terminal, disembarking passengers can board the Wiki Wiki Shuttle for a free lift closer to the baggage claim, although it's only a few minutes by foot.

Transportation options from and back to the airport include shuttles, taxis, limousines and sedans, the city bus, and rental cars. Some hotels may have a shuttle available to pick you up, so ask before you book other services. For general shuttle service to Waikīkī hotels, we recommend the state-approved **Airport Waikīkī Express** (866-898-2519; 954-8652; robertshawaii.com) coach. It stops at the baggage claim median every 20 minutes, 24 hours a day. Cost is about $10 per person one-way. Reservations away from the airport are not necessary, but do call at least 48 hours in advance to schedule a return to the airport. If you're staying at a condo in Waikīkī instead of a hotel, you can still arrange to be delivered to or picked up from the nearest hotel to you.

If you're staying outside Waikīkī, make reservations for a special shuttle pickup at the baggage claim median. Be prepared for significantly higher fares to locations outside Honolulu. Limousine and special sedan services must also be booked in advance.

Taxis are a good alternative both to Waikīkī and within the Honolulu area. Check in with dispatchers at the baggage claim area median and queue up. The cost to Waikīkī is approximately $35. See *Taxis, Sedans, Limos, Vans* in this chapter for recommendations and other details.

The city-operated public transportation system, called TheBus, operates only on the departure-level median. Information on luggage restrictions and fares is also listed later in this chapter, under *City Bus*.

All the major car rental agencies have pickup/drop-off locations at the airport and in Waikīkī and can provide directions to get you to your destination. Airport shuttles can take you to the rental counters.

Hawai'i Super Transit: 841-2928; 877-247-8737; hawaiisupertransit.com

O‘ahu Airport Shuttle: 681-8000; oahuairportshuttle.com
Airport-Island Shuttles: 521-2121; 800-624-9554; shuttleguys.com
Honolulu Airport Express: 226-6668; waikikiairportshuttles.com

MODES OF TRANSPORTATION Renting a car is the best way to experience O‘ahu's beauty and diversity. However, if you'd like to avoid driving, you can use O‘ahu's public bus system, TheBus. The Waikīkī Trolley is also available to take you to Honolulu highlights. Guided Island tours, even some of the smaller out-fits with modest vans, often charge enormous sums to visit sites you can easily reach on your own—although they do have the advantages of ease, keeping you and your belongings secure, and providing interesting histories and facts. We've listed several adventure-tour companies in the "Recreation" chapter.

We suggest not using a bike or moped as a mode of travel outside Waikīkī, Kailua, or the North Shore, and to definitely pass up hitchhiking (which is illegal on highways). A reasonably fit person can easily explore the breadth of Waikīkī entirely on foot, but will still need a lift to most other destinations.

RENTING A VEHICLE In Hawai‘i your best bet is to rent a low-key, modestly sized passenger car with good gas mileage. Our gas prices are some of the high-est in the nation, and flashy vehicles don't impress outside of town and even bring unwanted attention. Frequent rain showers and the searing Hawaiian sun negate some of the fun of convertibles and jeeps; and since most of the people driving them are visitors, they help identify you as a tourist and increase your risk for a break-in.

O‘ahu's traffic has crushed many a starry-eyed traveler expecting quaint tropical roads from a vintage postcard. Honolulu is a modern city filled with people going to work, taking the kids to piano lessons, visiting the dentist, shopping, and beachgoing—all by car. And although it has the same roadway density as other large American cities, the number of cars on the roads has skyrocketed, and twice as many people are forced to share its limited lane miles. It can be hard to accept the reality of bumper-to-bumper traffic in a place so beautiful, but try not to let it ruin your vacation.

All of the big rental car players have locations in both Waikīkī and at the airport, and shuttles to the airport lots pull up at the median outside the baggage claim. Be sure to compare prices and book before you arrive—prices vary significantly and great deals abound, especially online. All of them can direct you to roadside emergency assistance and set up vehicles for disabled drivers (with advance notice). Make sure they give you an O‘ahu *Drive Guide* magazine at car pickup. It contains excellent Island maps to help you get around.

Disabled drivers or passengers: Bring your handicapped parking placards from the Mainland, along with official proof that the placard belongs to you. The placards will be honored anywhere on the island. Visitors with physical disabili-ties may prefer to call **Access Aloha Travel** (545-1143; 800-480-1143; access alohatravel.com), a local travel agency that can rent you a wheelchair-accessible van and ramp.

If you dream of renting a Ferrari or other exotic vehicle and cost is no object, call **Luxury Rentals** (222-2277; hiluxurycarrentals.com), 2025 Kalākaua Ave., Waikīkī.

If you prefer the wind in your hair, rent a motorcycle for a country cruise. In Waikīkī check out **Big Kahuna Rentals** (924-2736; 888-451-5544; bigkahuna rentals.com), 407 Seaside Ave. They also rent mopeds and bicycles. See *Biking* in the "Recreation" chapter for more information on traveling by bicycle, more places to rent bicycles, and bicycle adventures.

Alamo: 877-603-0615; alamo.com

Avis: 800-321-3712; avis.com

Budget Car & Truck Rental: 800-527-0700; budget.com

Dollar Rent A Car: 800-800-4000; dollarcar.com

Enterprise Rent-A-Car: 800-736-8222; enterprise.com

Hertz: 800-654-3011; hertz.com

National Car Rental: 888-868-6207; nationalcar.com

Thrifty: 800-847-4389; thrifty.com

DRIVING IN HAWAI'I Show your aloha while here by driving "local style." Ease up on the gas pedal; invite others to merge in front of you or pass you; wave "thanks" when offered any courtesy on the road; avoid tailgating; honk only in urgent situations; stop for pedestrians (required by law); resist giving "stink eye" to bad drivers; and drive especially carefully in the country, where chickens, dogs, kids, coconuts, and deep potholes can be plentiful. Sightseeing down most remote rural roads is often seen as an invasion of privacy and is not recommended. Signs that say KAPU mean "keep out."

Seat belts are mandatory at all times for front-seat passengers; children under 18 must be belted in backseats. Children ages 4 through 7 must use a safety or booster seat unless they're more than 4 feet, 9 inches tall, or if the vehicle has lap-only seat belts in the rear seats. Driving with more than 0.08 blood-alcohol content is illegal. Cell phone use is also illegal, unless you're using a hands-free device.

Never leave valuables in your car, especially at beach parks and hiking areas, where break-ins are common.

UNDERSTANDING LOCAL DIRECTIONS Getting to O'ahu is easy. Finding your way around can present more of a challenge. Nearly 85 percent of our street and place-names are written in the Hawaiian language, seeming to always begin with a *k* and end with *a*.

Learn how to pronounce major highways you'll likely travel. These include Kalaniana'ole (kah-lah-nee-ah-nah-OH-leh), Kahekili (kah-heh-KEE-lee), Kamehameha (kah-meh-hah-MEH-hah), Likelike (lee-keh-LEE-keh), Pali (PAH-lee), and Farrington (that's an easy one!). In Waikīkī the three main through-roads are Kalākaua Avenue (kah-lah-KOW-ah), Kūhiō Avenue (koo-HEE-oh), and Ala Wai Boulevard (AH-lah-WHY).

O'ahu has four freeways: H-1, H-2, H-3, and the Moanalua Freeway (H-201/78). When it comes to freeway exit numbers, highway numbers, or mile markers, however, residents are clueless—we use road names and landmarks instead.

We combine them with the local directional terminology *mauka*, "toward the mountains" or "on the mountain-side of . . ."; and *makai*, "toward the ocean" or "on the ocean-side of . . ." In the Honolulu area, we also add *Diamond Head* or *'Ewa* to send you in these respective general directions.

Here's an example of how these all work together: "Go Diamond Head on H-1 to the Kāhala exit. Turn right just past the mall then left on Pueo. Look for our yard sale on the makai side of the street."

CITY BUS O'ahu's award-winning bus system **TheBus** (848-5555; thebus.org) stops at most of O'ahu's main attractions and beaches islandwide, although it often runs on "Hawaiian time." Nearly every bus in service is wheelchair-accessible, and all are air-conditioned and equipped with front-load bike racks. Luggage of airline carry-on dimensions are allowed (one per person), but must fit under your seat or in your lap. Although surfboards are not permitted, bodyboards are welcome.

PARKING IN PARADISE

Parking your car in Honolulu (and especially in Waikīkī) can be a challenge. Most hotels charge between $10 and $25 per day for guests to lodge their vehicles, with public lots in Waikīkī and downtown easily running up to $30 per day or more. Many restaurants and shops will validate or even valet park for free if you're visiting their establishments. Call your destinations to find out what they offer before heading out. Most meters—but not all—are free on Sundays and holidays. Keep quarters handy.

Eastern Waikīkī's best metered and free street parking is found at **The Honolulu Zoo**, 151 Kapahulu Ave., and around the enormous **Kapi'olani Park**, although they're long walks from central and western Waikīkī. In central Waikīkī, try the **Aston at the Waikīkī Banyan** (922-0555), 201 'Ōhua Ave., for excellent daily and weekly flat rates that include "in and out" privileges. The garage entrance is just off Kūhiō Ave. In western Waikīkī, park at the **Bank of Hawai'i Waikīkī Center**, 2155 Kalākaua Ave., and request the flat day rate.

In downtown, park at **Ali'i Place** (522-1285), 1099 Alakea St. Rates are per hour, cash only; on weekends, the moderately priced garage offers a great flat-rate deal. Or try the meters at **'Iolani Palace**. In Chinatown the "Smith-Beretania" **Chinatown Municipal Parking**, 1170 Beretania St., location is cheap and convenient, but bustling.

In Kailua, a public lot off **Aulike Street** offers three-hour metered blocks of time. Street meters and other free business lots are also plentiful.

Printed schedules are in stores and kiosks in Waikīkī and elsewhere, or call TheBus seven days a week for route assistance. Exact change in either coins or bills is needed for the $2.50 adult ($1 seniors and disabled adults, $1.25 ages 6–17) one-way fare, and must be paid at the front door upon boarding. Request a free two-hour transfer to switch buses. Visitors can also purchase a pass good for four consecutive days on TheBus for about $25 at ABC Stores in Waikīkī and at Ala Moana Center.

The following are a few key visitor-friendly routes to get you up and riding right away.

Buses 19 and 20 run about every half hour between the airport and Waikīkī, stopping at shopping meccas Ward Centers and Ala Moana Center, as well as downtown, on the way. The 20

CHINATOWN STREET SIGNS COMBINE ENGLISH, HAWAIIAN, AND CHINESE.

continues to the Pearl Harbor site hub as well.

The 8 and 13 travel the length of Waikīkī up to the zoo. The 2 does also, but instead of ending at the zoo, it circles Kapiʻolani Park. The 2 and 13 will also take you to downtown from Waikīkī. The 8 circles you between Ala Moana Center and Waikīkī.

Bus 22 travels between Waikīkī and Hanauma Bay; Routes 55 and 52, known as the "Circle Island" buses, depart Ala Moana Center for three-hour journeys that take in Windward Oʻahu, the North Shore, Central Oʻahu, and Chinatown/downtown. They return to Ala Moana.

THE WAIKĪKĪ TROLLEY If you have limited time, plan to pack a lot into your day, and don't care about appearing touristy, you might want to use the open-air **Waikīkī Trolley** (593-2822; waikikitrolley.com), DFS Galleria Ticket Counter, 330 Royal Hawaiian Ave., Waikīkī.

The four trolley lines stop at major attractions and hotels throughout the Honolulu area, including Bishop Museum, Hanauma Bay, Ala Moana Center, Sea Life Park, Diamond Head Crater, and the Honolulu Academy of Arts. You can jump on and off any of them as much as you want. One-day tickets cost $30 for adults, $20 for seniors, and $14 for ages 4–11. The four-day pass is a much better value at $52/$31/$20.

TAXIS, SEDANS, LIMOS, VANS Let someone else worry about the driving! Grab a cab or even hire a luxury sedan or limousine for special occasions.

TOWN AND COUNTRY

O'ahu has two states of mind: Town and Country. When we say "town," we mean the Greater Honolulu metropolitan area, including extended urban suburbs like Pearl City. When we say "country," we mean just about everywhere else on the island, except for a few non-rural bedroom communities like Mililani, Kailua, Kāne'ohe, and Kapolei, which float in the netherworld.

In town, anything goes day or night, from bare feet to pink stilettos. Outside town, the flashy look is frowned upon. Country's more "local style": old-model Toyotas with surf racks, backyard lū'au, homegrown chutney mangoes, T-shirts advertising local plumbing or plate-lunch businesses, dogs and kids riding in the back of the truck, run-down family markets, rubber slippers, spear fishing, auntie hanging out the wash, Budweiser and Primo beer (in the can). Of course, you might see all that in town, too. And that's just the way we we like it.

Taxis are readily available at major tourist hubs, like in Waikīkī and at Ala Moana Center, but may otherwise be difficult to find. Meter rates are city-controlled and set at $3.10. Additional charges accrue at $3.20 for every mile you travel. For service from the airport, cross to the median outside of baggage claim and speak to the dispatcher on duty.

Arrange any other type of transportation service in advance, including limo transfers to and from the airport. Costs are usually calculated by the hour, with a minimum charge. Many companies not only provide you with vehicle and driver, but also offer custom tours all over the island.

TheCab: 422-2222; thecabhawaii.com

Charley's Taxi & Tours: 531-1333; charleystaxi.com

Elite Limousine Service: 735-5159; 800-776-2098; elitelimohawaii.com

Carey Hawai'i Chauffeured Services: 572-3400; 888-563-2888; hawaiilimo.com

COMMERCIAL TOURS We're choosing to *not* promote large-scale tour companies in this book. Why? Because most of us know how annoying it is to be at a lovely beach, quiet lookout, or local food joint and suddenly have 40 strangers charge off a coach and swarm in. We also think your Hawai'i experience will be less personal (and perhaps less authentic) on large tours. Therefore, we recommend you consider small-scale adventure tours. Please see the "Recreation" chapter for our suggestions.

ON FOOT Honolulu's most interesting neighborhoods are walkable. These include the greater downtown area and Waikīkī. Be sure to press crosswalk buttons to activate walk signals or you might wait until the end of time to cross. See *Historic Walking Tours* and *Food Tours & Classes*, both in the Greater Honolulu chapter, for walking tour ideas.

CLASSIC "SCENIC O'AHU" DRIVES

"Circle Island" Drive. Take Like Like Hwy. (63) through the Ko'olau Range to the upper Windward Coast, traveling northward on Kahekili/Kamehameha Hwy. In Lā'ie, turn right at the only stoplight for photos at Lā'ie Point. Eat lunch at a Kahuku shrimp shack (try Romy's). Continue along to the North Shore, stopping at beaches and shopping in Hale'iwa. Return via Central O'ahu (99/H-2).

Southeast O'ahu Drive. Exit Waikīkī eastward via Diamond Head Rd., traveling along Kāhala Ave. and Kalaniana'ole Hwy. through Hawai'i Kai. Stop at Hanauma Bay (small parking fee), Lāna'i Lookout, and Makapu'u Point for photos. Continue through Waimānalo, returning to Honolulu via Kailua Rd. After the tunnels, stop at the Pali Lookout via Nu'uanu Pali Dr.

Tantalus/Round Top Drive. Follow directions up Makiki Heights Dr. to The Contemporary Museum for lunch and browsing. Then continue driving upward with the windows down to enjoy forest birdsongs and fragrances. Stop at Pu'u 'Ualaka'a Park for a panoramic city view. Continue in the same direction to wind back down the mountain.

CULTURE

Take a break from the beach and explore Oʻahu's cultural side. In this chapter we point you toward the arts, the bars, the events, and more in Honolulu and around the island, as well as many of our most significant historical sites. Even more details can be found under *To See* and *Entertainment* in each chapter.

One historic destination we highly recommend is **Pearl Harbor**. The *Arizona* Memorial, USS *Missouri*, USS *Bowfin*, and the new Pacific Aviation Museum make visiting this National Historic Landmark an educational and emotionally powerful experience for anyone. Kids will love exploring a real battleship and submarine, too.

Another essential is **Bishop Museum**, a natural history museum housing the world's premier collection of Oceanic cultural artifacts. Combine it with ʻIolani **Palace,** home of Hawaiʻi's last reigning queen. Add a walking tour of the historic downtown area, and you'll come away with a good breadth of knowledge of Hawaiʻi's history and period architecture.

On the subject of Hawaiiana, we suggest you attend an authentic hula or Hawaiian music performance. Waikīkī's hula mound, near the Duke Kahanamoku statue, features hula troupes several nights a week. Call 922-5331 for the schedule. Best bet: Speak with a hotel concierge for the latest schedule of classic Hawaiian performers in Waikīkī and around town. Tell them you'd like to experience musicians like the Mākaha Sons or slack-key guitarist Ledward Kaʻapana, or hula events like the Prince Lot Hula Festival, and they'll know you're looking for the real deal.

If you enjoy Western and indigenous arts and crafts, the **Honolulu Academy of Arts** is an absolute must. This gem of a museum also features an excellent café and gift shop. On the last Friday evening of every month, the house fills with hip happenings for ARTafterDARK.

On the first Friday of every month from 5 to 9 PM, thousands turn out for First Friday, a social event that revolves around independent art galleries in the Chinatown area. Pick up a gallery guide at **The ARTS at Marks Garage** or from HawaiiAlliance.org.

Since 1967 Hawaiʻi's government has required that at least 1 percent of the funds for new public buildings be used to purchase or commission art for public spaces. This was the first such legislation in the United States and it has resulted in a tremendous collection, as well as a more attractive Honolulu. Some of the collection is on display at the **Hawai'i State Art Museum**.

Regarding entry fees to places and events: If you're living in Hawai'i (and have a local ID), always ask if kama'āina rates are available. If you're active military personnel, you may also qualify for a discount. If you're neither of the above, grab a handful of free booklets from Waikīkī's sidewalk racks—they often have coupons. Steer clear of street peddlers with "great deals," which usually involve cheap-quality products or gimmicks.

As always, please call your destination in advance to check on the latest fees and hours of operation. Many close on state and federal holidays, as well as select days of the week.

ARCHITECTURE Like its culture, Honolulu architecture is a summary of many contradictory influences, resulting in what can sometimes amount to visual mayhem. If you haven't been here before, expect a strong, modern skyline rather than the thematic and feminine low-rise grace for which cities like San Francisco are noted. We're a chop suey of Japanese pagodas, Italianesque mansions, art deco government buildings, postmodern skyscrapers, 1950s box structures, and rustic wooden plantation houses, all framed by forested green mountains and sparkling blue sea. Somehow, it works.

THE BOLD LOOK OF HONOLULU'S MODERN ARCHITECTURE

No indigenous Hawaiian homes or structures remain intact on O'ahu. Built mainly of stone and pili grass, the majority were dismantled during a wave of Christian conversion in the 19th century and harvested for building materials into the 20th century. For information on visiting the remnants of several sacred heiau (stone temple sites), check the *To See* listings in each chapter.

O'ahu's Western-style 19th-century buildings can be found in the historic downtown area. The most significant of these include the Mission Houses, 'Iolani Palace, and Kawaiaha'o Church. Island architects Hart Wood, Charles Dickey, Alfred Preis, Oliver Traphagen, and Vladimir Ossipoff designed some of our most memorable 20th-century homes and buildings, including the Moana Surfrider hotel and Gump Building on Waikīkī's Kalākaua Avenue, the Alexander & Baldwin Building downtown, and the USS *Arizona* Memorial at Pearl Harbor. Dickey's Hawaiian-style hipped roof has proved to be an enduring trademark. Other internationally famous architects, such as Julia Morgan and I. M. Pei, have also left their stamps here.

The unique Hawaiian plantation home is prevalent throughout the Islands, although slowly disappearing. These humble, one-story wooden houses typically feature wide roofs with deeply bracketed eaves, plank walls, a square box layout, diminutive rooms, and porch fronts. They're often painted in earthy contrasting tones such as dark green with tan trim and landscaped with mature mango trees, tī plants, and banana. These older homes belonged to—and, in some cases, still belong to—the many thousands of plantation workers brought to Hawai'i over the decades, and thus stir strong nostalgic sentiment in local folks.

Twenty-first-century architecture in Hawai'i continues to pit form against function. Like Manhattan, Hawai'i real estate is always in style, even in a recession. In 2006 the Trump International Hotel in Waikīkī set a world record, selling all 464 units, worth a total of $700 million, in only eight hours—before it was even built! As long as the demand is here, we can expect architecture to respond to the needs of investors. But that isn't the whole story.

Architecture in Hawai'i author Rob Sandler writes that local architecture today "is expressing a renewed emphasis on 'appropriate' designs for indoor-outdoor living. Mediterranean-style masonry structures with tiled roofs, generous eaves, and shady arcades, or Hawaiian-Victorian buildings wrapped in broad lānai are again in favor."

The word *ho'okipa*, lately used in reference to modern architecture and meaning a "Hawaiian sense of place," is more than a new buzzword. It reflects years of reaction against Americanism both in aesthetics and mind—or, one could alternatively say, a re-embracing of Hawaiian values and knowledge. Today some structures, including large public and private buildings, will not break ground without a blessing ceremony conducted by a kahu (traditional Hawaiian priest). A door may be placed on a particular side of a house to allow for ancient warrior spirits to pass through without disruption. At the very least, these actions reveal a new way of thinking about the spaces we occupy.

PARADE PĀ'U RIDER (SEE *SPECIAL EVENTS*)

Check out the *Historic Sites* and *Historic Walking Tours* entries in "Greater Honolulu" to see the most interesting, significant, and inspiring architecture O'ahu has to offer.

CUISINE Food is a central theme of the local lifestyle. Hawai'i's cuisine is as diverse and colorful as our mixed culture, and a tribute to harmonious living.

BASIC FOOD GLOSSARY

Here is the approximate way residents pronounce typical local foods, followed by loose definitions.

adobo (ah-DOH-boh)—both a Filipino dish and a marinating and stewing technique

'ahi (AH-hee)—Hawaiian tuna, including albacore, bigeye, and yellowfin

aku (AH-koo)—skipjack or bonito fish

apple-banana—a small, sweet, firm variety of banana

a'ukū (ah-OO-koo)—swordfish

azuki (ah-ZOO-kee)—sweetened black or red bean (whole or paste)

bento (BEN-toe)—a boxed take-out meal

butterfish—black cod

crack seed—Chinese-style dried fruit (such as plums), seasoned sweet and/or sour

furikake (fur-ee-KAH-keh)—roasted seaweed, salt, and sesame seed flavoring

haupia (haoo-PEE-ah)—coconut pudding

huli huli chicken (HOO-lee)—barbecued chicken turned repeatedly while cooking

imu (EE-moo)—a traditional Hawaiian earthpit oven

kālua pig/pork (kah-LOO-ah)—a salty pork dish baked in an earthpit oven

kampachi (kahm-PAH-chee)—amberjack fish

kau kau (KAOO-kaoo)—a pidgin word meaning "food"

kiawe (kee-AH-veh)—a mesquite-related wood used in barbecuing

kūlolo (koo-LOH-loh)—taro root and coconut cream pudding

laulau (LAOO-laoo)—a packet of taro leaf and meat (often pork or butterfish) baked in an imu

li hing (lee-HING)—a blend of sugar, salt, and five-spice powder often used to flavor snacks

liliko'i (lee-lee-KO-ee)—yellow passionfruit

limu (LEE-moo)—commonly used to refer to seaweed

loco moco (LOH-koh-MOH-koh)—a fried egg/hamburger patty/white rice/gravy dish

lomilomi salmon (LOH-mee)—a salsa-like salted salmon, onion, and tomato dish *lumpia* (LOOM-pee-ah)—a spring-roll-like wrap with vegetables and bits of meat inside

lū'au (LOO-aoo)—now used to refer to a "traditional" Hawaiian feast and celebration

mahimahi (mah-hee-MAH-hee)—dolphinfish (not the mammal!)

malasada or *malassada* (mah-lah-SAH-dah)—a Portuguese ball-shaped doughnut rolled in sugar

manapua (mah-nah-POO-ah)—a steamed, moist bun usually filled with pork

mochi (MOH-chee)—a Japanese steamed rice flour cake

moi (MOH-ee)—threadfin fish

musubi (MOO-soo-bee)—a rice block, often topped with Spam (Spam musubi)

'ōhelo berry (oh-HEH-loh)—a native berry related to the cranberry

'ō'io (oh-EE-oh)—bonefish

okazuya (oh-kah-ZOO-yah)—a traditional Japanese take-out shop

onaga (oh-NAH-gah)—red snapper

ono (OH-noh)—a large mackerel-type fish

'ono (OH-noh)—a Hawaiian word meaning "delicious"

opah (OH-pah)—moonfish

'ōpakapaka (oh-pah-kah-PAH-kah)—blue snapper

phô (FUH)—Vietnamese beef and noodle soup

plate lunch—meat entrée, two scoops of white rice, and macaroni salad

pohā berry (POH-hah)—similar to cape gooseberry

poi (POH-ee)—a starchy, pudding-like main or side dish made from taro root

poke (POH-keh)—a marinated dish, usually of raw and diced tuna or octopus

Portuguese sausage—a garlic-heavy pork sausage, usually served at breakfast

pūpū (POO-poo)—a Hawaiian word used to mean "appetizer"

saimin (sye-MIN)—ramen-style noodles in dashi-flavored broth

sashimi (sah-SHEE-mee)—thinly sliced raw fish, usually tuna

shave ice—a local version of the snow cone (no *d* on *shave*)

shoyu (SHOY-yoo)—soy sauce

soba (SOH-bah)—narrow buckwheat noodles

tako (TAH-koh)—octopus

taro or *kalo* (TAH-roh or KAH-loh)—a tuber plant primarily used to make poi

tī or *kī leaf* (TEE or KEE)—the leaf of the tī plant, used to wrap foods and for other purposes

ulua (oo-LOO-ah)—selected species of crevalle, jack, or pompano fish

CULTURE

✳ Special Events

Below are some of the biggest and best annual events on Oʻahu, organized by month. For those events that are competitions, we assume you'll be a spectator, not participant, and so we post admission fee information based on that fact.

The phone numbers listed below tend to change frequently, as do the months the events take place. For up-to-the-minute calendar listings, check the *Honolulu Star-Advertiser*, the *MidWeek*, or the more "alternative" *Honolulu Weekly*. Online calendar resources include the Hawaiʻi Visitors and Convention Bureau (calendar .gohawaii.com), Hawaiʻi Events Online (hawaiieventsonline.com), and Hawaiʻi Public Radio (hawaiipublicradio.org).

January: **Sony Open in Hawaiʻi** (523-7888; sonyopeninhawaii.com). One of the PGA golf tour's most prestigious stops. Waiʻalae Country Club golf course, Kāhala. Admission.

February: **Chinese New Year Festival** (533-3181; chinatownhi.com). A daylong festival in Honolulu's Chinatown in commemoration of Chinese New Year, culminating with an exciting parade. Chinatown. Free.

March: **Honolulu Festival** (926-2424; honolulufestival.org). Promotes cultural exchange and harmony between Hawaiʻi and Asian-Pacific nations through weeklong events including a hula competition, a craft fair, and performances. It wraps with a colorful ethnic heritage parade through Waikīkī. Ala Moana Center and other Waikīkī-area locations. Free.

April: **Annual Easter Sunrise Service** (532-3720). For nearly 110 years, people of many faiths have gathered for this very special Easter sunrise service, which begins at about 6 AM. Parking is very difficult. National Memorial Cemetery at Punchbowl. Free.

May: **Lei Day Celebration** (692-5118; honolulu.gov/parks/programs/leiday). An event that honors the cherished local ritual of wearing fresh flower lei on May Day. It also includes our unique tradition of a full Hawaiian royal court, plus features some of Hawaiʻi's best entertainers. Kapiolani Park, Waikīkī. Free.

Local Motion Surf into Summer (523-7873). Kick off Memorial Day weekend with Hawaiʻi's largest amateur surf contest, presented by O'Neill. Sandy Beach. Free.

Memorial Day Ceremonies (532-3720). A full event that includes decoration of more than 35,000 graves with flower lei, government dignitary presentations, squadron jet formations overhead, and a 21-gun rifle salute. National Memorial Cemetery at Punchbowl. Free.

June: **King Kamehameha Floral Parade** (586-0333). Ongoing for more than 90 years. Although fewer floral floats appear each year due to budget shortages, the beautiful horseback pāʻū riders, royal court, and multitudes of flowers are still its signature. From the King Kamehameha statue downtown through Waikīkī. Free.

King Kamehameha Hula Competition (536-6540; tickets 800-745-3000; hula comp.com). If you really want to say you've seen hula, attend this multiday event and leave well educated. Blaisdell Arena. Admission.

Pan Pacific Festival and Parade (926-8177; pan-pacific-festival.com). An event that forges closer relationships between Japan and Hawai'i through hula. The weekend includes a ho'olaule'a (block party), a parade, and hula performances. Waikīkī and Ala Moana Center. Free.

July: **Hawai'i All-Collectors Show** (941-9754; ukulele.com). The largest collectibles/antiques show in Hawai'i. Sift through vintage Hawaiiana, plus estate jewelry, old postcards, coins, ivory, baseball cards, and more. Blaisdell Exhibition Hall. Admission.

Korean Festival (koreanfestivalhawaii.com). A bustling and colorful event with Korean foods, dance, and more in honor of Hawai'i's many Korean and Korean American residents. Kapi'olani Park, Waikīkī. Free.

Prince Lot Hula Festival (839-5334; mgf-hawaii.org). Immerse yourself in traditional Hawaiian crafts, hula dancing, and games. The setting is gorgeous and the attendees mostly residents. Moanalua Gardens. Admission.

WHAT IS "LOCAL" CULTURE IN HAWAI'I?

People in Hawai'i are proud to be "local," or distinctly different from folks on the Mainland. Ask a longtime resident to define what that means, and a long list unfurls.

A virtual emblem to our lifestyle is the rubber slipper, which conjures images of eternal summer, a relaxed attitude, simplicity, humble beginnings, and Asiatic influences. We wear slippers with pants or dresses, to school and to weddings. We always remove them before entering a home. If you see mountains of slippers in front of a doorway, you can guess a good party's inside!

Another very local feature is our unique dialect, which is a product of history, isolation, and mixed ethnic backgrounds. We call it "pidgin," but most linguists call it Hawai'i Creole English. If you hear someone say, "Howzit, brah!," you've heard pidgin.

Other classic customs? We eat white rice with almost everything; dance hula; wear aloha shirts to work; eat Spam musubi for breakfast; surf, race outrigger canoes, spearfish, or hunt wild boar; call anyone older than ourselves "auntie" or "uncle"; live with three or even four generations of our family; and, yes, we really do give flower lei to one another in celebration of birthdays, graduations, or other special events.

Most residents, though, would probably sum up local culture with the phrase *living with aloha*—in other words, living each day with respect, love, and gratitude for others and for our Island home.

August: **Bayfest Hawai'i** (254-7679; tickets 800-745-3000; bayfesthawaii.com). O'ahu's biggest summer extravaganza, with major fireworks exhibitions, carnival rides, live bands like the Black Eyed Peas, and more. Marine Corps Base Hawai'i, Kāne'ohe. Admission.

Duke's OceanFest (545-4880; dukefoundation.org). Celebrating the birthday of ultimate surfer boy and ocean enthusiast Duke Kahanamoku. The weeklong series of competitions includes events like paddleboarding, canoe racing, longboard surfing, tandem surfing, and ocean swimming, and it wraps with a block party. Kūhiō Beach, Waikīkī. Free.

Hawaiian Slack Key Guitar Festival (226-2697; slackkeyfestival.com). Showcasing Hawai'i's unique slack-key style of guitar playing. Roll out the beach blanket and listen to masters of the art perform all afternoon. Kapi'olani Park, Waikīkī. Free.

'Ukulele Festival (732-3739; http://roysakuma.net/ukulelefestival). Check out some of the best 'ukulele players in the world, along with Hawai'i's favorite entertainers. See why we love this little instrument and how it can shine. Kapi'olani Park, Waikīkī. Free.

September: **Aloha Festivals** (391-8714; alohafestivals.com). A multiday, multievent celebration of Hawaiian culture dating back more than 60 years. Highlights include a ho'olaule'a (block party) in Waikīkī and a parade full of Hawaiian-style pageantry from Ala Moana Park to Waikīkī. Free.

FOURTH OF JULY

Okinawan Festival (676-5400; okinawanfestival.com). It kicks off with a parade through Waikīkī and ends with a huge festival featuring stage performances, food booths, and *bon* dancing. Kapiʻolani Park, Waikīkī. Free.

October: **Louis Vuitton Hawaiʻi International Film Festival** (528-4433; hiff.org). Considered by many to be one of the best film festivals in the United States. Film selections focus on Asia, the Pacific, and North America. At selected Honolulu theaters. Admission.

Men's Molokaʻi to Oʻahu Canoe Race (http://molokaihoe.org). Local, national, and international teams race against one another in Hawaiian-style outrigger canoes across the rough, 40-plus-mile ocean channel from Molokaʻi to Oʻahu. A Hawaiʻi tradition in which residents take special pride. Duke Kahanamoku Beach, Waikīkī. Free.

November: **Mission Houses Museum Holiday Craft Fair** (447-3910; mission houses.org). In our opinion, the most charming and tasteful holiday fair on the island. Authentic Hawaiiana and artisan crafts include handmade wooden bowls, glass ornaments, jewelry, and Hawaiian feather lei hatbands sold by the artists themselves. Mission Houses Museum. Free.

World Invitational Hula Festival (486-3185; worldhula.com). Your last big chance of the year to get schooled in the art of hula. Troupes from around the world perform both ancient and modern styles. Waikīkī Shell, Waikīkī. Admission.

December: **Honolulu City Lights** (honolulucitylights.org). A good old-fashioned family tradition that centers on an enormous dose of Christmas-themed decorations and lights. The celebration kicks off the first weekend of the month with a parade and the official lighting of Honolulu Hale's holiday tree. Take an evening tour of the lights via trolley, antique fire truck, or horse-drawn carriage. Downtown Honolulu at Honolulu Hale. Free.

Honolulu Marathon (734-7200; honolulumarathon.org). Watch nearly 30,000 entrants from Ethiopia to Shanghai battle the 26-mile course. Ala Moana Park to Hawaiʻi Kai, ending in Kapiolani Park, Waikīkī. Free.

ALOHA FESTIVALS FLORAL PARADE

THE EDDIE AIKAU BIG WAVE SURF INVITATIONAL

BEYOND THE CENSUS: A RAINBOW OF PEOPLE

Hawai'i's modern culture is unique and colorful, resulting from centuries of immigration and intermarriage among peoples mostly from Oceania, Asia, and North America. Even today immigration is at a fever pitch: Nearly 25 percent of our current population was born not only outside Hawai'i, but also outside of the United States. As you might then guess, about half of Hawai'i's marriages occur between residents of differing ethnic backgrounds, and more than 20 percent of residents are of "mixed" ethnicity—compared with less than 3 percent nationwide. We're very proud of this. If someone tells you he or she is Chinese, Hawaiian, Japanese, Filipino, German, Samoan, and Portuguese, you can believe it.

During your stay, you may encounter terms of identification that have morphed beyond the grasp of a dictionary. None of them are considered by most residents to be derogatory by definition—it just depends on who uses them and how!

First of all, you might hear the word *haole*. All it really means today is "Caucasian." *Kama'āina* is used commercially to distinguish state residents from visitors, often for the purpose of price breaks, and to indicate born-and-raised residents (often of haole background) whose families have a long history in the Islands. *Malihini* refers to newcomer residents, or those who act as if they're "fresh off the boat." All people who live in Hawai'i are

Pacific Handcrafters Christmas Fair (254-6788; http://pacifichandcrafters guild.com). An excellent guild show featuring handcrafted treasures on sale by the artists themselves. Collect quality woodcrafts, pottery, glass items, and much more. Thomas Square. Free.

Vans Triple Crown of Surfing (637-2299; triplecrownofsurfing.com). One of the most prestigious surfing competition series in the world. Events include the Vans Hawaiian Pro, O'Neill World Cup, and Billabong Pipeline Masters, plus several women's events. Be sure to call ahead—the competitions stop and start according to surf conditions. It begins in November, but most events take place during December. Hale'iwa, Sunset Beach, and Banzai Pipeline, North Shore. Free.

Quiksilver in Memory of Eddie Aikau Big Wave Surfing Invitational (http://surf.quiksilver.com/events/index.aspx). An elusive, non-annual invitational surfing competition that opens in December then waits through February for winter waves to stabilize at 30-foot face heights or more. It's bigger than its name. If you're lucky enough to be here when it happens, go. Waimea Bay, North Shore. Free.

called Hawai'i residents; but only the approximately 20 percent of residents who claim Hawaiian ethnic heritage can also correctly be called Hawaiian, Native Hawaiian, or Kanaka Maoli. And although *Native Hawaiian* has found its place in the vernacular, referring to residents as "natives" is never appropriate.

Another subtly confusing term is *local*. Old-timers sometimes use it to describe "real Island-style," naturally darker-skinned residents who may appear to be ethnically Hawaiian—even if they aren't. *Local* can also be used as an adjective to signify anyone for whom Island customs are so ingrained that he or she cannot help but follow them, as well as in reference to authentic Island living and lifestyles. It can even jokingly refer to something that has been done or made in a very laid-back, homemade, amateur style instead of "Mainland professional."

Though perhaps not politically correct, in Hawai'i we often use ethnic background and "localness" as a way to describe ourselves or affectionately poke fun at one another. Some of the most beloved Island comedians have based their routines on caricaturizing the hilariously endearing interplay among Hawai'i's cultural groups. A classic skit recording still available in stores is Rap Replinger's *Poi Dog*, and *Pidgin to da Max* is a must-have "dictionary" that implicates every ethnicity in Hawai'i in its comic exploration of local language use and diversity.

HAWAIIANS TODAY It may sound dully obvious or even trite to say that in Hawai'i, we live within a Hawaiian culture—but the multicultural layers of modern life here often obscure this fact. We're talking about something more than the "mahalo" at the supermarket or giving lei at graduation ceremonies. Those are but minor notes of a much deeper rhythm that many Native Hawaiians, as well as perhaps others who've lived in Hawai'i for generations, feel just below the surface.

Yet even today, when traditional Hawaiian practices are experiencing a revival, the question is still being asked by Native Hawaiians in academia as much as by the visitor on the street: What does *Hawaiian* mean? Is it a blood quantum, a cultural history, a connection to a place, a state of mind? What does it mean to be Kanaka Maoli (Native Hawaiian) in the 21st century? Although we have no answers for you, we do believe that you're interested in learning about Hawaiian culture and that we might serve as a first bridge for your exploration.

Below we present several core elements considered classically Hawaiian and how they manifest in today's world (if at all). We hope this chapter will inspire you to see Hawai'i and its people in a new way and to learn more. For a short list of recommended reading, please see "Information."

GENEALOGY

I am a Native Hawaiian, he Kanaka Maoli, 'ōiwi maoli au. This is a simple enough assertion, the meaning of which is as clear as water when it springs from the rock. I belong here, not just to the land but to the other Kanaka Maoli of this 'āina, and they belong to me. . . .

Many think that asserting our Nativeness is merely about claiming entitlements. Having identified themselves with America, most residents of Hawai'i do not understand that our self-definition as Hawaiians has little to do with trying to gain political and economic advantage over them. It has everything to do with kinship. In the same way, our goals have much less to do with resources than with inheritance, even less to do with money than with dignity.

WINDWARD O'AHU TARO FARM

—University of Hawai'i at Mānoa professor Jonathan Osorio from his book, Dismembering Lāhui: A History of the Hawaiian Nation to 1887

About 20 percent of Hawai'i's 1.3 million people, or about 250,000 of our residents, are Native Hawaiian. According to the 2006 Native Hawaiian Data Book, another 160,000 Native Hawaiians live on the Mainland, with more than 60,000 in California alone. After a radical decline in the 1800s the number of Hawaiians is growing; and although 99 percent of today's Native Hawaiians are of mixed heritage, a Hawaiian bloodline is highly valued.

Scientifically speaking, ethnic Hawaiians are a branch of the greater Polynesian family, which includes Maori, Samoan, Tongan, Marquesan, and Tahitian. They, in turn, may have originated in Southeast Asia or Indo-Malaysia, settling Polynesia 3,500 years ago or more. It's believed that Marquesans were the first to inhabit the Hawaiian Islands, followed by Tahitians; today's Native Hawaiians are the descendants of these groups of people. Their contact with Tahiti seems to have ended as early as the 1200s, leaving Hawaiians in isolation until the arrival of Western explorers in the late 1700s. Estimates made both then and recently suggest the population count of Hawai'i was anywhere between 300,000 and 1 million.

Various oral chants describe Hawaiian genealogy and cosmology. The most cited is the Kumulipo, a 2,077-line chant that stretches from the creation of lower life-forms and the spirit world to the world of living men and specific family lineage. Genealogy and kinship are central to traditional Hawaiian life; like ancient Egyptians, the ali'i (high chiefs) traced their lineage to gods themselves. Some genealogy chants account for 40 different generations, back to Tahitian chiefs of a millennium ago. Several relate that the "father and mother" of Hawaiian people, or perhaps of all people, are Wākea, god of light and the heavens, and Papa, goddess of the earth and the underworld.

THE HISTORIC POLYNESIAN SAILING VESSEL *HŌKŪLE'A* RETURNS FROM TAHITI.

LAND *"Ua mau ke ea o ka 'āina i ka pono"*—"the life of the land is perpetuated in righteousness." These were King Kamehameha III's words upon the restoration of the kingdom of Hawai'i after a brief coup in the name of Britain in 1843. It's safe to say that when he spoke of 'āina, or "the land," he meant something of much greater significance than the return of "property." The Hawaiian people considered themselves related to the land, and the concept of mālama 'āina, caring for the land, was ingrained in their spirit. Traditional Hawaiians were animists— that is, they believed spirits existed in the wind, rocks, water, fish, and other animate and inanimate creations of nature. In Hawaiian culture, nature was not something that could be owned.

In pre-contact times, each Hawaiian island was divided into moku (districts). Within each moku were a series of typically triangular-shaped ahupua'a—land divisions—extending from mountain crestlines to beyond the reef. The name of one ahupua'a was Waikīkī; it stretched from today's Waikīkī beachfront all the way into Mānoa Valley. The ahupua'a system united various ecosystems into a complete, sustainable unit of resources that all shared. The king and chiefs were stewards for the resources and people on it, who worked the land—but the system differed in many ways from Europe's feudal system. During Makahiki, a festival period lasting about four months each year, all unnecessary work was disbanded, including the planting of crops.

In 1848, under pressure from foreigners in the kingdom who felt disadvantaged by the traditional land system, King Kamehameha III enacted legislation called the Great Mahele. This slowly divided the landscape. A million acres of land were directed into the king's possession, although they could be sold, leased, or mortgaged at will. Called the Crown Lands, they became part of the public domain upon annexation of Hawai'i. The Mahele established 1.5 million acres of land as Government Lands, intended to produce revenue for the operation of the government. Some of this land was sold to foreigners or Caucasian residents of Hawai'i to help with expenses. Another 1.5 million acres became Konohiki Lands, under the control of chiefs.

LIMITED LAND MEANT LIMITED RESOURCES FOR HAWAIIANS.

Courtesy Hawai'i State Archives

Hawaiian commoners were invited to stake claims upon the lands they currently resided on, but the system was so foreign to them that many did not step forward. By the time the offer was withdrawn, fewer than 10,000 Hawaiians had been granted deeds on a total of 30,000 acres, called the Kuleana Lands.

Those Hawaiians who did claim land found that without the ahupua'a system, little could be done with it. Their small plots did not necessarily include fishing rights, access to irrigation, or use of grazing pastures. Many eventually abandoned their land and—not knowing what do without it, either—attempted to eke out urban livings in Honolulu. By 1936 records show that only 6 percent of Kuleana Lands were still owned by Hawaiians.

Foreigners and naturalized Hawaiian citizens, who fully understood the value of purchased land in a Westernized economy, went quickly to work to obtain as much as possible. A mere four years after the process of distribution began, no less than 16 members of the Congregational Mission held an average of 500 acres of prime lands each—many of which are still owned by their descendants today and worth countless millions of dollars.

In 1920—more than 70 years after the Great Mahele took place—Prince Kūhiō established the Hawaiian Homes Act in order to offer a total 200,000 acres of land for homesteading and cultural revival for modest prices to Hawaiians of any blood quantum. At the time, 22,500 Hawaiians still existed, down from 80,000 during the Mahele. Non-Hawaiians, concerned over losing acreage to Hawaiians, pressured Kūhiō to require applicants to possess at least 50 percent Hawaiian heritage—a standard they hoped few would eventually be able to meet as the race died away.

The program exists essentially as it was drawn in 1920. Despite Kūhiō's noble intentions, it has been abysmally managed, with only 7,200 leases awarded in 85 years; many people died long before their names were ever called. As of 2004, the waiting list held more than 20,000 names. In the last several years, the department has been working hard to rectify the outrageous lag.

RELIGION AND THE KAPU The religious system in which Hawaiians once lived infused every aspect of life with spiritual value, from fishing to hula to sacred births.

Four main gods, also worshipped in other areas of the Pacific, were primary in this belief system: Kū, Kanaloa, Lono, and Kāne. Kū is commonly described as the god of war; heiau dedicated to Kū could call for human sacrifice. Kanaloa was called the god of the ocean. Lono was considered the god of peace, agriculture, and fertility, as well as of other natural elements. Kāne was the procreator, the provider of sunlight, water, and life substances. These four gods, in turn, were multiplied into many forms; they could even appear as humans and take part in earthly living.

Numerous lesser gods, as well as demi-gods, also populated Hawaiian life. These include well-known gods such as Pele, goddess of the volcanoes; Laka, goddess of hula; and Kamapua'a, a pig demi-god. Even today, selected gods are honored; Pele, for example, is given offerings to curb her fury.

'Aumakua, or "ancestor gods," were often relations no longer living. They took

Courtesy BIVB

HAWAIIAN REFUGE PU'UHONUA O HŌNAUNAU, ON THE ISLAND OF HAWAI'I

the shape of a lizard, shark, owl, or other animal and worked to help their descendants. Some Hawaiians today still honor their 'aumakua through private communication, as well as through respect for animal forms they take.

The kapu or taboo system was a central layer of fabric intertwined with the greater Hawaiian perception of the world, including religion. Often described simply as a strict code of laws, the kapu revolved around the concept of pono—righteousness, "rightness," and balance within the greater cosmology. Kapu implied sanctity, danger, and things off-limits. Certain stones, bones, trees, or even names could be kapu. If a kapu was broken, it could upset the natural order. Someone could be put to death for breaking kapu in events as seemingly simple as a woman eating a banana or a man's shadow falling upon the cloak of a great chief.

However extreme it sounds today, the system was meant to protect the people, rather than punish them. And there was a loophole for kapu breakers. If the offending citizen could manage to reach a designated pu'uhonua, or "place of refuge," he or she would earn sanctuary and pardon within its walls. In Kona, on the Big Island of Hawai'i, you can visit a beautifully restored pu'uhonua. O'ahu had at least one pu'uhonua as well.

In 1819 King Liholiho and several high chiefesses dared to challenge the kapu system. Forty years of Western influence in the Islands were bearing down upon tradition; and they had heard that in Tahiti, the kapu had been recently broken. When Hawai'i's ali'i openly defied the kapu and witnessed no discernible punishment from the gods, the crack that had been forming gaped wide open. That same year, New England missionaries arrived as if on cue to replace the kapu system with Christianity.

HAWAIIAN LANGUAGE Languages are much more than words; they're fluid data banks of unique cultural knowledge. The Hawaiian language belongs to the Polynesian language family. Traditionally an oral language only, missionaries in the 1820s grafted it onto a Latin alphabet to enable Hawaiians to read the Bible. Ironically, this action helped preserved what would soon become a dying language. Because of their efforts, we have thousands of samples from early post-contact years exemplifying communications in Hawaiian.

On the other hand, the choices missionaries made in interpreting Hawaiian have also meant some language information has been lost. For example, the missionaries waffled as to whether they were predominantly hearing a *v* or a *w*, an *1* or an *r*. The letters *w* and *1* won, although historical information suggests the truth might lie somewhere in between. Without the use of diacritics in early writing, we have also lost the correct pronunciations and meanings of a number of words.

Use of the Hawaiian language fell into steep decline in the late 1800s, and in 1896, after Hawai'i was annexed by the United States, English was designated the primary language of instruction in every school. Speaking Hawaiian became shameful, or only for private family communication. A 1983 survey estimated that out of more than 1 million Hawai'i residents, only 1,500 people still spoke Hawaiian at home; most of them were elderly, and many native speakers lived on the isolated island of Ni'ihau.

With the resurgence of ethnic pride, Hawaiian is "back in business." It shares a place with English as an official language of Hawai'i, and the number of second-language speakers of Hawaiian is on the rise. More than 30 Hawaiian immersion charter schools now teach only in Hawaiian, and they pair language learning with intensive Hawaiian cultural learning. At the University of Hawai'i's Mānoa and Hilo campuses, students can now major in or pursue graduate degrees in Hawaiian studies and the Hawaiian language, and programs are packed with participants from Hawai'i, the Mainland, and abroad.

ARTS AND CRAFTS "Pre-contact" Hawaiians possessed advanced skills in many crafts, including house building, outrigger-canoe building, mat and basket weaving, rope making, wooden bowl carving, net making, cloth making, feather work, jewelry making, and more. The volcanic Hawaiian Islands contained no metals, so the people used bones, teeth, woods, hair, shells, stones, plants, and other natural materials to create everything they had.

One of the crafts in which Hawaiians excelled over other Pacific cultures was barkcloth, called kapa (also tapa). Only women were permitted to make kapa, which requiring stripping and soaking bark from selected trees and beating it with progressively grooved and patterned wooden implements of infinite designs. Some kapa was worked until it was as light and pure as lace; many were grooved as if they'd been ironed into patterns, and most were dyed or block printed in reds, browns, blacks, and various other shades and color combinations. The making of kapa required a great deal of time and effort, and the end products were treasured goods that served as shoulder cloaks, wrap skirts for women, and loin-cloths for men, as well as bedding covers.

We have intact examples today of Hawaiian feather work, including capes, cloaks, and helmets created for the ali'i. Several are on display at Bishop Museum in Greater Honolulu. Capes and cloaks, called 'ahu'ula—or "red garment," a symbolic color for gods and high chiefs throughout Polynesia—were made of red feathers from both the native 'i'iwi and 'apapane birds. Rare yellow feathers from the 'o'o and both yellow and black feathers from the mamo provided contrasting colors. A yellow cloak once belonging to King Kamehameha I, now in the possession of the museum, is estimated to contain no less than 450,000 feathers tied in tiny bunches to a fine mesh framework. These artifacts were considered extremely valuable in traditional times and are priceless today.

It's easy to find newly made traditional handcrafts at fairs or high-end shops. The most common include handmade wooden bowls, bone pendants, and shell lei, as well as post-contact, missionary-era-style crafts such as Hawaiian quilting.

FISHING AND FARMING As you would expect from a seafaring people surrounded by water, Hawaiians were absolute masters of everything related to the ocean, from swimming and diving to surfing, canoeing, and fishing. Fish (and other seafood) of all kinds made up a large part of traditional diet, and were caught through a variety of methods: spear fishing, fishing by hand, fishing with a slip noose, net fishing, fish stunning, and fishing with a hook and line. One of the most interesting and enduring methods Hawaiians devised, however, was the fishpond.

Hawaiians built larger and more fishponds than any other Pacific culture. Ponds still standing today are of varying ages, with some 800 or more years old. The typical fishpond was built along a coastline, sometimes at the mouth of fresh water. Rock walls up to several thousand feet in length created an enclosure, punctuated by sluice gates. The gates permitted small fish to enter, but were crafted to prevent them from leaving once fattened.

The southern coast of Moloka'i once had more than 70 fishponds. Many still remain and are being brought back to life by students and other dedicated volunteers. Kauai's Menehune Pond is legendary for its beauty and construction. On O'ahu, prominent fishponds are still visible on the Windward Coast.

Agriculture was central to the Hawaiians' way of life, and their knowledge of and skill in growing taro, sugarcane, sweet potato, coconuts, breadfruit, banana, and other plants was tremendous and laden with ritual. In Hawai'i, taro in particular was a central element of life; in fact, taro is said to be the ancestral older sibling of the Hawaiian people. Recent attempts by the University of Hawai'i to experiment with the genetic modification of taro met with protest and outrage.

Today tending a taro patch, or lo'i, is becoming more common as the demand for poi and the desire to learn traditional ways increase.

HULA is probably Hawai'i's most recognizable and celebrated cultural treasure, although it has long been misunderstood and caricatured by the West. Dances performed by men and women unfolded tales that honored the gods as well as the ali'i, and were accompanied by offerings and prayers to the goddess of hula, Laka.

MOKOLI'I FISHPOND

During much of the 19th century, missionary disapproval of hula kept the practice underground, until King Kalākaua encouraged its revival toward the end of the century. At that time, modern styles of hula were born that incorporated tī-leaf and grass skirts, melodious music, and a lighter attitude that appealed to visitors and suited festivities.

Hula in old Hawai'i was accompanied by chanting, or *mele*—a word that in modern times has come to mean chanting and singing both, as well as song. In Old Hawai'i, melody and meter served more to assist chanters in recalling lengthy chants that recounted genealogies, battles, tales of love, and other histories and beliefs, which hula helped to convey in bodily form. Melodic hymnals introduced by Western missionaries profoundly shaped the future of Hawaiian music.

In the 1970s Hawai'i experienced a tremendous resurgence in interest in both traditional (kahiko) and modern ('auana) styles of hula, as well as in modern Hawaiian music—a broad category that includes everything from slack-key guitar to hapa-haole vintage songs to falsetto singing. Nowadays it seems everyone takes hula (or even "hulacise"), and hālau have spread across the Mainland and Japan. But hula is a serious business; it's an art form that requires years of study under the training of a kumu hula (master). It's a way of life.

HAWAIIAN GOVERNANCE IN THE 21ST CENTURY Hawai'i has been an American state since 1959, with two senators and two representatives serving us in Washington. A semi-autonomous and controversial government body, the Office of Hawaiian Affairs (OHA), was created in 1978, instilled with the mission of "righting" all types of injustices to, and creating opportunities for, the

THREE KUMU, ON HULA

In 2010 the Hawai'i State Art Museum held a beautiful exhibition: Ho'oulu, the Inspiration of Hula. Among other displays, walls were lined with photos of many of the 20th century's most important kumu hula, or hula masters/teachers, with personal stories. We extracted a few of their comments to give you an idea of the role of hula in Hawaiian culture even today.

> Robert Cazimero: *"Hula is the art of Hawaiian dance, expressing everything we hear, see, smell, taste, touch, and feel."*

> Keli'i Taia: *"My approach was to show that hula was physical and demanding, and required dedication and learning."*

> Louise Beamer: *"In our family, hula is a way of life. . . . It has never been a question of choice but commitment to our culture."*

To go deeper into the world of hula and for additional resources, visit the Hula Preservation Society at HulaPreservation.org.

SACRED HULA AT 'IOLANI PALACE

Courtesy HTA/Tor Johnson

Hawaiian community. Residents disagree, however, on whether OHA does too much for the people (its existence has even been challenged in court), or too little.

The trustees of OHA, the local and federal governments, Hawaiian advocacy groups, activists, and students continue to debate the subject of new political structures that could restore Native Hawaiians' rights as self-determining people, and what would be legal, practical, and desirable. Possible solutions have ranged from a "nation-within-a-nation" status to complete independence from the United States—an idea particularly fueled by the US government's official apology to Hawai'i in 1993 for its role in what it acknowledged as an unrightful usurpation of a sovereign nation in 1893.

One of OHA's tasks is to encourage ethnic Hawaiians from all over the world to "kau inoa," or register their names with OHA, so they may one day participate in the reshaping of Hawaiian governance.

A bill that has garnered heavy media attention in Hawai'i and on the Mainland for more than a decade is the Native Hawaiian Government Reorganization Act (also known as the "Akaka Bill"), reintroduced in 2009 after failure to win over Washington in previous sessions. The bill would accord a process of reorganization and U.S. federal recognition of a Native Hawaiian governing entity. Hawai'i residents themselves have been hotly divided over it, with concerns ranging from reverse racism to disappointment in its willingness to compromise. As of late 2010, the bill had passed the U.S. House and was awaiting a vote from the Senate.

To hear Native Hawaiian community leaders discuss a broad range of subjects impacting Native Hawaiians today, tune into KKNE AM 940's 6:30–9 AM daily radio broadcast *Nā 'Ōiwi 'Ōlino* (People Seeking Wisdom), launched by OHA in 2006. OHA's Web site, oha.org, features extensive information and news updates, as well as an online version of its Hawaiian topical newspaper, *Ka Wai Ola*.

Our local PBS station and other local cable channels (see "Information") also frequently run quality programming covering Hawai'i's complex political, social, and cultural issues.

Another excellent introduction to Hawaiian culture is the documentary *The Hawaiians: Reflecting Spirit*, by Edgy Lee (2006). Her Web site (PacificNetwork.tv), billed as "the Native Hawaiian portal to the world," is chock-full of educational Island news, stories on Native Hawaiian issues, and beyond.

RECREATION

Hawai'i is an "outdoors" kind of a place. Warm weather, rippling ocean waves, and soaring green mountains are the perfect ingredients for a year-round active lifestyle. In fact, on the whole, Hawai'i's population is one of the fittest in the United States, and we have the longest life spans. Now's your chance to soak up the same energy forces. Try some outdoor adventures, like kayaking to sea islets, or indoor adventures like a tī-leaf body wrap in a luxury spa, and you'll return home glowing inside and out.

Please remember that we all play a role in Hawai'i's future. Some activities, even those mentioned in certain other guidebooks, may not be healthy for our environment—or even entirely safe for you. With this in mind, we've done our best to only include high-quality, conscientious, local-oriented activities and vendors in this chapter. We encourage you to let any guides or operators you do book with know that you're in support of authentic and respectful practices.

In this chapter we dig deeper into a variety of Hawai'i-style activities, plus recommend outfits that provide quality adventures across the island. Be sure to also check out the locale-specific adventures described under *To Do* in each chapter of the book.

AIRPLANE & HELICOPTER RIDES Try viewing Hawai'i from the air for a new perspective on Pearl Harbor, remote mountain peaks, hidden waterfalls, and spectacular coastlines. Unless otherwise indicated, the operators below take off from small strips surrounding Honolulu Airport. Be sure to ask for directions. Each outfit can fly you over any region of the island; some will even fly you inter-island.

Islandwide Service
Blue Hawaiian Helicopters (831-8800; 800-745-2583; bluehawaiian.com), 99 Kaulele Pl., airport area. Blue Hawaiian operates across Hawai'i and has a great safety record. They fly "quiet technology" Eco-Star helicopters over sights and landmarks of O'ahu, and have provided service for studios filming in the Islands. Purchase a video of your aerial adventure when you land.

Island Seaplane Service (836-6273; islandseaplane.com), 85 Lagoon Dr., airport area. Years of flying experience and an excellent safety record make this company a great choice for a seaplane trip. The owner, Pat Magie, was named National Seaplane Pilot of the Year in 2000 and has flown planes in television shows, commercials, and films. Take off from the waters of Honolulu Bay for an air tour of major Island sights.

Makani Kai Helicopters (834-5813; 877-255-8532; makanikai.com), 130 Iolani Pl., airport area. This locally owned tour operator features six-seat helicopters and has several O'ahu tours to choose from, including flights over Hanauma Bay, waterfalls, and the North Shore. Flight times range from 30 minutes to an hour. They can also offer customized inter-island trips, including to Kalaupapa on Moloka'i, wedding packages, and charter excursions.

Paradise Helicopters (293-2570; paradisecopters.com), Turtle Bay Resort, 57-091 Kamehameha Hwy., Kahuku. These guys are located out on the North Shore, which allows you to choose a short flight and still see lots of countryside. Their four-seat helicopter cruises waterfalls and valleys along the Windward Coast as well as the North Shore, town, and the central plains. They can take the doors off for better viewing, and headsets enable you to communicate easily with the pilot and other passengers.

SAILING OFF WAIKĪKĪ

Stearman Bi-Plane Rides (637-4461; peacock.com/biplane), Dillingham Airfield, Hanger B6, Mokulēi'a. Be an original—suit up in a leather helmet and goggles for a North Shore or Pearl Harbor air tour in one of two fully restored, open-cockpit biplanes dating from 1941. If your stomach's strong, you can do full rolls and more. All pilots are also licensed commercial airline pilots. Located on the North Shore.

BIKING Despite traffic and poor bike lanes, O'ahu does offer decent recreational biking, including both beach cruising and mountain biking. In Waikīkī, try Kapi'olani Park, following Kalākaua Ave. up and over Diamond Head Road. Kailua is generally bike-friendly as a whole, and renting a beach cruiser to in fact cruise to the beach is a fun idea (lock it up, though!). On the North Shore, the ultimate "beach cruiser" path is a bike and pedestrian lane that winds the coastline from Sunset Beach to Waimea Bay. There are some good mountain trails on the North Shore, too, which your bike rental facility can tell you about. TheBus system features bike racks on the front of every bus so you can haul your bike where you like. Contact the **Hawai'i Bicycling League** (735-5756; hbl.org) if you need more information, are looking for bike route maps, or want to find out about the league's weekend rides.

For guided bicycle adventures in exotic settings around the island, call **Bike Hawai'i** (734-4214; 877-682-7433; bikehawaii.com), owned by John Alford, who also authored several good books on mountain biking in the Islands. Adventures include dirt mountain biking on scenic private ranchland and other trips that combine biking with hiking, sailing, or snorkeling. You can even arrange for a private, more intensive trail ride.

BODYBOARDING, STAND-UP PADDLING, & SURFING Bodyboarding (also called boogie boarding) is fun, high energy, and easy for even kids. The foam boards are extremely buoyant and attach to your ankle by a tether. With a pair of fins, you can kick fast enough to catch the lip of a wave and propel forward for a fantastic ride, belly-down. Rent a board and fins up and down Waikīkī Beach, or at one of the several shops we mention in regional chapters. In Waikīkī try the beginner- and intermediate-level breaks at the Kūhiō Groin, where Kalākaua Ave. meets Kapahulu Ave. On the Windward side try Waimānalo Bay State Recreation Area.

If you haven't yet heard, stand-up paddling is the new hot thing. It reportedly started right here on O'ahu in the 1960s, with Waikīkī beach boys who found it easier to monitor and photograph their surfing students while standing on their boards. Stand-up paddleboards have much larger dimensions than regular surfboards and come equipped with, you guessed, it, a paddle. You paddle while standing on the board, easing along for the fun of easing along, and maybe catching a small wave or two. It's more of a workout than it appears. Find rentals and lessons on Waikīkī Beach and almost everywhere surfboards and other ocean equipment are available. See the shop listings in individual locale-specific chapters.

If you're serious about stand-up paddling and want an experience to write home about, head over to Ala Moana Regional Park weekdays and ask the lifeguard if China Uemura's around. A guru of stand-up paddling and a surfing legend (if it's July, he'll be busy with the annual China Uemura Longboard Surfing Classic competition, in Waikīkī), China gives free stand-up paddling advice—and a *free lesson*—to anyone. If you're lucky enough to be one of his students, be sure to proffer a million thanks.

And then there's the granddaddy of Hawai'i water sports: surfing. Ancient Hawaiians invented surfing, and it was one of their favorite pastimes. Waikīkī even once had a heiau, or temple site, at which you could pray for good waves. But like many traditional activities, by the early 1900s it had nearly died out in the wake of Westernization. Then along came Waikīkī beach boy and Olympic medalist Duke Paoa Kahinu Mokoe Hulikohola Kahanamoku—"The Duke"—who helped popularize surfing worldwide and gave it the touch of glamour it retains today.

O'ahu is the ultimate destination for surfing, as well as the unofficial headquarters of the surfing world. On the North Shore in winter, many of the sport's biggest stars can be spotted on the waves or grabbing a bite at unobtrusive lunch wagons. More than 1,700 named surf areas exist across the state. Some were named for old landmarks, like "Publics" in Waikīkī, which recognized the public baths that once stood just onshore; others, like "Himalayas" and "Slaughterhouse" on the North Shore, characterize area wave height or behavior—or what might happen to you!

In the last 15 years surfing has really caught on worldwide. It seems every visitor to Hawai'i now wants to learn to surf, and surf schools have sprouted up on every corner. With it, lesson prices have skyrocketed, large student groups have replaced private tutoring, and already crowded surf spots have become virtually unmanageable. Some spots are unofficially considered "locals only," and you'll feel it if you try to invade, especially as a beginner. If you take a lesson, ask for the scoop on where you can continue practicing afterward—that is, places easy to surf and out of the way of the regulars. Waikīkī Beach is still one of the easiest spots to learn and the most tolerant to visitors in training wheels. Try the surf breaks in front of the Moana Surfrider hotel and Kūhiō Beach.

Below we list outfits that offer surf lessons and even surf camps for kids and adults in more than one area of the island, or that can transport you from Waikīkī to their "secret spots." We highly recommend them all. Additional recommendations are listed in regional chapters, including where to rent your own board.

Islandwide
✪ **Girls Who Surf** (371-8917; girlswhosurf.com). This chick-founded surf school teaches all levels of surfing and ocean knowledge to the entire family. Transportation and equipment are included, and all instructors are lifeguard,

DAD AND SON HIT THE WAVES.

CPR, and first-aid certified, as well as licensed to teach by the state. Group and private lessons are available in Waikīkī, in the Leeward area, or on the North Shore; or you can just rent surfboards from them.

◒ **Hawaiian Fire** (737-3473; hawaiianfire.com). Let a member of the Honolulu Fire Department teach you surfing and water safety on a secluded beach with gentle beginner waves and no crowds to worry about. Both group and individual lessons are available, and all equipment, as well as transportation from and back to Waikīkī, is included.

◒ **Hans Hedemann Surf School** (924-7778; hhsurf.com). Pro surfer Hans Hedemann has two surf school locations on Oʻahu—one in Waikīkī and one at Turtle Bay Resort on the North Shore—from which his trained instructors lead group and individual lessons. You can also take bodyboarding or stand-up paddling lessons, sign up for a surf camp, rent a board, or take private lessons with the master himself.

CLASSIC SURF FILMS

Big Wednesday (1978)
A primarily fictional account of the lives of three California surfers dealing with issues of the era, such as the Vietnam War. Features high-quality surf cinematography of top pros.

Blue Crush (2002)
Three surfer girls battle life and the waves of the North Shore. Fictional, but with surprisingly genuine lifestyle details alongside some corny story elements. Goes way beyond Gidget to inspire a generation of female surfers.

North Shore (1987)
A cult classic about a surfer from Arizona trying to make it on the North Shore. A homespun 1980s film, but with plenty of heart—as well as many of the day's top surfers both behind it and in it. The director did a great job capturing local life.

Riding Giants (2004)
An excellent documentary chronicling the history of surfing, and in particular big-wave surfing. Awesome footage.

Step into Liquid (2003)
An insider's exploration of the real world of surfing. *Rolling Stone* calls it "the best surfing documentary ever made." A beautiful film.

The Endless Summer (1966)
An oldie but a goodie, and the ultimate classic surf documentary. Follow two California surfers as they circle the globe in the quest for the perfect summer wave.

CAMPING Camping on Oʻahu is common and coveted among extended local families, some of whom, until restrictions in recent years, would seem to spend entire summers living under makeshift tarps at Windward beach parks. In our opinion, having grown up around those parks, it's a modern extension of traditional village life and a major way people here bond.

You might imagine, then, that camping in Hawaiʻi would be very different in style and mind-set than it might be at some Mainland campgrounds. Here's a snapshot of a possible scenario: Up early to go spear fishing, unchain the pit bull companions to run loose around the grounds, perhaps smoke a bit of pakalōlō, and fire up the hibachi. It's a private realm that's very "un" Frisbee games and Patagonia equipment, and not always welcoming to outsiders.

So: Although you *can* camp at many beach parks on the island, we've restricted the lists we provide in each chapter to only the most safe and welcoming-to-tourists sites—which happen to be some of the most beautiful sites, too. If you're up to the experience, it could very well turn out to be the most wonderful aspect of your visit. (PS: A six-pack or freshly cooked burgers go a long way in making new campground friends!)

Camping site permits range from free to about $20 per night, and a five-night maximum stay is typical. Each location has different regulations and requirements; be sure to call as far in advance as possible for information on how you can arrange your stay. Some permits can be arranged online.

Contact the **Department of Land and Natural Resources** (587-0300; hawai istateparks.org) regarding camping at state parks. County parks across the island are under the jurisdiction of the **City and County of Honolulu** (768-3003; honolulu.gov/parks).

Bring all your own equipment or buy it locally. At the time of writing (as well as for some time prior), nobody offers rental camping gear on Oʻahu.

CANOEING & KAYAKING Even in the excitement of riding a wave, kayaking or outrigger canoeing can be a calming, spiritual encounter. Today's kayaks are stable, relatively lightweight, and manageable for anyone with moderate upper-body strength and a touch of determination. Oʻahu doesn't have any significant rivers to comb, so kayakers cruise the coastlines in one- or two-seaters.

In Hawaiʻi outrigger canoeing is more than a sport—it's been a way of life for thousands of years in the Pacific. The only canoe form historically used in Hawaiʻi is the outrigger canoe, which features a balancing arm connected to the boat by two beams, keeping it upright even against strong waves. Knowing how to paddle an outrigger canoe well is a quick way to earn respect in the Islands; many kids and adults are members of paddling teams.

In Waikīkī check in with the beach boys at the 50-year-old **Waikīkī Beach Services** (542-0608; waikikibeachservices.com), Outrigger Waikīkī, 2335 Kalākaua Ave., located on the beach in front of the hotel. They offer outrigger canoe rides most of the day. Booking in advance is a good idea. They're also found on the beach in front of the Outrigger Reef (352-2882), 2169 Kalia Rd.

Hawaiian Oceans Waikīkī (306-4586) offers canoe rides. Visit their shack on Kūhiō Beach near the Duke Kahanamoku statue. With both outfits, you'll be expected to help paddle.

CATAMARAN & SAILING EXCURSIONS Spend a couple of hours off the sand and on the water. Sailing off the coast is so much fun, and it offers a beautiful view of our island. In Waikīkī you can do it surprisingly cheaply. Along Waikīkī Beach you'll find at least four catamarans pulled up onto the sand and loading passengers up for a ride (the trips often also include dudefest vibes and flowing drinks).

You can also book a more formal, traditional sailing excursion through charters—an incredible adventure you'll never forget.

Islandwide Services

Hawai'i Sailing Yachts/The Sailing Club Hawai'i (222-9768; 800-908-5250; hawaiiansailingcharter.com; http://hawaiiyachts.com), 350 Ward Ave., Kaka'ako. The ultimate experience! Charter a licensed yacht or sailboat from the same company that has provided service to presidents and celebrities. They have the largest fleet of private boats in Hawai'i and full crews, and can take you wherever you want to sail within the Islands, for as long as you want. They can even connect you to land with special high-end car services, to the air by private jet, and other treatments.

Royal Hawaiian Catamaran (593-9993; royalhawaiiancatamaran.com). For a high-end Hawai'i adventure, book a shared or private charter on this lovely, 52-foot, custom-designed yacht. Rent her for the day, the week, or the month and direct her wherever you please.

DOLPHIN-, SHARK-, & WHALE-WATCHING If you've fantasized about swimming with dolphins, you're not alone. Entire organizations are dedicated to the spiritual healing that this experience can reputedly bring. Hawaiians recognized the power of dolphins as well and considered them a form of mighty Kanaloa, god of the sea.

Four species of dolphin are typically found in Hawai'i: Pacific bottlenose; rough-toothed; spotted; and spinner. None is considered threatened or endangered, but they've all been gradually changing their habits in response to encroaching human activity. The National Marine Fisheries Service (NMFS) advises people to keep at a distance of 150 feet or so from wild dolphins. This does not mean, however, that the dolphins cannot come to you—and they sometimes do, curious creatures that they are. Outfits on the North Shore and Leeward side do a good job combing for pods without being too invasive. See those chapters for details.

If you must actually touch a dolphin, as opposed to just being near one, consider **Dolphin Quest O'ahu** (739-8918; 800-248-3316; kahalaresort.com), Kāhala Hotel & Resort, 5000 Kāhala Ave., Kāhala. For a hefty fee you'll get right into the hotel's lagoon and interact with its resident Atlantic bottlenoses. Even though it's not in the wild, for many it's still an incredible experience.

From November through March or early April, more than 5,000 humpback whales loll about in Hawaiian waters. They swim several thousand miles from Alaska, bask in the warmth of the lower latitude, mate, and give birth before trekking all the way back with babies in tow. The 1,400-square-mile **Hawaiian Islands Humpback Whale National Marine Sanctuary** helps to protect these still-endangered 45-foot-long creatures. Although the gargantuan humpbacks are local stars, Hawai'i also has sperm whales, Hawaiian pilot whales, and Hawaiian melonhead whales in its waters.

Maui has some of the best whale-watching in the state, but you can often spot whales off O'ahu from Diamond Head, Turtle Bay Resort, and Makapu'u Point, as well as on a whale-watching boat excursion. We've even seen them spouting in Waikīkī just off the Hilton Hawaiian Village. The law requires you to stay at least 300 feet from humpbacks for your safety as well as theirs. See regional chapters for recommended tour operators.

Hawai'i has about 40 different species of sharks, from the 8-inch pygmy shark to the 50-foot whale shark. Eight can be aggressive to humans and are occasionally seen close to shore. But it's the massive tiger shark that perpetrates Hawai'i's extremely rare attacks (out of many millions of dips taken in Hawaiian waters each year, only a few folks get nibbled).

Several well-meaning tour companies have been offering North Shore "shark encounters." Their point of view is that it's educational, which is most certainly true. The opposing point of view, shared by many surfers, area residents, and ocean organizations, is that these outfits are illegally feeding the sharks, disrespecting the animals, and creating a potential problem that will end with increased attacks. These are good points, too. Bills keep coming and going that address these issues.

Recent impact study findings conclude that the potential risk to humans is probably negligible. Still out for debate, however, is whether the practices of the shark tours are ethical, and whether they're hedging feeding laws. Whale tour boats hit several whales every year and dolphin encounter boats disrupt dolphin behavior, so nobody's perfect. The best we can do is to follow the rules, and make nature-viewing choices that are conscientious and low-impact.

See the operators listed in the North Shore and Leeward Coast chapters.

FISHING The Kona Coast on the island of Hawai'i is renowned for marlin fishing and big-name competitions. However, fishing on O'ahu is also pretty good, and there are plenty of deep trenches or coastal regions to explore. Note that the time of year will dictate which fish are available. On sportfishing tours, you might not be permitted to keep what you catch.

You don't need a permit in Hawai'i for basic rod-and-reel ocean fishing or to spend the day fishing from a licensed vessel. You can also let the locals take you wade fishing or boat fishing for smaller game fish.

Islandwide Services

Shoreline Adventures (428-4680; bonefish808.com). Oliver Owens offers customized, personal, nontouristy visitor adventures built around catch-and-release fly- and light-tackle fishing (under 30 pounds) and environmental and cultural awareness. He'll take you all over the island for the best bonefish and other catches. A great choice for a unique experience.

FITNESS Return from your vacation in better health than when you arrived! If you're into walking or jogging, the best places are Kapiʻolani Park and Diamond Head Rd. in Waikīkī, and Ala Moana Park just outside it, next to Ala Moana Center.

For other workouts in Waikīkī, try **24-Hour Fitness** (923-9090; 24hourfitness .com), Pacific Beach Hotel, 2490 Kalākaua Ave. The **Waikīkī Community Center** (923-1802; waikikicommunitycenter.org), 310 Paokalani Ave., features a schedule of creative pay-as-you-go classes such as Big Band dance, gentle yoga, hula, and Okinawan karate. **Yoga Under the Palm Trees** (373-8833) takes place on the grass between the Waikīkī Aquarium and Natatorium on Kalākaua Ave. 8–9 AM Mon. A donation of $7–15 is about right.

Just outside Waikīkī members of the Y can work out, swim, or take classes at the **Central YMCA** (941-3344; ymcahonolulu.org), 401 Atkinson Dr., Ala Moana.

In Kailua, **Bikram's Yoga College of India** (262-6886; bikramyoga.com), 600 Kailua Rd., Suite 205, Kailua, limbers you up in 100-degree-plus yoga rooms. They're also on the North Shore, behind the Waialua Library (637-5700), 67-208 Goodale Ave., Suite 2, Waialua.

If you're visiting Oʻahu with a large group, make arrangements with the ✍ **YMCA Camp Erdman** (637-4615; ymcahonolulu.org), 69-385 Farrington Hwy., Waialua, on the North Shore for use of their ropes courses.

GAMES In Waikīkī, try the unusual ✍ **Big Kahuna's 3D Glow Golf** (924-3030; bigkahunasglowgolf.com), Waikīkī Shopping Plaza, 2250 Kalākaua Ave., open daily. And yes, it is glow-in-the-dark miniature golf.

There's more going on in metropolitan Honolulu. **Aiea Bowl** (488-6854; aiea bowl.com), 99-195 Aiea Heights Dr., Aiea, is far from Waikīkī, but it's the latest cool hangout with great local food. Closer in, head to ✍ **Dave & Busters** (589-2215; daveandbusters.com), Ward Entertainment Center, 1030 Auahi St., Kakaʻako, for outrageous video games, pool, and other games. **Hawaiian Brian's Billiards** (946-1343; hawaiianbrians.com; 1680 Kapiʻolani Blvd., Ala Moana, is within walking distance of Waikīkī, and it's the best pool hall on the island. ✍ **Jungle Fun** (949-4905), Ala Moana Center, 1450 Ala Moana Blvd., Ala Moana, is at the mall, and mostly a kid-oriented video and parlor game room surrounded by a squawking pack of plush animal critters.

In addition to the ideas above, game-heads might check local papers for Scrabble, chess, and backgammon club gatherings.

GOLF Golf has been played in Hawaiʻi since the late 1890s. After statehood in 1959 the sport boomed, and we now have more than 80 courses throughout the

Islands. If you're here in January, get tickets for the famous **Sony Open** (sony openinhawaii.com), a PGA event running for about 40 years at the prestigious (and private) Wai'alae Country Club golf course.

In the 1980s the Japanese discovered Hawai'i's perfect golfing climate, and they arrived in droves to play and open their own courses and clubs. Perhaps because of the number of visiting golfers from Japan, our green fees can be high. The golf courses listed in each chapter include green fees calculated without carts, unless carts are required, for the cheapest time of day or day of the week to play, and for the full course. Call ahead for your tee time and to see what special deals are being offered, especially if you're a resident with local ID.

Want to pick up a set of clubs or even an individual club at a good price? Here's a local secret for used and new equipment both: **Roots & Relics** (538-3311), 249 Merchant St., downtown.

GUIDED ADVENTURES For those who feel that adventures can only be had through independent travel, guided excursions may not be for you. However, one of the advantages is that you'll visit multiple destinations safely and easily all in one day, plus learn some history and enriching facts along the way. Some companies will even take you to spots you wouldn't otherwise find on your own.

There are numerous tour companies on O'ahu, but only a few keep it low-key, environmentally and culturally conscientious, and real. Here are several of the very best. We're sorry to say that this list has thinned since our last edition, with the economy running small-scale ecological businesses into the ground.

We've listed them in alphabetical order islandwide, since all will pick you up wherever you're located and take you around.

Islandwide Services
Annette's Adventures (235-5431; annettesadventures.com). Native Hawaiian O'ahu resident Annette Kaohelauili'i has spent 25 years understanding, interpret-

THE SONY OPEN

ing, and protecting Hawai'i's cultural and natural resources. She's the founder of the Hawai'i Ecotourism Association and also leads trips for the Sierra Club. Annette creates discriminating, custom ecotours for visitors and specializes in birding experiences.

Bike Hawai'i (734-4214; 877-682-7433; bikehawaii.com). O'ahu boy John Alford has written several great books on mountain biking in Hawai'i and has earned a good reputation in the community for his conscientious approach to trail exploration. He and his team lead biking tours, as well as several other low-impact nature adventures, across the island. If you want to do biking off-road, you'll be in the hands of an expert. Bike Hawai'i is recognized by the Hawai'i Ecotourism Association.

O'ahu Nature Tours (924-2473; oahunaturetours.com). This company takes groups of up to 14 at a time in their vans for standard to more original bird-watching trips, hikes, and scenic sightseeing islandwide. Some of their guides were born and raised in Hawai'i; most have degrees in natural sciences, or expertise in mountain climbing and other outdoor sports. The company participates in various projects that help restore natural habitats and is recognized by the Hawai'i Ecotourism Association.

HANG GLIDING, PARAGLIDING, GLIDERS, & ULTRALIGHTS These four activities get the wind in your hair without the distraction of roaring engines.

Almost everyone is familiar with hang gliding, in which you jump from a high point and coast along on the wings of your lightweight equipment. O'ahu's safe hang gliding spot is at the 1,200-foot Makapu'u cliffs, which jut above the ruggedly gorgeous Makapu'u Beach.

The lesser-known paragliding involves parachuting from a high-altitude location and then maneuvering your equipment to float along in the air.

Ultralights are lightweight, small-engine-powered flying machines. You can choose how long you stay in the air and exactly where you'll go.

Gliders (also known as sailplanes) are towed up and then uncoupled for an engine-free ride. Hawai'i is one of the world's best locations for gliding, and views can reach 40 miles distant and farther. All glider planes on O'ahu leave from Dillingham Airfield in Mokulē'ia on the North Shore.

HIKING O'ahu has amazing hikes of all kinds. Because Honolulu is so urban, it's easy to forget that most of the island is rural and mountainous. Even our most popular trails introduce you to bamboo thickets, giant ferns, forest birds, trickling waterfalls, sand dunes, sensual aromas of wild ginger and guava, and sweeping valley or coastal views. The trails and trail systems we've suggested here and in each place-specific chapter are all family-friendly, relatively easy, and generally safe. We also point you to opportunities for more serious hiking adventures.

There are two trail systems we'd particularly like to recommend. In Honolulu, the spectacular and underutilized **Lyon Arboretum** (988-0456; hawaii.edu /lyonarboretum), 3860 Mānoa Rd., Mānoa, has a network of short, easy-to-moderate mountain trails for guided or independent hikes/walks. Wear plenty of mosquito repellent here and prepare for possible rain showers. Open Mon.–Sat.

On the North Shore, ✆ **Turtle Bay Resort** (293-6000; turtlebayresort.com), 57-091 Kamehameha Hwy., Kahuku, also has an underused trail system with about 12 miles of trails winding along coves and grassy beach dunes and through coastal groves. Do not disrupt the dunes, which have historical significance.

Check newspaper calendar listings for upcoming hikes led by the local **Sierra Club** (538-6616; sierraclubhawaii.com), **The Nature Conservancy of Hawai'i** (537-4508; nature.org), or the **Hawaiian Trail & Mountain Club** (htmclub.org). Not only are they knowledgeable about conditions and the environment, but they also have special access to trails normally off-limits to the public.

Serious hikers will want more information than we present in this book. Although not revised since 2000, the undisputed bible of O'ahu hiking is Stuart Ball's *The Hiker's Guide to O'ahu.* He covers more than 50 trails from beginning difficulty to advanced, and in great detail. Maps and trail descriptions are available online through **Hawai'i's Division of Forestry and Wildlife** (587-0166; hawaii .gov/dlnr/dofaw). Information on selected trails is also available online at **Nā Ala Hele** (hawaiitrails.ehawaii.gov), the state of Hawai'i's trail and access system.

Hawai'i is free from many of the creepy crawlies and poisons of the Mainland and elsewhere, with no poison ivy or oak, Lyme disease, malaria-carrying mosquitoes, worrisome snakes, or deadly spiders. If you run into wild fowl or boars, let them pass undisturbed.

KITEBOARDING, PARASAILING, & WINDSURFING O'ahu is one of the world's best windsurfing locales, with Kailua Beach, Diamond Head, and the North Shore reigning supreme. This sport is harder than it looks—but even a beginner can have a good time taking a lesson or two. Serious enthusiasts will have a great time.

The relatively new sport of kiteboarding is exactly what it sounds like: A large crescent-shaped kite pulls you across the water on a board for an exhilarating rush. Kailua is the perfect place to try it.

Although there are several outfits from which you can rent and take lessons, the best is **Naish Hawai'i** (262-6068; naish.com), 155 Hāmākua Dr., Kailua. Robbie Naish grew up on O'ahu, and by the age of 13 had already won an amateur windsurfing world championship. He eventually turned pro and is well respected in the field as both a competitor and a maker of quality boards. He opened his windsurfing school nearly 25 years ago. Rent windsurfing equipment or take lessons. They can also hook you up with kiteboarding.

Parasailing is an activity is in which skydiving and water-skiing meet. You'll head out on the water in a sports boat and be strapped to a parachute that, when the boat speeds up, lifts you as far as 600 feet high into the air. Awesome views abound. You can touch down either in the water or on land. The actual time in the air is short, running 5 to 10 minutes.

SAFETY ON THE TRAIL

Hawai'i has real-life wilderness with unique environmental elements, some of which can pose dangers as well as delights. We'd like to prepare you for safe and happy hiking during your stay, so please heed the following information.

First, stick to marked trails. While stumbling upon a closely guarded pakalōlō field might be unlikely, an off-trail romp could anger a private landowner, set you out on treacherous older trails, place you in the crosshairs of a boar hunter, or get you desperately lost. Rescues are fairly common here, and once in a great while missing hikers are never found.

Hawai'i trails are hikable year-round, but heavy rains can turn valley trails into mud and streams into flash floods. Swimming in local streams and waterfall pools may also put you at slight risk for leptospirosis, a bacterial infection. If you do swim, keep clear of cliff overhangs—O'ahu's porous lava boulders are prone to crumbling, sometimes onto your head while you're waterfall bathing.

Wear sunscreen, especially on coastal hikes. Wear mosquito repellent, too, especially on mountain and valley hikes. Bring plenty of drinking water. If you're parking at a trailhead, leave no valuables in your car. Always hike with a buddy, and leave early enough to complete the trail long before dusk, which falls quickly in the tropics. Clean your shoes before and after the hike to prevent the spread of invasive species. And of course, keep voices soft while on trails and leave nature exactly as you found it.

For parasailing off Waikīkī, contact either **Diamond Head Parasail** (597-8646) or **Hawaiian Parasail** (591-1280), both at 1085 Ala Moana Blvd. in Kaka'ako. Each can pick you up at your hotel and take you out from nearby Kewalo Basin.

SCUBA DIVING & SNORKELING About 2 percent of the world's oceans contain coral reefs, which house a diversity of life second only to tropical rain forests. Coral is made from the calcareous skeletons of thousands of tiny, stinging critters called polyps. Extremely fragile, they require certain conditions to thrive.

More than 500 different kinds of fish—plus turtles, rays, sea urchins, dolphins, whales, seals, sea cucumbers, anemones, hermit crabs, eels, lobsters, snails, octopus and sea stars—thrive in and around Hawai'i's coral reefs. Don't miss the opportunity to see them in their own habitats via snorkeling or scuba diving. You can rent or purchase a snorkel, mask, and fins or book a snorkel trip, which includes all the equipment you'll need. The latter is best if you're uncomfortable in the ocean or new to snorkeling.

To go it on your own, visit one of the beach boy shacks on Waikīkī Beach to rent equipment. Or visit **Waikīkī Diving Center** (922-2121; waikikidiving.com), 424 Nāhua St., Waikīkī.

In Greater Honolulu get rentals at **Snorkel Bob's** (735-7944; snorkelbob.com), 700 Kapahulu Ave., Kapahulu. In Kailua visit **Aaron's Dive Shop** (262-2333; hawaii-scuba.com), 307 Hahani St. On the North Shore head to **Deep Ecology** (637-7946; deepecologyhawaii.com), 66-456 Kamehameha Hwy., Hale'iwa, or **Surf N Sea** (637-9887; surfnsea.com), 62-595 Kamehameha Hwy., Hale'iwa. On the Leeward Coast, get equipment at **Hale Nalu** (696-5897; halenalu.com), 85-876 Farrington Hwy., Wai'anae.

Many of these vendors, as well as most local bookstores and sundry shops, carry marine life identification guides. ABC Stores also sell inexpensive "underwater" cameras.

There are many good snorkeling spots that are also safe. In Waikīkī try the marine conservation zone at Queen's Surf Beach, just past the zoo. In Greater Honolulu you should really visit Hanauma Bay, despite its crowds. Equipment can be rented on site. On the North Shore try Kuilima Cove at Turtle Bay Resort, as well as Sharks Cove at Pūpūkea Beach Park. On the Leeward Coast head to the lagoons at Kō 'Olina Resort. The first and second lagoons are the best for snorkeling. Read more about the above beach sites under *Beaches* in their respective chapters.

For your safety, even at these mild-mannered spots, always snorkel in sight of a buddy. For the safety of the ocean critters, never stand on or touch live coral reef, or kick sand up around it. Human activity has destroyed more than 35 million acres of reef to date worldwide, so let's keep preservation in mind. That goes for fish and other sea life—feeding and otherwise disturbing their habitats are harmful to them.

Scuba diving tours will unfold greater depths of amazing. Beginners can opt for dives in shallow or moderately deep waters filled with thousands of colorful fish. Certified divers can go deeper to explore marine life around sunken ships and World War II aircraft wrecks. Several companies also offer full certification courses that you can complete in a week's time.

We've listed several companies below that offer either snorkeling tours, scuba dives, or, in some cases, both. All visit different sites around the island, instead of sticking to one region. Also see regional chapters for area information. Keep in mind that trips run only when weather conditions permit and, of course, that viewing sea life is an unpredictable endeavor.

Islandwide Service

Aaron's Dive Shop (262-2333; hawaii-scuba.com), 307 Hahani St., Kailua. This 40-year-old company is well known for leading snorkeling and other tour operations islandwide, but their specialty is scuba diving; owner Jack can cite an impressive list of celebrities who have relied on his team for safe dives. They also sell equipment.

Deep Ecology (637-7946; deepecologyhawaii.com), 66-456 Kamehameha Hwy., Hale'iwa. An environmentally conscious organization focusing on scuba dives on the North Shore and around the island. Snorkeling trips are also available. They have an amazing selection of courses and options, from PADI certification to cavern and night diving.

Surf N Sea (637-9887; surfnsea.com), 62-595 Kamehameha Hwy., Hale'iwa. All things surf-n-sea-related happen at this 40-year-old North Shore fixture, from equipment rentals and sales to snorkel and scuba diving trips to Leeward O'ahu or on the North Shore, as conditions permit.

Waikīkī Diving Center (922-2121; waikikidiving.com) 424 Nāhua St., Waikīkī. This 30-year-old company offers intimate, interesting scuba and snorkel dives around the island; a warm, well-trained team; certifications; and competitive prices for trips and equipment.

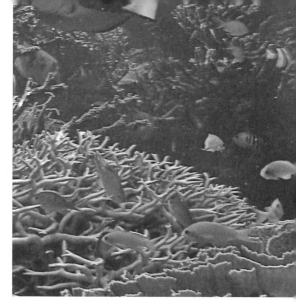

EXPERIENCE THE UNDERSEA WORLD.

FUN ON A BUDGET

Put away the credit card for these simple—and simply wonderful—little adventures. All are free to the public. Be sure to check ahead to confirm happenings.

Fireworks at the Beach. Waikīkī's Hilton Hawaiian Village (949-4321) launches TGIF fireworks every Friday, usually around 7:45 PM. Grab ice cream from Lappert's (near the lobby) for the beachfront show.

Tank o' Fish. The Oceanarium Restaurant at Waikīkī's Pacific Beach Hotel (923-4511) is so named for its two-story aquarium, home to 400 fish and rays. You don't have to eat in the restaurant to view the tank.

First Friday. Join thousands of artsy and artless folks in Chinatown for First Friday (521-2903), a sociable art gallery walk held 5–9 PM every first Friday of the month.

Royal Hawaiian Band. Enjoy a free concert by Honolulu's municipal band (922-5331), founded in 1836 by King Kamehameha III. They perform most Sundays at 2 PM at Waikīkī's Kapi'olani Park Bandstand and most Fridays at noon at downtown's 'Iolani Palace.

Observe the Law. The Hawai'i State Legislature (Senate 586-6720; House 586-6400) is in session Jan.–Apr., and visitors are welcome to observe proceedings in the State Capitol Building.

See Stars. The Hawaiian Astronomical Society (hawastsoc.org) busts out the "big gun" telescopes once a month at Kāhala Field, near Waikīkī, and at Dillingham Airfield in Mokulēi'a.

SPORTING EVENTS Because Hawai'i has no professional teams, our college sports—and even high school sports—are a big deal. At the University of Hawai'i at Mānoa (UHM), the women's volleyball team is renowned and the girls are local stars. Catch a game if you can. Contact the **University of Hawai'i at Mānoa** (tickets 944-2697; 24-hour Rainbow Sports Hotline 956-4481; hawaiiathletics.com) for information and tickets for college-level volleyball, basketball, baseball, football, and so forth. All take place at the campus in Honolulu.

Polo has a long history in Hawai'i, and even Prince Charles has played here. Dress is totally casual, and pre-game tailgating encouraged. On Windward O'ahu the **Honolulu Polo Club** (521-6927; honolulupolo.com) plays Sun. at 2:30, June–Oct., at the Waimānalo polo grounds on Kalaniana'ole Hwy. (the entrance is across from McDonald's). Gates open at 1 PM.

On the North Shore the **Hawai'i Polo Club** (637-8401; hawaiipolo.com) plays every Sun. at 2 PM from around March through September at the Mokulē'ia Polo Field off Farrington Hwy. (930). Gates open at 11, and they have food vendors as well as a bar.

SUNDAY POLO

Waikīkī 1

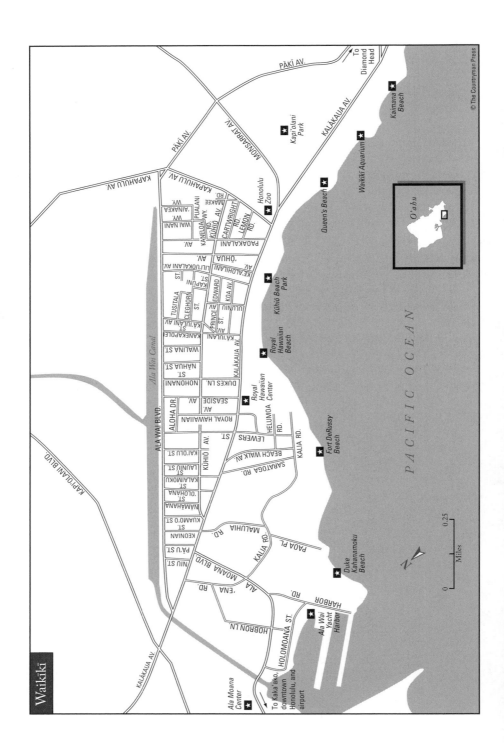

Waikīkī

PĀKĪ AV.
PĀKĪ AV.
KALAKAUA AV.
To Diamond Head
Kaimana Beach
Kapi'olani Park
MONSARRAT AV.
Waikīkī Aquarium
KAPAHULU AV.
KAPAHULU AV.
Queen's Beach
MAKEE WY.
'AINAKEA WY.
WAI NANI WY.
PUALANI RD.
KANELOA RD.
KŪHIŌ AV.
CARTWRIGHT RD.
LEMON RD.
Honolulu Zoo
PAOAKALANI AV.
'OHUA AV.
KE'EAUMOKU AV.
LILI'UOKALANI AV.
KAPUNI ST.
KOA AV.
Kūhiō Beach Park
KAI'ULANI AV.
TUSITALA ST.
CLEGHORN ST.
EDWARD ST.
PRINCE AV.
ULUNIU ST.
Ala Wai Canal
KA'IULANI AV.
KANEKAPOLE ST.
Royal Hawaiian Beach
WALINA ST.
KALAKAUA AV.
NAHUA ST.
NOHONANI ST.
DUKES LN.
ALA WAI BLVD.
ALOHA DR.
SEASIDE AV.
Royal Hawaiian Center
ROYAL HAWAIIAN AV.
HELUMOA RD.
LEWERS ST.
KAI'OLU ST.
KŪHIŌ AV.
BEACH WALK AV.
Fort DeRussy Beach
KAPI'OLANI BLVD.
LAUNIU ST.
SARATOGA RD.
KALIA RD.
'OLOHANA ST.
KALAIMOKU ST.
NAHUA ST.
NAMAHANA ST.
KUAMO'O ST.
KEONIANA ST.
MALUHIA RD.
KALIA RD.
PĀ'U ST.
PAOA PL.
Duke Kahanamoku Beach
NIU ST.
ALA MOANA BLVD.
'ENA RD.
HOBRON LN.
HOLOMOANA ST.
HARBOR RD.
Ala Wai Yacht Harbor
KALAKAUA AV.
Ala Moana Center
To Kaka'ako, downtown Honolulu, and airport

PACIFIC OCEAN

O'ahu

N

0   0.25
Miles

© The Countryman Press

WAIKĪKĪ

Waikīkī, Honolulu's most illustrious neighborhood, is a virtual brand name for classic tropical getaways. More than a century of postcards have captured its gently curving shoreline, glistening waves, and iconic Diamond Head backdrop, enchanting generations of dreamers and doers. Once the center of pre-contact Hawaiian rule and dotted with sacrificial stone temples, grass dwellings, taro paddies, footpaths, and coconut groves, Waikīkī still carries a powerful mana, or "spiritual power." Walk along its beaches on a moonlit night, and you might feel it.

As modern tourism took hold in the mid-20th century, Waikīkī built up then collapsed into a swap meet of wet T-shirt contests, coconut-bra hula reviews, mai tai hangovers, and other clichés of "life in paradise." In the 21st century, however, entire blocks of the neighborhood have been erased and replaced by upscale shops, hip hotels, and new cafés. While it hasn't shaken off every ounce of kitsch, Waikīkī rises again as a bold destination still surprisingly rich in natural beauty.

MEDICAL TREATMENT CENTERS Doctors on Call (971-6000), Sheraton Princess Ka'iulani, 120 Ka'iulani Ave., Lobby Level. Open 24/7.
Urgent Care Clinic of Waikīkī (924-3399), Kalākaua Business Center, 2155 Kalākaua Ave., Suite 308. Mon.–Fri. 8:30 AM–6:30 PM, Sat.–Sun. 8:30–4:30.

✳ To See

ARCHAEOLOGICAL AND SACRED SITES Healing Stones of Kapaemahu, east of the police station on Kalākaua Ave. These four enormous bell stones brought down from the mountains are said to carry the mana—sacred power—of four ancient kāhuna from Tahiti. Considering that connections between Tahiti and Hawai'i are believed to have ended by about AD 1200, the healers probably visited O'ahu long before that date. The kāhuna transmitted their mana to the stones before returning home, burying idols and the sacrificed body of a young chiefess beneath one of them.

The stones are not in their original placement. Two may have initially been closer to the shoreline, or in the water. According to some reports, the location of at least one stone was unknown for years, eventually turning up not far from its current home during excavation on the property of Princess Ka'iulani.

HISTORIC SITES Moana Surfrider, A Westin Resort & Spa (922-3111; moana-surfrider.com), 2365 Kalākaua Ave. On the National Register of Historic Places. Opened in 1901, the Moana is the oldest standing hotel in Waikīkī and one of the most beautiful. Its long client history includes Hollywood stars, royalty, and American tycoons, and it's officially listed as one of the Historic Hotels of America. In the 1990s it underwent a $50 million renovation that restored its former glory and earned it numerous national awards. Free guided tours of the hotel are offered Mon., Wed., and Fri. at 11 AM.

The Royal Hawaiian (923-7311; royal-hawaiian.com), 2259 Kalākaua Ave. On the National Register of Historic Places. Painted in deep pink, The Royal Hawaiian is reminiscent of the Beverly Hills Hotel in style and often called the "Pink Palace of the Pacific." After its opening in 1927, the hotel immediately attracted the famous and wealthy; pineapple juice reportedly flowed from its fountains. Both the interior and grounds still exude the luxury and soft atmosphere of the past. Free guided tours of the hotel are offered Tue., Thu., and Sat. at 2 PM.

MUSEUMS & GALLERIES US Army Museum of Hawai'i (955-9552; hiarmy museumsoc.org.), Battery Randolph, 2161 Kalia Rd. Open Tue.–Sat. 9–5. Free admission; on the National Register of Historic Places. What happens when you try to knock a 1911 military battery down with a wrecker ball, but it won't budge? You turn it into a super-cool and original museum that happens to be right on prime beach property in Waikīkī. Before you even enter, enormous military equipment will salute you. When you do enter, you'll find a dark, cell-like

OLD-WORLD GLAMOUR AT THE ROYAL HAWAIIAN

Courtesy Starwood Hotels & Resorts Hawai'i

atmosphere—the belly of an antique coastal defense system. Every exhibit within its walls is presented well and covers everything from ancient Hawaiian warfare (including rare artifacts) to Pearl Harbor attacks and the Vietnam War. Worth a visit. Gift shop.

✳ To Do

Also see the "Recreation" chapter for islandwide activities.

BICYCLE CRUISING Big Kahuna Motorcycle Tours & Rentals (924-2736; 888-451-5544; bigkahunarentals.com), 407 Seaside Ave. Mopeds, trek mountain bikes, and beach cruisers are on the menu, in addition to big-gun motorcycles.

BODYBOARDING, STAND-UP PADDLING, & SURFING Beach boys and gals working Waikīkī's beach equipment booths are always happy to give a lesson or rent you a board. Better yet, call a surf company for quality lessons that put fun and safety first. (See "Recreation.") If you already know how to surf and want the latest conditions, check out the **Surf News Network** (596-7873; surf newsnetwork.com).

To rent a surfboard at a better rate than the beach boys offer, or for a longer time, try **Koa Board Sports** (923-0189; koaboardsports.com), 2420 Koa Ave. They're only a block from Kūhiō Beach, in Waikīkī.

Just outside Waikīkī, even better surfboard rates (plus a car rack) can be had from **Blue Planet** (922-5444; blueplanetsurf.com), 813 Kapahulu Ave., Kapahulu. They also rent stand-up boards. **Hawai'i Surfboard Rentals** (672-5055; hawaiisurfboardrentals.com) has a two-day minimum on surfboards, but they'll deliver quality rental boards directly to you (with an optional car rack) at a great price.

CANOEING & KAYAKING In Waikīkī, check in with the beach boys at the 50-year-old **Waikīkī Beach Services** (542-0608; waikikibeachservices.com), Outrigger Waikīkī, 2335 Kalākaua Ave., located on the beach in front of the hotel. They offer outrigger-canoe rides most of the day. Booking in advance is a good idea. They have a second location on the beach in front of the Outrigger Reef (352-2882), 2169 Kalia Rd. **Hawaiian Oceans Waikīkī** (306-4586) also offers canoe rides. Visit their shack on Kūhiō Beach near the Duke Kahanamoku statue. With both outfits, you'll be expected to help paddle.

CATAMARAN & SAILING EXCURSIONS Gay Hawai'i Cruise (923-0669; hulas.com). The famed Hula's Bar and Lei Stand offers a 90-minute Saturday cruise for gay men and women off Waikīkī and Diamond Head, with unlimited tropical cocktails and a great price. The 45-foot boat is fast and furious. Pick up tickets in person at the bar, and several days in advance.

Maita'i Catamaran (926-5665; leahi.com). The Maita'i 44-foot catamaran sets out several times a day for offshore cruising and one sunset sail. Find Maita'i parked on the sand between the Halekūlani and Sheraton Waikīkī hotels.

Na Hoku II Catamaran (nahokuii.com). This perky, 45-foot catamaran takes a 90-minute cruise along Waikīkī and past Diamond Head five times per day, right up through sunset. Pick up a ride on the beach just west of the Moana Surfrider hotel.

Outrigger Catamaran (922-2210; outriggercatamaranhawaii.com). The fastest of the Waikīkī Beach bunch is—in our opinion, and because it belongs to Outrigger Hotels—slightly more family-friendly and classy than the other beach catamarans. You can book a snorkel sail, a "speed sail," or sunset sail. Catch it in front of the Outrigger Reef hotel.

FOR FAMILIES For family fun away from the beach, try the well-known Oʻahu adventure parks listed below.

✄ ✪ **Honolulu Zoo** (971-7171; honoluluzoo.org), 151 Kapahulu Ave. Our zoo's beginnings date to the Victorian era, and perhaps a few of the enclosures still reflect the limited space it occupies (as well as its funding challenges). But years of gradual renovations, still ongoing in some areas, have created an overall excellence in presentation, and its hundreds of temperate-zone animals are well cared for.

THE HONOLULU ZOO

Explore the African Savanna, Tropical Forest, Pacific Islands, and the wonderful new Children's Zoo, where interaction with critters is encouraged. Animals range from the orangutan and rare crocodilian gharial to the Surinam toad and turtledove. Peafowl that wander the grounds are said to be descendants from Princess Kaʻiulani's collection.

Special zoo programs include stargazing, night tours and sleepovers, week-long day camps, and summer concerts. Open daily 9–4:30. Basic admission $12 adults, $3 ages 4–12.

✄ ✪ **Waikīkī Aquarium** (923-9741; waquarium.org), 2777 Kalākaua Ave. Founded in 1904, this small, education-oriented facility is part of the University of Hawaiʻi. It's no Sea World, and we think that's a good thing. Enjoy the aquarium's artistically presented space filled with more than 2,500 colorful sea creatures and plenty of educational facts. Fun nature-oriented activities include a guided night exploration of the coral reef fronting the aquarium and even sleepovers. Open daily 9–4:30. Basic admission for adults is $9, with a range of cheaper prices for kids.

GARDENS & PARKS Kapiʻolani Park (begins at Kalākaua Ave. and Kapahulu Ave., eastern edge of Waikīkī). This is Honolulu's oldest city park and one of the island's best. With 200 beachfront acres, it's popular with visitors and residents both. The park was established in 1877 through the goodwill of King Kalākaua, and originally held a horse racetrack. Today it features tennis courts, sports fields, the Kapiolani bandstand, the Honolulu Zoo, the Waikīkī Aquarium, and the Waikīkī Shell concert arena. It also hosts major festivals and events like the Honolulu Marathon, as well as almost every Frisbee game or birthday party in town.

SALONS & SPAS Keep a smile on your face with a massage, nail treatment, or hair trim. Our biggest hotels each have a spa, with special services that often incorporate Island-style treatments. Try a traditional Hawaiian lomilomi massage, which involves long, rhythmic strokes that release tension and free energy.

Abhasa Waikīkī Spa (922-8200; abhasa.com), The Royal Hawaiian, 2259 Kalākaua Ave. This 10,000-square-foot spa offers eight outdoor treatment cabanas, Hawaiian sea salt scrubs, reflexology, deluxe men's facials, wraps, and more.

Mandara Spa (945-7721; mandaraspa.com), Hilton Hawaiian Village, 2005 Kalia Rd., Kalia Tower. Stone therapy, a private whirlpool and sun terrace, massage from two therapists at once, and tandem massages culminating in playful chocolate body application are just some of your options.

Moana Lani Spa (237-2535; moana lanispa.com), Moana Surfrider, 2365 Kalākaua Ave. This new 18,000-square-foot spa has already ranked as a top spa in Hawaiʻi and in the top 50 nationwide. It's also the only one with selected rooms looking directly onto the beach.

Na Hoʻola Spa (237-6330; hyatt regency.com), Hyatt Regency, 2424 Kalākaua Ave. Choose from a lomilomi facial, skin brightening, seaweed wrap, macadamia nut body scrub, shiatsu massage, or just about any other luxurious body treatment you can imagine.

Paul Brown's Spa Olakino (924-2121; paulbrownhawaii.com), Waikīkī Marriott, 2552 Kalākaua Ave. Island salon star Paul Brown has a special Waikīkī location offering full-service hair and nail care, body wraps, eyelift treatments, massages, facials, and more.

SpaHalekūlani (931-5322; halekulani.com), Halekūlani, 2199 Kalia Rd. Reflexology, Thai massage, massage for pregnant women, body scrubs and wraps, facials, nail care, waxing, and even child manicures are available.

Waikīkī Plantation Spa (926-2880; 866-926-2880; waikikiplantationspa.com), Outrigger Waikīkī, 2335 Kalākaua Ave. The relatively new Waikīkī Plantation spa is earning great reviews for its services, which include firming marine body masks, pre- and postnatal massages, solar manicures, and more.

SCUBA DIVING & SNORKELING Outrigger Catamaran (922-2210; out riggercatamaranhawaii.com). The catamaran, which belongs to Outrigger Hotels, offers a simple snorkel trip just off Waikīkī. Catch it in front of the Outrigger Reef hotel.

TENNIS Space-starved Waikīkī has very few hotel tennis courts. Contact **Miles James** (551-9438), who ranked for many years as Hawai'i's number one player; he can reserve court time for you and your friends on a private Waikīkī court at a great rate, provide rental equipment, give you lessons, or even just bat (or power-house!) the ball around with you.

Try the **Diamond Head Tennis Center** (971-7150), 3908 Paki Ave. These 10 unlit courts are run by the City and County of Honolulu. Just across the park and near the aquarium, the popular **Kapi'olani Tennis Courts** (971-2510), 2740 Kalākaua Ave., are open 24 hours a day.

✳ Beaches

What defines Waikīkī? **Waikīkī Beach**. Actually, Waikīkī Beach is a string of individual beaches running the length of the district. Most are named for a notable home, hotel, landmark, or person associated with the area. The individual characteristics of each beach also attract various types of sun worshippers.

For much of the 20th century, Waikīkī was famous for its "beach boys"—a collection of young, fairly glamorous men who taught surfing to visitors as well as stoked the social scene. Several of the original legendary watermen are still around, but most beach boys (and girls) today have more limited duties, which are restricted to surf lessons, catamaran rides, outrigger canoe rides, and beach equipment rentals. You'll find them at tents and booths along the main strip of Waikīkī Beach. One of the best activity rental booths is located in front of the The Royal Hawaiian hotel.

Box jellyfish can wash into Waikīkī beach areas about 10 days after a full moon; if lifeguard-posted signs indicate they're present, stay out of the water. Their sting is very painful.

The beaches we list below primarily make up that 2-mile stretch we call Waikīkī Beach, starting from the west end and traveling east.

Kahanamoku Beach lies at the westernmost end of Waikīkī, fronting the Hilton Hawaiian Village. A wide beach, and a tad rubbly and dry, it's dotted with hotel umbrellas and visiting families. The water conditions are shallow with very few waves. Just west of the beach, the newly restored, man-made Duke Kahanamoku Lagoon is perfect for infants and inflatable-mat naps.

Fort DeRussy Beach is separated from Kahanamoku Beach by the Atlantis Submarine pier. This stretch has a bit more spunk, although the beach and water conditions are similar. Resident volleyball games seem to run continuously, and the nearby military hotel Hale Koa creates a relatively heavy concentration of service personnel. A nice people-watching walkway runs the length of both beaches, then picks up again along a seawall until the next significant stretch of sand west.

Royal Hawaiian Beach, or Royal Moana to some, is the slender strip of sand fronting the Moana Surfrider and Royal Hawaiian hotels. Fashionable resident and visitor bodies line up here towel-to-towel. The water can have more of a kick, with small-wave action that encourages hundreds of first-time surfers.

Kūhiō Beach stretches all the way to the Kapahulu Groin, a cement walkway extending like a pier into the water with a shaded hut on the tip. Low seawalls run parallel to the beach and create placid, shallow bathing segments. Narrow Kūhiō Beach is a free-for-all, with local families, fresh-off-the-boat tourists, style slaves, and plenty of neighborhood kids bodyboarding and hanging out.

Queen's Surf Beach combines beach with park life. It also fronts the Waikīkī Marine Life Conservation District, a pretty good place for snorkeling. When the water's calm, walk out on the rock piling near the snack bar and you'll see loads of large reef fish below you. The east side of Queen's is popular for large-scale picnics. The west side has a long history as a gay area, although homeless encampments are increasingly crowding it out.

Kaimana's is the beach just beyond the Waikīkī Aquarium and the War Memorial Natatorium, an aging, condemned saltwater swimming facility built to honor World War I's fallen men. The beach is also known as San Souci. With a long channel through the reef perfect for distance swimming, an ocean temperament at once relaxed but not wimpy, and close proximity to two exclusive private membership clubs, Kaimana's attracts a relatively stylish and athletic resident crowd.

KŪHIŌ BEACH

✳ Lodging

Waikīkī has recently upped its trendy factor with unprecedented renovations both within hotels and across entire city blocks. Many of the larger hotels now offer full spas, wedding planning, vow renewal ceremonies, activity desks, and cultural learning opportunities, and even the smaller ones are embracing fully nonsmoking facilities, free WiFi, plasma televisions, seated check-in, trendy Balinese-inspired

STAYING COOL AT THE BEACH

Hawai'i visitors are often surprised to discover how intense our sun can be, and lobster-fried faces are only the beginning when it comes to a tropical-latitude burn.

As for surf, waves and swells are a product of seasonal weather. In summer our south and east shores can kick up frisky to heavy waves. In winter the North Shore and the west side can get crazy big—even up to 25 feet or higher.

About 60 people drown in Hawai'i every year, many of them visitors. Hundreds more are pulled from the water alive, but a bit wiser. Here are a few tips to keep the fun quotient high and the damage low. For great information on local beaches, safety conditions, and more, visit the **Hawaii Lifeguard Association** at aloha.com~lifeguards.

- Use waterproof sunscreen with a high SPF, even when it's cloudy; reapply often.
- Keep clear of shore breaks when swells and waves seem high.
- Stick to shallow areas with on-duty lifeguards.
- Stay out of the ocean when red beach flags are posted.
- Avoid stepping on coral and leave sea life undisturbed.
- Always swim with a friend.
- Have plenty of drinking water on hand.

decor, and spa touches. Because Waikīkī is long and narrow, you'll never be far from a beach, no matter which hotel you choose.

Aqua Bamboo & Spa (922-7777; 866-326-8423; aquaresorts.com), 2425 Kūhiō Ave. Moderate. Totally overhauled several years ago, the petite Bamboo hits targets such as "trendy" and "refreshingly intimate." The location is quite good—on the quieter end of Waikīkī's main strip but near enough to the action, and about a block to the beach. Hip 20-, 30-, and 40-somethings on a moderate budget, as well as the relaxed older set, enjoy the 32-inch LCD televisions, free in-room high-speed Internet access, basic spa services, private

balconies, and a striking "Zen" backyard with a saltwater pool, sauna, hot tub, and mini waterfall. Basic rooms are very small at 170 to 214 square feet, and offer clean, sleek Bali-modern decor that looks a bit more IKEA than truly upscale. Larger studios and suites are also available, although expensive. Room views might be of a wall, courtyard, or the city, and street noise can be a problem. Car parking is cramped and limited. Continental breakfast is included, and a laundry is available.

Aqua Waikīkī Wave (922-1262; 866-326-8423; aquaresorts.com), 2299 Kūhiō Ave. Inexpensive–moderate. If you'd like to set yourself in the very middle of Waikīkī without breaking the bank, the Waikīkī Wave may be the right choice. An un-family-style hotel that's still perfect for the family, it's next door to the trinket-souvenir paradise of International Market Place, and only a block from the beach. As with most of Kūhiō Avenue, however, late-night street traffic can include a few dressy hookers. Although the lobby is unremarkable, the hotel's 247 recently renovated rooms are comfortably sized with Asian-inspired, and even artistically vogue, decor. Balconies look out onto modest city views, peekaboo ocean views, or wide ocean views, depending on your room choice. All are air-conditioned and feature flat-screen TV and WiFi. A small swimming pool is on the property.

✒ Aston at the Waikīkī Banyan

(922-0555; 877-997-6667; aston waikikibanyan.com), 201 ʻŌhua Ave.

Moderate. The Waikīkī Banyan is popular with visitors from the Mainland as well as with residents coming to Oʻahu from neighboring islands, and its many amenities make it a good choice for families in particular. The hotel is on a quieter street about two blocks from the beach. Its classic Hawaiiana lobby is one of the prettiest in Waikīkī, with an open-air front, a small waterfall and koi pond meandering through, Balinese-inspired furnishings, stone and dark wood trim elements, tropical plants, and oversized Honolulu landscape paintings and photographs. Two guest room towers are linked by a recreation area with an older tennis court, large pool, jet spas, a sauna, putting green, and more. All units are one-bedroom suites with about 600 square feet of space, full kitchen, air-conditioning, high-speed Internet access, and sizable balcony. Upper-story views can

AQUA BAMBOO & SPA

be impressive, including interesting views of Diamond Head. Because each unit is privately owned, decor can vary, but the hotel is responsible for keeping them clean, which they do. Parking rates are very reasonable.

Aston Waikīkī Beach Hotel (922-2511; 877-997-6667; astonwaikiki beach.com), 2570 Kalākaua Ave. Moderate–expensive. The Waikīkī Beach Hotel on Kalākaua Avenue underwent a relatively recent $60 million renovation, then switched back from the ResortQuest to Aston brand. It features 644 smoke-free, air-conditioned guest rooms, 85 percent of which have partial or full views of Waikīkī Beach. The hotel sits directly across the street from the beach and no hotel fronts it, so rooms facing the water have remarkable panoramic vistas. Festive Hawaiiana decor creates a fun beach-extension atmosphere with peppy neon surfboards, tiki torches, bamboo, and tapa prints. The well-known Tiki's Grill & Bar restaurant (see *Where to Eat*) is located next to the pool and can be a bit loud, although this is a hotel to have fun at, not find sanctuary. Rooms are small but intense and original, with dark Indonesian teak furniture, eye-popping bedding, and bamboo-bead closet curtains, plus plasma television. Many also feature doors that connect two or more rooms together.

✪ **Aston Waikīkī Beach Tower** (926-6400; 877-997-6667; astonwaikiki beachtower.com), 2470 Kalākaua Ave. Expensive–very expensive. We really like this little condo property across the street from Waikīkī Beach. Before you balk at the price category, check out what you get. The smallest unit is a 1,050-square-foot, one-bedroom apartment that can sleep up to four people. Bump up to a two-bedroom, two-bath for even more luxury and space. Every unit features an elegant, full kitchen with all the extras, including a blender, dishwasher, rice cooker, and china for six; air-conditioning; a washer and dryer; bathrobes; a DVD player; a Bose wave radio; a flat-screen TV; marble and granite surfaces; weave carpets; and high-speed Internet access. Some have wet bars, and housekeeping service is provided twice daily. Decor is modest contemporary and a touch worn, but tasteful and clean. If that's not enough, add to it unobstructed, to-die-for, sweeping beach and ocean views from enormous balconies, plus a hotel pool, Jacuzzi, sauna, complimentary valet parking, and a personal concierge. A secret bargain when you add it all up. Book a high floor on 02 or 03 stacks for the best views and most quiet.

Aston Waikīkī Circle Hotel (923-1571; 877-997-6667; astonwaikiki circle.com), 2464 Kalākaua Ave. Inexpensive–moderate. When decor and hotel amenities are less important than budget and a location across from the beach, The Circle may be for you. The lobby's more of a desk window, the hotel has no pool, and the rooms are tiny and motel-style simple, but 85 percent of them have partial or full ocean views because of the tower's circular shape. Just roll out of bed, drop into the elevator, and step across the street to fall back asleep on the sand. Rooms do have high-speed Internet for a fee, plus flat-screen TV, and parking's reasonable. Staff is friendly, and mats, floats, and other beach gear are yours for the borrowing.

Best Western Coconut Waikīkī Hotel (923-8828; 866-326-8423; aquaresorts.com), 450 Lewers St. Inexpensive–moderate. With an extensive renovation now complete, the Aqua-property Coconut Waikīkī is getting rave reviews from visitors for being clean, unpretentious, tastefully decorated, and well priced. The hotel sits two blocks from the beach and one of Waikīkī's best new shopping strips, Waikīkī Beach Walk. It faces northward over traffic along Ala Wai Boulevard and the meandering Ala Wai Canal, but the city and mountain views are very pleasant. Relatively spacious rooms feature airy and fresh decor with mod touches, free WiFi, and 40- or 42-inch LCD TV; some rooms have a balcony. Amenities and services include a fitness center, swimming pool, barbecue grill, and complimentary breakfast. Service is attentive.

🐾 **The Breakers** (923-3181; 800-426-0494; breakers-hawaii.com), 250 Beach Walk St. Inexpensive–moderate. Right in the middle of Waikīkī and only a block from the beach is a charming, Elvis-era hotel that will appeal to those who love the low-key, low-tech, and authentically retro. The Breakers has survived the urban high-rise takeover through the rare fortune of land ownership and has a serious following of Canadian snowbirds who return every winter for lengthy stays. The hotel (which really looks more like a motel) is built ranch-style around a swimming pool. The local staff members are easygoing and helpful, and the ambience is peaceful, slow paced, very clean, and even humble. Most rooms are plain but feature atmospheric shoji (sliding Japanese rice-paper doors) and look out onto a central courtyard, where free WiFi is accessible. A small Japan-

THE BREAKERS

ese bistro is on site, poolside. Parking is very limited.

Cabana Vacation Suites (926-5555; 877-902-2121; cabanavacationsuites .com), 2551 Cartwright St. Inexpensive–moderate. Welcome to Waikīkī's only openly gay-friendly, gay-owned, and gay-operated little motel, just around the corner from the beach (including Queen's Surf, a gay men's strip) and the famous Hula's hangout. The place has recently traded in cocktail hour and a hot tub for more self-sufficient rooms. All are now stylishly upgraded one-bedroom suites featuring king-sized beds, fully equipped kitchens, and entertainment systems. The building's a walk-up. Most of the guests are men, but the hotel avoids that South Beach pickup scene—instead you'll enjoy down-to-earth comfort, privacy, and camaraderie. The hotel even organizes some fun trips for guests.

Courtyard by Marriott Waikīkī Beach (954-4000; 877-995-2638; marriott.com), 400 Royal Hawaiian Ave. Moderate. The 405-room Courtyard recently took over the short-lived Wyland Waikīkī. The open-air lobby is overall contemporary and hip, with two gargantuan G5 Macintosh computers available to guests free of charge. Teen angst is resolved in the lobby's special chill room, where kids can hang out in beanbag or massage chairs and play Xbox on flat-screen televisions while parents loll at the nearby pool. All guest rooms have a balcony, flat-screen television, and jumbled Island-pop furnishings, although mostly very modest views onto the street.

Embassy Suites Waikīkī Beach Walk (921-2345; 800-362-2779; embassy suiteswaikiki.com), 201 Beach Walk St. Expensive. Embassy Suites is the cornerstone of the new Beach Walk

COURTYARD BY MARRIOTT

shopping development in Waikīkī and just a few steps from the beach. With two towers serving up 369 one- and two-bedroom suites, you'll have enough space for family and friends (the latter may enjoy the in-room wet bars). All other convenient amenities are here, such as the 24-hour fitness center, no-charge business center, high-speed Internet access, and swimming pools. Overall a solid choice, although perhaps cookie-cutter.

'Ewa Hotel Waikīkī (922-1677; 800-359-8639; ewahotel.com), 2555 Cartwright Rd. Inexpensive–moderate. The 92-unit 'Ewa Hotel is a good budget choice for mellow singles and couples. A tidy micro-lobby leads to tiny rooms of about 200 square feet, or to larger studios and suites, which have a balcony and kitchenette (although they charge extra for microwave, rice cooker, and coffeemaker). Overall the rooms are simple and clean, with old-style rattan furnishings. Hair dryers, air-conditioning, WiFi, voice-mail phone, and other basic features make long-term stays popular. Some rooms may still permit smoking. There's no pool, and views from the low-rise look out onto back alleyways, but you're right around the corner from the beach. A sundeck, laundry facilities, and an Internet café are available on site.

Hale Koa Hotel (955-0555; 800-367-6027; halekoa.com), 2055 Kalia Rd. Moderate. Since 1975, this beautiful, 817-room beachfront hotel has exclusively served members of the US armed forces and their families—so unless you fall into one of those categories, you can stop reading right here. Located adjacent to Fort DeRussy, which now consists mostly

of a large beach park and the interesting Army Museum, the hotel has one of the best locations in all of Waikīkī and views to match. Its 72 acres of landscaped grounds feature a variety of well-tended tropical foliage, winding paths leading to the beach, and a large swimming pool. The café and bar surrounding it are popular with younger guests as the night falls. The restaurant Bibas has a great reputation, and all food on the property is relatively inexpensive. Room rates are likewise an incredible bargain based on rank and room category.

✪ **Halekūlani** (923-2311; 800-367-2343; halekulani.com), 2199 Kalia Rd. Very expensive. Begun as a beachfront bungalow guesthouse more than 100 years ago, the Halekūlani ("house befitting heaven") has grown into an internationally renowned five-star hotel and member of the Leading Hotels of the World. You'll step into understated, lap-of-luxury living with excellent service that borders on geisha-like graciousness and professionalism. The hotel's creamy, contemporary, open-air, wood-trimmed architecture complements a groomed grass courtyard and sophisticated floral arrangements in unobtrusive elegance. Prices tend to attract a largely Japanese clientele.

Prepare for a dream stay filled with full spa services, swimming in an orchid-mosaic oceanfront pool, and dining at the Five Diamond French restaurant La Mer (see *Where to Eat*). The 519-square-foot-plus "basic" room offers a flat-screen television, Sony MP3 docking station, entertainment center, WiFi, deep soaking tub, pure cotton robes, and twice-daily housekeeping. Nearly all rooms have

Courtesy Hotels & Resorts of Halekūlani

HALEKŪLANI

ocean views. Not big enough for you? You can keep upgrading all the way to the Royal Suite, which offers more than 4,000 square feet and a personal butler. Tack on one of the hotel's available Bentleys, Lotuses, or Maseratis for the full experience.

If you can't afford the Halekūlani, you can still enjoy the hotel's several excellent restaurants and bars, which all offer complimentary hotel valet parking.

Hawai'i Prince Hotel Waikīkī and Golf Club (956-1111; 888-977-4623; princeresortshawaii.com), 100 Holomoana St. Expensive. The Hawai'i Prince Hotel's twin towers are new landmarks of the western entrance to Waikīkī, just steps from Ala Moana Center and the vast Ala Moana Regional Park. Glass elevators travel the outside of each tower, showcasing city and mountain views. A grand, modern lobby leads to contemporary, sleek rooms with floor-to-ceiling windows that all look directly onto a yacht harbor and the ocean. A swimming pool overlooks the harbor. The touted golf club aspect of the hotel is in fact an Arnold Palmer course many miles west of Honolulu. The hotel attracts a large percentage of Japanese visitors, but you'll see local residents at the Prince Court restaurant for business lunches and its excellent Sunday brunch service.

Hilton Hawaiian Village Beach Resort & Spa (949-4321; 800-345-6565; hiltonhawaiianvillage.com), 2005 Kalia Rd. Expensive. The Hilton Hawaiian Village is Waikīkī's only mega-resort, with nearly 3,000 rooms spread across 22 oceanfront acres of land secured back in the 1950s. The most outrageous place to stay in its early days, it hosted celebrities such as Elvis as well as politicians and other wealthy visitors. It still wins international awards today, especially as a family-friendly destination. The resort overall isn't about outstanding service, although it's good; it's about total-package ease. The property is a labyrinth of five towers, plus shops, bars, lobbies, hula shows, penguin and flamingo ponds, cultural activities, swimming pools, and several award-winning restaurants, all on a grand scale—plus an on-site chapel, fitness center, full spa, and lagoon. The beach fronting the resort is wide and the water placid and shallow, perfect for kids. Whether you stay here or not, pick up ice cream at Lappert's and head to the beachfront for the hotel's free Friday-night fireworks.

Hilton Waikīkī Prince Kūhiō (922-0811; 888-243-9252; waikikiprince kuhio.hilton.com), 2500 Kūhiō Ave. Moderate–expensive. With the amenities and professionalism of a business hotel and the benefits of a location only a block from Kūhiō Beach, the Prince Kūhiō is a strong new addition to the Hilton family. In the main lobby area glamorous contemporary wood and marble notes mesh with atmospheric, golden lighting. At the Lobby Bar a trendy ambience in burgundy, soft peach, and pale green prevails. Down the hall you'll find the award-winning pop-age diner MAC 24-7 (see *Where to Eat*), which will send food up to your room at any time of the day or night. A complimentary 24-hour business center is at your beck and call. All of the rooms are nonsmoking and were completely renovated several years ago. They are chic and sleek, each with a balcony, 42-inch plasma television, high-speed Internet, Hilton Serenity Beds, Crabtree & Evelyn toiletries, and an awesome "GuestLink" system that enables you to use the television screen with your laptop, video camera, MP3 player, and more. Last but not least are the views, which on higher floors give way to spectacular ocean or mountain vistas.

✪ **Hotel Renew** (687-7700; 888-485-7639; hotelrenew.com), 129 Paoakalani Ave. Moderate. Just half a block from the beach you'll find the 72-room boutique Hotel Renew, where internationally acclaimed San Francisco designer Jiun Ho has melded a very hip, mod-Asiatic ambience with sophisticated and luxuriously minimalist statements. No kids screaming poolside or wicker furniture here—the hotel is deep spa-groove, and a surprising, almost secret find in Waikīkī. The lobby sets the tone with a water-lily stone fountain and Lounge Renew, a chic side nook serving everything from organic teas to signature cocktails depending on the hour. Smallish guest rooms upstairs are offset by sleek tailoring in richly dark woods, graphic creams, hints of red, and black trim. Extra touches include decorative trays peppered with spa treats, WiFi, shoji-style blackout

HILTON WAIKĪKĪ PRINCE KŪHIŌ

Courtesy Lew Harrington

screens, dimmers, and 50-inch flat televisions. Good ocean views are had from south-facing rooms above the fifth floor. North-facing rooms have mediocre city views. The hotel does not feature a pool.

Hyatt Regency Waikīkī Beach Resort & Spa (923-1234; 800-233-1234; hyatt.com), 2424 Kalākaua Ave. Expensive. Step into one of Waikīkī's grandest hotels, just across from an unobstructed stretch of kid-friendly beach. Modern, massive, and architecturally striking with a spaceship-sized, open-air atrium separating two tall towers, the Hyatt is late-20th-century mega-glamour at its best. It's especially popular with Japanese visitors. The more than 1,200 rooms are attractively furnished and spacious with balconies and high-tech amenities. Front-facing rooms have beautiful

HOTEL RENEW

Courtesy Hotel Renew

views of the ocean and coastline. The hotel also has a gorgeous swimming pool and Jacuzzi, plus a large spa.

ʻIlikai Hotel & Suites (949-3811; 866-326-8423; ilikaihotel.com), 1777 Ala Moana Blvd. Moderate. The iconic ʻIlikai is a tri-star-shaped hotel and condo overlooking a lagoon, a yacht harbor, and the ocean. On the far west end of Waikīkī, it dominates a traffic-heavy, harbor-front strip between Waikīkī Beach and the huge Ala Moana Park, which also boasts a great family beach. Either one is about a five-minute walk. Also five minutes away by foot is Ala Moana Center, Honolulu's largest shopping center. The hotel has the enjoyable notoriety of being in the opening credits of the original *Hawaiʻi Five-0*. Reemerged from foreclosure in 2009, the ʻIlikai is now under the management of Aqua Resorts. Rooms are very spacious at 600-plus square feet; some also have a kitchen. The rooms themselves are clean and modern, but balconies and the building exterior are a bit run-down.

ʻIlima Hotel (923-1877; 800-801-9366; ilima.com), 445 Nohonani St. Moderate. This 93-room hotel is located in central Waikīkī along the Ala Wai Canal, about a two-block walk from the beach, with views either toward Diamond Head or downtown. The lobby is cute and clean, and staff is friendly, warm, professional, and helpful. The best bet are the hotel's 530-square-foot studios with full kitchen, balcony, air-conditioning, and enough room for a family. Larger suites and even penthouse accommodations come with a soft price tag. Definitely shop online with ʻIlima—they offer significant Internet discounts. The room decor is old-school rattan and floral. Little touches such as a free daily newspaper make you feel at home, and a heated dipping pool, fitness room, sauna, and laundry facilities make it hard to leave. A limited number of parking stalls are available for free.

Island Colony (923-2345; 866-326-8423; aquaresorts.com), 445 Seaside Ave. Inexpensive–moderate. This 44-story Aqua condo hotel has improved over the years and gets high marks from many guests. It's a good value, very clean, and view-friendly, with hotel-style rooms, studios with kitchenette, and one-bedroom suites—plus translucent balcony railings. Decor is tired and variable, with much of the typical old white rattan, floral-pattern furnishings. Although located several blocks from the beach and on a busy roadway, you're removed from the bustle of Waikīkī just enough to feel relief, and within it enough to feel hooked up. Vistas from most rooms run from good to stupendous—sometimes even panoramic. The pool is spacious and very nice, with a wide sunning deck and jet spa.

The Lotus at Diamond Head (922-1700; 800-367-5004; thelotusat diamondhead.com), 2885 Kalākaua Ave. Moderate–expensive. A 50-room boutique hotel formerly of the W Hotel family, The Lotus is now under the management of Castle Resorts & Hotels and prices have come way down. Its super-trendy style has been perfectly preserved, however, right down to the Zen-boudoir lobby, creamy dreamy rooms, and pillowy beds. The location is one of our favorites—the hotel is nestled among a handful of exclusive, quiet buildings

Courtesy Castle Resorts & Hotels

THE LOTUS AT DIAMOND HEAD

at the foot of Diamond Head and surrounded by parkland, trees, and ocean. Central Waikīkī is a 10-minute beachfront walk away, which at night can be a little sketchy due to homeless encampments. The hotel has no pool or other amenities, but the beach is a mere 50 steps from the lobby and much less touristy than you'd find deeper into Waikīkī. The building faces east, so no rooms look directly to the ocean except the 360-degree penthouse (which is duly fabulous). Choose a higher-floor room for a nice Diamond Head and coastal view from room and balcony. At the time of writing, the stylish Diamond Head Grill and renowned hipster club WonderLounge are closed down; an upscale fish restaurant and new club zone are reportly taking their place.

Moana Surfrider, A Westin Resort & Spa (922-3111; 866-716-8112; moana-surfrider.com), 2365 Kalākaua Ave. Expensive. On the National Register of Historic Places and often called "the First Lady of Waikīkī," the 793-room beachfront Moana Surfrider has entertained the rich and famous since 1901, with a guest history that includes Frank Sinatra, Lucille Ball, Amelia Earhart, Prince Edward of England, and Joe DiMaggio. It was also once home to the world-famous radio program *Hawai'i Calls*, which was broadcast to more than 30 countries from 1935 to 1975 and sort of a *Grand Ole Opry* for Hawaiian music of the day.

The hotel is built around a courtyard and historic banyan tree of incredible size. The lobby is a masterpiece of Italianate style, and the entire building has an almost feminine, delicately ornate plantation quality now rare to find. Recline on the veranda or sip drinks under the yawning limbs of the banyan at the Beach Bar. Afternoon tea on the veranda is legendary. On the second floor, artifacts tell the history of the area and the hotel.

The rooms vary—in the original wing windows are small, walls are thin, and space is limited. But it's charming. In the newer towers standard modernism, albeit with some good ocean views, seems to contradict the hotel's original glamour. A redo on a middle-aged wing may be in the works, so ask for a construction update before booking. An 18,000-square-foot oceanfront spa is the latest addition to the premises.

New Otani Kaimana Beach Hotel (923-1555; 800-356-8264; kaimana .com), 2863 Kalākaua Ave. Moderate–expensive. The 1964 beachfront Kaimana is one of the better boutique choices in Waikīkī, even though it retains some outdated elements. Undoubtedly the best aspect of the Kaimana is the location. Because it's one of just a handful of buildings along the "Gold Coast" section of Waikīkī, you'll be a pleasant 10-minute parkland stroll from the crowds and cradled between Diamond Head Crater, beautiful Kapi'olani Park, and the sparkling sea.

Room decor is muted and simple with hints of rattan and floral, and wall-to-

THE MOANA SURFRIDER, A WESTIN RESORT & SPA

Courtesy Starwood Hotels & Resorts Hawai'i

wall glass doors lead to private balconies. Standard park-view rooms run on the moderately expensive side, with partial-to-full ocean-view rooms definitely costing some bucks—but if you splurge on the oceanfront deluxe, the vista from your room and balcony are unparalleled and totally romantic. If you go for it, request a corner room. Steer clear of the park-view studios.

The hotel has no pool, but it sits right on the sands of an excellent beach. Use caution walking after dark in the park area, as drifters have become more common.

Outrigger Luana (955-6000; 800-688-7444; outriggerluanawaikiki .com), 2045 Kalākaua Ave. Moderate. A nice surprise: Luana Waikīkī, standing alone along a hotel-less stretch of park a few steps west of the action. Not much from the outside, and in fact fronting traffic-heavy Kalākaua Avenue, the lobby is cool, quiet, clean, and spacious, with marble, stone, and wood touches. This midpriced hotel/condo is highly recommended by many guests and one of the better values in Waikīkī. Rates can vary widely; some are even a downright steal. Choose from freshly decorated hotel rooms, studios with kitchenettes, and one- or two-bedroom units with complete kitchens, including a dishwasher. A small pool, fitness center, laundry services, and a sufficient business center in the lobby make it a great choice for an easy and affordable long- or short-term stay. WiFi is available only in common areas. All units are nonsmoking and air-conditioned, plus feature balconies with nice views onto the 70-acre Kuroda Field, the city, or distant ocean. The closest beach access is about a two-block walk through the park.

Outrigger Reef on the Beach (923-3111; 800-688-7444; outriggerreef .com), 2169 Kalia Rd. Moderate–expensive. The Outrigger Reef recently completed a $110 million total renovation that bumped it from worn-down and cheesy to contemporary and interesting. The new lobby is inspired by traditional Hawaiian *hale*, the crowning touch being a 100-year-old Hawaiian koa-wood canoe hanging from the eaves. It sets the tone for the entire hotel. All 639 rooms have been redone, and the ocean-view rooms are stellar, with totally modern amenities and provisions. Decor is more vintage Hawaiiana than trendy. The location is great—next door to the famed Halekūlani and a park, and right on the beach. The quality of its restaurants could improve.

Outrigger Waikīkī on the Beach (923-0711; 800-688-7444; outrigger .com), 2335 Kalākaua Ave. Moderate–expensive. On prime beachfront between two of O'ahu's most beautiful historic hotels, the Outrigger Waikīkī offers more than 500 air-conditioned, nonsmoking rooms with free WiFi, flat-screen television, and balcony. Tastefully tropical rooms range from modest city views to one-bedroom deluxe oceanfront views that will blow you away. The hotel underwent renovation several years ago, and the main upstairs lobby is truly beautiful. The new Waikīkī Plantation Spa at the penthouse level also gets high marks. The downstairs lobby and shops are still unimpressive. Duke's, a restaurant and bar right on the beachfront, has become a landmark dudefest destination. The excellent Hula Grill, just above it, has great breakfasts, even better views, and more class. (See *Where to Eat* for both.)

Park Shore Waikīkī (923-0411; 866-372-1732; parkshorewaikiki.com), 2586 Kalākaua Ave. Inexpensive–moderate. Certain views from this hotel are amazing, considering the reasonable price. High-floor east- and south-facing rooms offer uninhibited, glamorous views of open ocean, the zoo, Kapiolani Park, Diamond Head, and the coastline. Room interiors are unimpressive with snug dimensions, humble decor, and street noise floating up to balconies. However, they do offer mini refrigerators, air-conditioning, and 42-inch flat-screen TVs in selected rooms, as well as overall cleanliness. Many of the rooms have been recently "refreshed." High-speed in-room Internet comes at a charge.

Queen Kapi'olani Hotel (922-1941; 800-533-6970; queenkapiolani.com), 150 Kapahulu Ave. Inexpensive–moderate. This 19-story, midsized hotel is a very economical choice with some ridiculously fabulous views if you get a high floor on the southeast side. It changed hands in 2009, so badly needed renovations are underway. The tropical dinginess of 1970 should be going, but hopefully the lobby's atmospheric Victorian-style paintings of Hawaiian royalty are staying. Until the redo, rooms are tiny, tired, and bland, but air-conditioned and sufficient, and many have a balcony. High-speed Internet in rooms is a new surprise, and they do have a pool. Guests are a mix of tour bus groups and independent travelers. Shop online for best rates.

The Royal Hawaiian (923-7311; 866-716-8110; royal-hawaiian.com),

VIEW FROM PARK SHORE WAIKĪKĪ

2259 Kalākaua Ave. Very expensive. There are few other hotels in Hawai'i that command respect like The Royal Hawaiian. Built in 1927, this historic building hosted the era's most glamorous icons, including Douglas Fairbanks, Shirley Temple, Clark Gable, the Fords, and the Rockefellers. Spanish-Moorish in design and similar to the Beverly Hills Hotel, it also uses pink as its trademark color, earning it the name "Pink Palace of the Pacific."

One of the three "grande dame" hotels of Waikīkī, it spreads out beachfront within an ancient coconut tree grove. In the lobby grand arches frame richly ornate Oriental-style carpets, natural lighting, and elegant shops. Two swimming pools, the new restaurant Azure (part of a recent and hefty property restoration; see *Where to Eat*), the Mai Tai Bar, and Abhasa Spa ensure total comfort.

The hotel has 529 rooms, with 6 floors in the historic section of the building and 17 in the more modern tower. The most modest of them are graceful and sophisticated garden rooms with flat-screen television, iPod alarm clock, high-speed Internet, lush bath accessories, and Luxury Collection beds. The top-of-the-line option, the Kamehameha Suite, shimmers in teak and koa woods, and opens onto a 26-by-38-foot balcony with unparalleled ocean and Diamond Head views.

✪ **Sheraton Waikīkī** (922-4422; 800-325-3535; sheraton-waikiki.com), 2255 Kalākaua Ave. Expensive. The centrally located beachfront Sheraton has ramped up from a middling hotel to a powerhouse. The massive modern structure looms over the adjacent antique hotels, and its unusual tri-star shape means that most of its nearly 1,700 attractive rooms have at least partial views of the ocean—some downright magnificent. Despite its lack of Old World grace and ambience, the recent $190 million renovation resulted in modifications that really stand out. They include a new adults-only infinity pool overlooking the ocean, the trendy oceanfront bar RumFire, a kid-friendly super pool with a 70-foot slide, Spa Khakara, and impressive redesigns of the open-air lobby.

Trump International Hotel, Waikīkī Beach Walk (683-7777; 877-683-7401; trumpwaikikihotel.com), 223 Saratoga Rd. Very expensive. The new kid on the block is hardly a kid. Understated sophistication pours from every corner of Hawai'i's only Trump, a 462-room tower just across the street from the beach. This private world begins on the sixth floor, in a darkly elegant open-air lobby that

THE ROYAL HAWAIIAN
Courtesy Starwood Hotels & Resorts Hawai'i

Courtesy Trump Hotels

TRUMP INTERNATIONAL HOTEL, WAIKĪKĪ BEACH WALK

looks out on ocean and park. We toured all types of rooms on your behalf and discovered deep closets and tubs, state-of-the-art kitchens, generous views from floor-to-ceiling glass walls, and a decidedly high-end apartment decor in each. Not all rooms are large—they start at a decent 355 feet—but each feels like home, especially the suites. A full spa, an infinity pool, and fine-dining choices add up to total luxury.

Waikīkī Beach Marriott Resort & Spa (922-6611; 800-367-5370; waikikibeachmarriott.com), 2552 Kalākaua Ave. Expensive. Across the street from a building-free strip of Waikīkī Beach, the Beach Marriott is a 33-floor, twin-tower complex of 1,300 rooms and all the features and amenities you'd expect, including two heated swimming pools, a full spa,

and a 24-hour fitness facility. A decentralized building design creates a more informal atmosphere, although it feels somewhat stark. Rooms are contemporary Hawaiiana and feature Marriott's Revive Bedding Collection, 37-inch HD flat-screen TVs, and private balconies. Selected rooms have incredible ocean and Diamond Head views. Try the Marriott's excellent on-site restaurants, including the award-winning Sansei (see *Where to Eat*), d.k. Steak House, and Arancino di Mare. The shops are unimpressive.

Waikīkī Grand Hotel (923-1814; 888-367-5003; waikikigrand.com), 134 Kapahulu Ave. Inexpensive– moderate. A mix of privately owned hotel rooms and condo studios, the Waikīkī Grand can be a gamble. Some units have been decorated well, and some have not. Castle Resorts &

Hotels manages about 40 of the rooms directly through the above contact information.

Why stay here? For gay visitors, on-site access to Honolulu's best loved gay bar, Hula's. For everyone booking an east-facing room, inexpensive, smokin' views of Diamond Head, Kapiolani Park, the zoo, and the ocean, plus a killer rooftop sundeck. You're also practically across the street from the beach, and a stone's throw from a gay-friendly stretch of sand and park.

Waikīkī Parc Hotel (921-7272; 800-422-0450; waikikiparc.com), 2233 Helumoa Rd. Moderate. This 297-room, Halekūlani-operated hotel tucked around the corner from the action experienced a complete renovation several years ago. Formerly an elegantly staid, Hawaiiana-themed boutique, it has transformed into a trendsetter, perfect for business travelers and the chic set. An exceptional level of personal service is its trademark.

In the immaculate, unfussy lobby, stone flooring and mood lighting con-

Courtesy Hotels & Resorts of Halekūlani

WAIKĪKĪ PARC HOTEL

trast with candy-colored pop-art furnishings. After passing through sleek hallways and into your ocean- or mountain-view room (go above the eighth floor for fabulous vistas), you'll find sharp, traditionalist decor with flat-screen televisions, high-speed Internet access, deliciously comfy beds, and sliding shutters that add just the right touch of charm.

Waikīkī Parc also has a fitness center, business center, impressive pool, and a location right across from the beach, as well as a 7,500-square-foot glamour restaurant, Nobu Waikīkī, owned by one of the world's leading Japanese fusion chefs (see *Where to Eat*).

✳ Where to Eat

DINING OUT Arancino (923-5557; arancino.com/en), 255 Beach Walk. Open daily for lunch and dinner. Moderate–expensive. Arancino is tucked into a cozy space on Beach Walk (a block away from Waikīkī

VIEW FROM WAIKĪKĪ GRAND SUNDECK

Beach Walk, the shopping strip). It's tidily rustic and easygoing, yet stylish, busy, and professional enough to make a visit special. If there's a wait, write your name on the list posted at the door; once inside, your food will likely come quickly and without a fuss. Napoli-style thin-crust pizzas are excellent, with fresh topping mixes like asparagus, fresh tomato, and Gorgonzola cheese, or Italian prosciutto and arugula. We expected personal-sized pizzas and were pleased to find they can feed two average appetites. Other dishes have included linguine with tiger shrimp, Maine lobster, and risotto with five different types of mushrooms. Wine selections are good. Prices have jacked way up since our last edition of the book—the heavily Japanese clientele may have something to do with it. The lunchtime set menus are the best deal. Reservations are accepted between 5 and 6 PM, or call ahead to put your name on the wait list.

Also check out Arancino's sister restaurant, **Arancino di Mare** (931-6273), Waikīkī Beach Marriott Resort & Spa, 2552 Kalākaua Ave. It's less pastoral, but offers sidewalk dining.

Azure (921-4600; royal-hawaiian .com), The Royal Hawaiian, 2259 Kalākaua Ave. Open daily for dinner. Expensive–very expensive. Reservations recommended. Located beachfront at The Royal Hawaiian, Azure opened in 2009 to high reviews. We like to describe the interior as "Mediterranean cabana" meets contemporary Pacific; it marries Turkish-style lanterns, airy ceiling heights, luxurious banquettes, and an overall white palette accented with crisp dark trim detail. Fresh fish and other

seafood are prominent on the menu, and presented with flair by esteemed local chef Jon Matsubara. Try dishes like sake-steamed Manila clams, torched wagyu carpaccio, a selection of freshly caught fish, Shanghai-style crispy lobster, or rib-eye steak.

BLT Steak (683-7440; bltsteak.com), Trump International Hotel, 223 Saratoga Rd. Open daily for dinner. Expensive–very expensive. Reservations recommended. BLT—as in Bistro Laurent Tourondel—is one of Waikīkī's newest high-end restaurants. Its location on the ground floor of the Trump International Hotel is the first indicator of quality. Tourondel blends the delicious elements of the American steak house and the French bistro with the same success as that of his restaurants on the Mainland and elsewhere.

The restaurant interior reflects the spirit with the dark woods of a clubhouse, tempered with murals and flower arrangements. The menu includes Kamuela tomato salad, lobster Cobb salad, creamed spinach, a porterhouse steak for two, sautéed Dover sole, fresh local fish dishes like moi and 'ōpakapaka, and crêpe soufflé with passion fruit sauce. An award-winning wine list offers perfect pairings to your meal.

❧ **Duke's Waikīkī** (922-2268; dukes waikiki.com), Outrigger Waikīkī, 2335 Kalākaua Ave. Open daily for all three meals. Moderate–expensive. Reservations are recommended for lunch and dinner. This Waikīkī Beach hangout has become almost as iconic as its namesake, famed local swimmer and surfer Duke Kahanamoku. The breakfast crowd is a cattle call of tourists, all of whom have arrived for

two reasons: the "pretty good" all-you-can-eat buffet, and picture-perfect, open-air views directly onto Waikīkī Beach's busiest stretch. Lunch is generally busy, but as cocktail hour approaches, the sand-level deck opens and the place explodes with energy and crowds that don't ease up until long past the dinner hour. The menu goes a fairly standard "tropical Americana" route with crab and macadamia nut wontons, mango barbecue ribs, tuna melts, prime teriyaki sirloin, and shrimp scampi. Considering this is not an award-winning restaurant, dinner prices are high. Many of the restaurant's entertainers, however, are top local performers, and the vintage Hollywood-Hawaiiana decor infused with memorabilia of "The Duke" and other beach boys is festive, fun, and unpretentious.

✪ **Hau Tree Lānai** (921-7066; kaimana.com), New Otani Kaimana Beach Hotel, 2863 Kalākaua Ave. Open daily for all three meals. Moderate–expensive. Reservations are recommended. In Waikīkī you pay a premium for perfect settings. The Hau Tree Lānai sits right on the sands of Diamond Head's Kaimana Beach, framed by an old railing dating from the graceful estate that sat here, and shaded by the same gnarled hau tree that Robert Louis Stevenson reputedly enjoyed sitting under while he wrote. All tables are on a charming (dare we say magical?) open patio, with beautiful ocean and sunset views.

The restaurant serves American-style dishes strongly infused with Pacific influences. We wish the lunch and dinner fare were better—most dishes are pretty good, but sometimes lackluster. Residents still love to have

business lunches here or bring out-of-towners. Menu items range from poi pancakes, seafood omelets, crabcakes Benedict, Portuguese bean soup, and papaya chicken salad to escargots, steamed snapper, Cajun 'ahi sashimi, and Colorado lamb chops.

✪ **House Without a Key** (923-2311; halekulani.com), Halekūlani, 2199 Kalia Rd. Open daily for all three meals. Moderate–expensive. No reservations. We can't say enough about the setting of this world-class hotel's patio restaurant. Immortalized in a 1925 Charlie Chan novel, House Without a Key is quintessential Hawai'i glamour—and its many decades of delighting residents and visitors attest to its perfect atmosphere. The setting is spacious, mellow, and resort-casual, with wide-open views onto the ocean and Diamond Head in the distance. From late afternoon until early evening, soothing vintage Hawaiian performances will transport you back in time.

The food—well, not quite as good as the views, but mostly pretty good. They serve a relatively expensive, all-you-can-eat, American-influenced buffet at breakfast. Lunch and dinner are the best bets, with items such as frisée and apple salad, romaine hearts salad, organic spaghetti, braised lamb shank, sashimi, Maui onion soup, and signature coconut cake.

🍴 **Hula Grill Waikīkī** (923-4852; hulagrillwaikiki.com), Outrigger Waikīkī Hotel, 2335 Kalākaua Ave. Open daily for breakfast and dinner; also Sun. brunch. Moderate. Reservations are recommended. Hula Grill, up on the second floor of the Outrigger, gets our vote as the best place in Waikīkī to eat breakfast. A Maui-born restaurant with a softly contemporary, native-wood plantation ambience, it offers open-air seating, views that span Waikīkī Beach all the way to Diamond Head, all-in-all good food, a mellow atmosphere, and amazingly reasonable prices for the package. Breakfast includes items such as traditional buttermilk pancakes with bananas and macadamia nuts, applewood-smoked bacon, and vegetarian omelets.

Dinner is on the high end of moderately priced, with Pacific-oriented fare like macadamia nut crusted mahimahi, baby back barbecue ribs, and pineapple coconut crème brûlée. If you don't mind sitting at the bar, however, you can opt for lighter (and less expensive) fare like Baja fish tacos, sashimi, and pork ribs. They've also recently begun Sunday brunch, with a rotating menu of fresh selections. Live Hawaiian music happens daily from 7 to 9 PM. Validated parking is offered at the hotel.

Hy's Steak House (922-5555; hys hawaii.com), Waikīkī Park Heights, 2440 Kūhiō Ave. Open daily for dinner. Very expensive. Reservations recommended. Recognized nationally by *Zagat* as a top Hawai'i steak house and voted O'ahu's best steak house by *Honolulu Magazine*, Hy's is a worthwhile splurge if you'd like to step outside of the tropical Hawai'i box and indulge your deepest red-meat fantasies.

The ambience is a plush, softly lit, Victorian gentleman's library of sorts, where tuxedoed waiters move quietly among white-cloth tables. The menu is traditional and quite large for an upscale steak house, with prime beef cuts dry-aged and trimmed right on

the premises. Dishes include selections such as seafood and avocado salad, filet mignon tartare, caviar, beef tenderloin with black truffle sauce, roast rack of lamb, kiawe-broiled steak, chateaubriand for two, Hawaiian snapper, and strawberry flambé prepared at your table. They also have a children's menu.

Add an extensive and award-winning wine list recognized by *Wine Spectator* magazine that focuses on savory California reds, after-dinner drinks such as Remy Martin Louis XIII, and noted Island performers, and you'll experience an evening to remember. Valet and self-parking are available. Collared shirts are required for men.

Kai Market (921-4600; sheraton -waikiki.com/kaimarket.html), Sheraton Waikīkī, 2255 Kalākaua Ave. Open daily for breakfast and dinner. Moderate–expensive. Reservations recommended for dinner. The new Kai Market is wonderfully different. Yes, you'll pay a lot up front for breakfast and dinner, although *kama'āina* and kids get substantial discounts. But nowhere else in Waikīkī, or Honolulu, or even in other cities will you have the chance for a fresh, all-you-can-eat, healthy, almost entirely locally grown, Island-style buffet.

Chef Darren Demaya has created a farm-to-table presentation that incorporates seven primary cultures that have influenced Hawai'i since the earliest plantation days, with no skimping. For breakfast, we're talking kim chee Portuguese sausage fried rice, rambutan, guava and taro breads, Molokai sweet potato hash browns. For dinner, miso fish, 'alaea prime rib, soy-sake braised beef short ribs, tako poke, Kahuku shrimp, sashimi, oysters, and berry tartlets, with dishes rotating daily.

The waterfront space opens up to views of the big blue, with nightly Hawaiian entertainment on the lānai below.

✪ **Keo's Thai Cuisine** (951-9355; keosthaicuisine.com), 2028 Kūhiō Ave. Open daily for dinner. Moderate. Reservations recommended. More than three decades in business, Keo's grew from a small neighborhood eatery to one of O'ahu's best-loved restaurants, Thai and otherwise. *Newsweek* has called it "one of the choicest dining spots in Honolulu," *Gourmet* has bestowed it with the Top Table Award, and *Bon Appétit* named it America's Best Thai Restaurant. Restaurateur Keo Sananikone is so insistent on fresh herbs and spices that he grows some of them himself on his North Shore farms.

The entryway is layered with auto-graphed photos of celebrity diners. Within, the mood is deeply exotic, even perhaps gaudily luxuriant, with fanciful sprays of orchids, dim light-ing, and bronzed sculptures. Wall doors fold open to the street (unfor-tunately, a loud one).

At the time of writing, breakfast was on hold—if it returns, we hope it will be better than the weak American-style dishes previously offered. Dinner is usually excellent, with everything you're looking for: Thai ginger soup, string beans with ginger and chili, cashew nuts with chicken, Panang curry, shiitake mushrooms with snow peas, grilled country game hen, Bangkok duck, apple-banana in coconut milk. The portions are medi-um in size and meant to be served family-style. Dress is casual, and free valet parking is available.

✪ **La Mer** (923-2311; halekulani .com), Halekūlani, 2199 Kalia Rd. Open daily for dinner. Very expensive. Reservations recommended. In our opinion, high-end dining doesn't get better than this. La Mer is the signa-ture restaurant of the world-renowned Halekūlani hotel, and until recently it was the only restaurant in Hawai'i to earn Five Diamonds.

La Mer's service is high art, with you at the center. Its dreamscape decor—glowing polished woods, golden Japanese teahouse screens, and opium-den lighting—contrast beauti-fully with the cool tones of an ocean-front setting and distant Diamond Head. Although decidedly reserved in

LA MER

tone, it exudes more feminine grace than stuffiness. The food is solidly impressive, with menu items such as Big Island lobster medallions, caviar, filet mignon of venison, bouillabaisse, and Grand Marnier soufflé, all accompanied by an award-winning wine list.

We've heard comments from some that the restaurant didn't meet expectations for the price, and it's certainly possible that La Mer doesn't always deliver. We've found it to be consistently worthwhile, however, and consider it perfect for a wedding anniversary—especially table 25.

A jacket is no longer required for men, but strongly suggested; a collared long-sleeve shirt is required. The hotel offers free valet parking.

Michel's (923-6552; michelshawaii .com), Colony Surf, 2895 Kalākaua Ave. Open daily for dinner; brunch is served on the first Sunday of the month. Expensive–very expensive. Reservations recommended. Another of Honolulu's treasured restaurants is Michel's, which opened in 1962 and was an instant star. Eventually it sold to a series of owners who couldn't keep up the magic; in recent years it has come to rest once again in the care of a master restaurateur and it's better than ever.

You'll be transported into casual luxury at this romantic, open-air, ocean-front retreat (perhaps a bit 1980s in decor). Arrive shortly before sunset to breathe in the outstanding panoramic view of shimmering waves, tiki torches, and endless horizon—then settle in for an evening of five-star service and cuisine. Although the waiters wear tuxedos, you don't have to;

upscale resort attire is very welcome as are hearty laughter and large groups.

Please your senses with dishes like Big Island abalone, Helix escargots Bourgogne, Kobe steak tartare, blackened yellowfin 'ahi, crisp Island 'ōpakapaka, steamed onaga, bouillabaisse, chateaubriand for two, and cherries jubilee, among other tantalizing selections. An extensive wine list offers plenty to pair with, and subdued entertainment includes a Grammy-winning slack-key guitarist and a harpist. Our Euro-inlaws were impressed.

The Sunday brunch at Michel's is an institution. Valet parking is available.

Miyako (921-7077; kaimana.com), New Otani Kaimana Beach Hotel, 2863 Kalākaua Ave. Open daily for dinner. Moderate–expensive. Reservations are accepted. Choose your level of comfort: a simple, Western-style dining room that deemphasizes decor and instead lets pure ocean views speak; a table on the open-air balcony high above the beach; or seating in a traditional tatami room. Kimono-clad servers will bring you made-to-order selections wherever you are. Choose from a variety of dishes, such as fresh Island tuna with Japanese yams, oyster platter with butter-herb sauce, lobster tempura, beef tataki with ponzu sauce, red soybean soup, and sushi rolls. You can also go prix fixe with appetizer, soup, entrée, and dessert.

Nobu Waikīkī (237-6999; nobu restaurants.com), Waikīkī Parc Hotel, 2233 Helumoa Rd. Open daily for dinner. Expensive. Reservations recommended. Japanese chef Nobuyuki Matsuhisa now has restaurants around the world, after founding a successful eatery in Beverly Hills and then partnering with Robert De Niro on the first Nobu. Culinary recognition of both Chef Nobu and the restaurant Nobu is too extensive to begin describing.

After hearing all the hype, we'd been expecting glitz and some attitude. Instead we experienced an upscale, cordial, bustling atmosphere; welcoming and well-informed servers; and food that actually lived up to the name. Your server will be key in ordering; the restaurant serves dishes tapas-style to share (Nobu lived in Peru and takes tips from its cuisine), and he or she can advise you on which items may be right for your taste and how much to order.

The menu is diverse: bigeye tuna tataki with ponzu, yellowtail sashimi with jalapeño, lobster seviche, shiitake salad, eggplant miso, baby abalone with garlic sauce, king crab tempura, asparagus bigeye tuna sushi roll, banana coffee brûlée.

The bar/lounge, in a separate room, oozes a little more swank and also serves the full menu.

Orchids (923-2311; halekulani.com), Halekūlani, 2199 Kalia Rd. Open daily for all three meals; Sun. brunch. Expensive–very expensive. Reservations are recommended, especially for Sunday brunch. Yet another Honolulu winner is the Halekūlani's Orchids, right on the oceanfront. The ambience is light, bright, clean, and understated elegance, with fresh orchid sprays enveloping patrons in delicate colors. It's a quiet restaurant, with a strong Japanese clientele.

Lunch and dinner are very good, with dishes such as shutome, scallop-and-shrimp curry, miso lobster consommé, seared jumbo scallops, Kona lobster, and moi. Breakfast Mon.–Sat. is upscale à la carte, but Sunday is when Orchids is in highest demand. Residents and visitors come together to enjoy its award-winning, all-you-can-eat brunch, complete with flute and harp accompaniments. (If you're thinking this would be the perfect place for Mother's Day brunch—and it is—call immediately. They take reservations for the occasion up to a year in advance.)

Dinner service requires collared shirts and slacks for men. The hotel offers free valet parking.

Roy's (923-7697; roysrestaurant.com), Waikīkī Beach Walk, 226 Lewers St. Open daily for lunch and dinner. Expensive. Reservations recommended. Roy Yamaguchi is known internationally as a culinary pioneer; *Gourmet* magazine has even called him "the father of modern East–West cooking." Although he now owns upscale restaurants across the Mainland, his very first restaurant was here in Hawai'i, where fusion-style cuisine has a long history of appreciation.

This is the newest of his several O'ahu locations, and the only one in Waikīkī. Inside, the atmosphere is stylishly contemporary and simple. The kitchen opens onto a fairly loud main room with a bustling bistro feel. A narrow patio area faces the street.

We have always been impressed by the quality of service at Roy's. It's professional all the way—which is saying a lot in Hawai'i, where it can often be too laidback or uneven. The food is equally excellent, with items like lobster bisque, pūlehu-smoked sirloin steak, island 'ahi poke, Hawaiian style misoyaki butterfish, and Roy's signature melting-hot chocolate soufflé. All dishes emphasize high-quality, fresh local ingredients. The award-winning and impeccable wine list will add to an already perfect evening. Validated valet parking is available at Embassy Suites on Beach Walk.

Sansei Seafood Restaurant & Sushi Bar (931-6286; sanseihawaii.com), Waikīkī Beach Marriott Resort & Spa, 2552 Kalākaua Ave. Open daily for dinner. Moderate–expensive. Reservations recommended. In this award-winning sushi-and-more restaurant founded by local celebrity chef Dave (D. K.) Kodama, freshness and a fusion of original flavors are par for the course. The menu features dishes such as Japanese calamari salad, mango crab-salad hand roll, seared foie gras nigiri sushi, lobster-and-blue-crab ravioli, asparagus tempura spears, chili porcini mushroom crusted filet of beef tenderloin, and tempura-fried macadamia nut ice cream. The seafood and sushi are the special draws. On Friday and Saturday nights between 10 PM and 1 AM, many dishes are half price. Hawai'i has only a handful of master sommeliers, and one of them, Chuck Furuya, presides over the stellar wine selection. *Wine Spectator* has given it an award of excellence. Validated parking, including valet, is available at the hotel.

Singha Thai Cuisine (941-2898; singhathai.com), 1910 Ala Moana Blvd. Open daily for dinner. Moderate–expensive. Reservations recommended. Opened by Chai Chaowasaree in 1988, Singha has earned numerous accolades both locally and overseas over the years, and it's the only Thai restaurant in Hawai'i to be certified by the Royal Thai Government. The restaurant is beautifully decorated in rich woods, orchid bouquets, and bronze and wood Buddha sculptures. Thai dancers add to the flavor.

Dishes include Thai curry puffs, fresh 'ahi katsu, Thai yellow curry with pineapple and potato, fresh mahimahi, and spicy Siamese fighting fish, all meant to be shared at the table. Follow them with mochi ice cream with fresh berries or fried caramelized banana cream cheese puffs with Grand Marnier sauce. Singha also offers prix fixe dinners crafted for two to five people and a large selection of wines, tropical drinks, sake, and micro-beers. Free validated parking is available in the building.

The restaurant once hit mostly high marks, but we're hearing mixed reviews these days on the quality of both food and service.

Tiki's Grill & Bar (923-8454; tikisgrill.com), Aston Waikīkī Beach Hotel, 2570 Kalākaua Ave. Open daily for lunch and dinner. Moderate–expensive. Reservations recommended. Tiki's is popular with residents and visitors, as ideal for families as it is for 20- and 30-somethings wanting to have a great time. Its open-air design features sweeping views across Kalākaua Avenue and Waikīkī Beach, and the festive interior shapes trendy, South Pacific retro style around the classic icon of tiki carvings. They've won several local and national awards, including "best new restaurant," "most spirited staff," and "good neighbor"—the last relating to its commitment to community development.

We would not call Tiki's gourmet dining, but the Island-casual food is pretty good: coconut shrimp, fried green Waialua tomato sandwich, calamari katsu, seared 'ahi skewers, guava-glazed baby back ribs, macadamia nut crusted mahimahi, and mochi ice cream are just a sampling. Several prix fixe menus help offset costs. Add local entertainment, a few drinks, and free validated parking at the hotel, and you're set for the evening.

Todai Sushi and Seafood Buffet (947-1000; todai.com), 1910 Ala Moana Blvd. Open daily for lunch and dinner. Inexpensive–moderate. Reservations are accepted. Todai is an international chain featuring an American-style, all-you-can-eat sushi and seafood spread that, at a whopping 160 feet long, rivals Las Vegas buffets. Cafeteria-bustling in mood, it's "every eater for himself." They offer 40 different kinds of sushi, plus snow crab legs, prime rib, and an endless array of other hot entrées, salads, and desserts. Add on wine, imported beer, and Japanese sake to wash it all down.

Lunch costs less than dinner, and during the week both are a little bit less expensive than on weekends. They offer special pricing for kids under 12, according to height. There may be a crowd outside when you arrive, but the large interior ensures a reasonable wait. Validated parking is available in the building.

EATING OUT Our island is rich with humble drive-ins, roadside shrimp trucks, holes-in-the-wall, burger quickies, noodle shops, plate-lunch take-outs, delicatessens, and other homey "quick and not-so-quick" affordable eats. This is how most residents eat day-to-day. Some, you'll fall in love with and keep returning to. Others may tide you over on the way home from the beach. Most are inexpensive. We hope you'll enjoy!

✒ **California Pizza Kitchen** (924-2000; cpk.com), Center of Waikīkī, 2284 Kalākaua Ave. Open daily for lunch and dinner. Moderate. Reservations are accepted. We said we'd try to steer you clear of chains, but this is a particularly good family choice in Waikīkī. Food's fresh and relatively healthy. The menu is huge, with items such as pear-and-Gorgonzola pizza, ginger salmon, and Waldorf salad. The kids' menu includes basic salads and Hawaiian pizzas. The best part: It's located right in the middle of Waikīkī on the main drag, making it an easy choice for dining without heavy fuss.

✒ 🐾 **Cha Cha Cha** (923-7797), 342 Seaside Ave. Open daily for lunch and dinner. Inexpensive–moderate. Reservations are accepted, except on Tue. Tucked away in the middle of Waikīkī, this perky little Carib/Tex-Mex spot has both a colorful personality and pretty tasty food for the price. You'll find a creatively casual menu with Jamaican jerk chicken burritos, mahimahi quesadillas, garlic soup served with tortilla strips, blackened fish Caesar salads, and more—plus happy hour 4–6 PM and again 9–11 PM. May we call that double happiness?

A kids' menu with "itty bitty" burritos and other goodies, super-friendly local-style service, a shorts-and-slippers attitude, and a streetfront outdoor patio make it a great place for an unpretentious and enjoyable evening with the gang or to hang out with your sweetie.

✇ **Cheesecake Factory** (924-5001; thecheesecakefactory.com), Royal Hawaiian Center, 2301 Kalākaua Ave. Open daily for breakfast (from 11 AM, but served all day), lunch, and dinner; Sun. brunch. Moderate. No reservations. Simply put, Waikīkī has few middle-income places to eat—so when this chain opened several years ago, visitors and residents went nuts. It's centrally located along the strip and stylishly pulled together. In fact, of the many Cheesecake Factory restaurants in the United States, this one's is a powerhouse, and waits can be extremely long. The menu features huge portions of more than 200 items, such as crispy artichoke hearts, hibachi steak, pear and endive salad, crabcake sandwich, wasabi-crusted 'ahi tuna, and chocolate cheesecake. On Sundays they offer a brunch menu 10–2.

✪ **Cream Pot** (429-0945; creampot honolulu.com), Hawaiian Monarch Hotel, 444 Niu St. Open for breakfast every day except Tue. Inexpensive-moderate. Reservations are recommended. If there's an antithesis to the biker bar, it's this sweet little French country kitchen on the ground floor of a not-so-sweet hotel. And guess what—the food is delicious. Each Belgian waffle, strip of maple bacon, banana crêpe, baked egg, cheese omelet, and serving of eggs Benedict is as thoughtfully prepared by owner Nathan Tran and team as the detailed

room decor. Some portions run small, like the bacon, but are high in flavor. It's popular with young Japanese but catching on with everyone else. Open through the lunch hour. All in all we consider this a secret breakfast gem.

Eggs 'n' Things (949-0820; eggsn things.com), 343 Saratoga Rd. Open daily for all three meals. Inexpensive. No reservations. Longtime Waikīkī favorite Eggs 'n' Things has recently stepped it up from a late-night/early-morn breakfast haunt to full service at "normal" hours. This has reduced its color somewhat—it used to host tourists in the morning, and off-duty cops and strippers in the wee hours. It must be listed in every Japanese guidebook or be on every bus tour route, because by midmorning an army of young Japanese tourists stretches out the door for breakfast. Dinner draws locals back in. If you've been here before, note that Eggs has changed locations (again), and it's way cuter—open-air, with a little outdoor counter terrace. Check-in is downstairs. Breakfast and lunch include 'ahi tuna steak, crêpes, omelets, waffles, and pancakes, served anytime. Dinner is limited to a few meaty specials. Frankly, we don't get the hype.

✇ **Hyatt on the Beach** (924-8646), 2453 Kalākaua Ave. Just across the street from the Hyatt—and, you guessed it, right on the beachfront—this snack bar deluxe is perfect for grabbing a bite while on the sand. Food choices include plate-lunch specials, hot dogs, and shave ice.

Le Jardin (921-2236), Hyatt Regency, 2424 Kalākaua Ave. Located in the beautiful Hyatt lobby, the petite Le Jardin features fresh juices, sandwiches, açai bowls, and crêpes.

MAC 24-7 (921-5564; mac247 waikiki.com), Hilton Waikīkī Prince Kūhiō, 2500 Kūhiō Ave. Open 24/7. Moderate. Reservations are accepted. This is definitely a fun, hip place to eat, with both residents and visitors as regulars. MAC 24-7 stands for "modern American cooking" and full service around the clock—a bonus not lost on Waikīkī crowds that often keep nonconformist hours. It should also stand for monstrous portions, officialized by the Travel Channel's *Man v. Food* show.

Big often means bland—but we've found the food here to be quite good. Attempt to work your way through creative takes on comfort foods, like the "Elvis"—chunky peanut butter pancakes swirled with crispy bacon— or pecan praline French toast, a Reuben corned beef sandwich, spicy tuna poke, bathtub-sized portions of saimin, and giant cupcakes. Order anything off the menu at any time.

We love the streamlined pop-art coffee-shop feel, eye-candy decor, lush garden view, and full bar with a flat-screen TV. The hotel offers validated valet parking.

Panya Waikīkī (791-2969; panya bakery.com), 2233 Kalākaua Ave., Building B. High-quality salads, sandwiches, and smoothies await at this "mini" Panya, little sister of other town locations. A great choice for take-out.

Teddy's Bigger Burgers (926-3444; teddysbiggerburgers.com), Hyatt Waikīkī Grand Hotel, 134 Kapahulu Ave. One of Hawai'i's favorite burger joints builds quality burgers and all the extras—even peanut butter shakes. It's a local favorite.

Ramen Nakamura (922-7960), 2141 Kalākaua Ave. At this classic little Japanese noodle joint, patrons are mostly from Japan. Great ambience and eats, if you can get a seat at the bar.

Ruffage Natural Foods (922-2042; ruffagenatural.com), 2443 Kūhiō Ave. A hidden gem, Ruffage makes great smoothies and all-natural sandwiches, very homemade. A little patio gives you room to eat lunch and dinner.

MAC 24-7

Courtesy Lew Harrington

♫ **Wailana Coffee House** (955-1764), 1860 Ala Moana Blvd. Open 24/7. Inexpensive. Reservations are accepted for groups of eight or more. A landmark 1960s coffee shop with decent food, yesteryear pricing, and friendly wahine servers; you'll think you're in the small-town Midwest until you see Spam, fried saimin, and papaya on the menu. Other standard local fare includes omelets, paniolo burgers, mahimahi sandwiches, and hot fudge ice cream cake. Service is fast and the atmosphere is easy-going; locals line the bar reading their morning papers, and in the booths brightly clad visitors discuss the day. The best part: This is a 24-hour diner with validated parking in the building.

Wolfgang Puck Express (931-6226; wolfgangpuck.com), Aston Waikīkī Beach Hotel, 2570 Kalākaua Ave. For gourmet on the go, try Wolfgang's, across from the beach. You'll find excellent thin-crust pizzas, rosemary rotisserie chicken with garlic mashed potatoes, and more.

AFTERNOON TEA The Veranda (921-4600; moana-surrider.com), Moana Surfrider, 2365 Kalākaua Ave. Honolulu was once as British as it was American, so the tradition of afternoon tea—finger sandwiches, scones with cream, freshly brewed teas, and other tiny treats—has a long history here. You can expect Old World plantation glamour and ease at the Veranda's daily seaside event. Light lunch items can be added on, as well as champagne. Dress the part: They've been serving tea here for 100 years.

SWEETS & TREATS ♫ ✪ **Lappert's Ice Cream** (944-9663; lappertshawaii.com), Hilton Hawaiian Village, 2005 Kalia Rd. Although now in locations on the Mainland, Lappert's was founded on Kaua'i by a retired Austrian. Some of the creamiest, chunkiest ice cream this side of Europe. Try our favorite flavor, Kaua'i Pie.

TEA & COFFEE Honolulu Coffee Co. (533-1500), Moana Surfrider, 2365 Kalākaua Ave. A local fave, tucked into a street-view wing of the hotel. Try their breakfast waffles or coffee and gelato in the afternoon.

✪ **Starbucks** (926-4863), DFS Galleria, 330 Royal Hawaiian Ave. Hidden at the very back of a designer shopping gallery, with a full open-air patio under yawning trees. Perfect for a mellow evening with friends and open from 8 AM until 11 PM.

WINE BARS A wine bar is the perfect place for good drinks, a sophisticated atmosphere, and tasty food.

Pane e Vino (923-8466; 408 Lewers St.). At this rustic, soothing, and Italian-owned establishment (Fabrizio Favale also owns Café Mediterraneo in Makiki), you'll have a hard time believing you're in Waikīkī. Open until it seems time to close.

✳ Entertainment

O'ahu has a pretty mellow night scene, but it still offers good diversity within the city limits. From surf bars to cocktail lounges, dance clubs to jazz taverns, your poison is here. We've organized the nightspots below according to type. Cheers!

LEWERS LOUNGE

DANCE CLUBS Level 4 (946-3100; 14Waikiki.com), Royal Hawaiian Center, 2233 Kalākaua Ave. Level 4 is local-style Vegas, youthful and hard-hitting edgy-fashionable. Occupying the shell of a short-lived fantasy stage production, it's built to impress.

Zanzibar (924-3939; zanzabarhawaii .com), Waikīkī Trade Center, 2525 Kūhiō Ave. Faux-Egyptian glitz and groove collide, as do a mixed crowd of residents, military, and tourists. One of Waikīkī's longer-running clubs, with themes and music styles changing every night.

GAY BARS Fusion (924-2422; fusionwaikiki.com), 2260 Kūhiō Ave. Get into Fusion's weekly guest DJs and notorious *Paper Doll Revue*, billed as Hawai'i's longest-running female illusionist show.

Hula's Bar & Lei Stand (923-0669; hulas.com), Waikīkī Grand Hotel, 134 Kapahulu Ave. Hula's is one of the longest-running clubs of any kind in Honolulu, and an institution in the gay scene worldwide. Day or evening, you can drink, dance, Web-surf, play pool, make new friends, or just enjoy the remarkable ocean view.

In-Between (926-7060), 2155 Lau'ula St. A mixed scene with mostly men, this hard-to-find little karaoke and cruise bar near Prada welcomes everyone. Happy hour specials run until 8 PM.

RUMFIRE

Wang Chung's (921-9176; wang chungs.com), 2410 Koa Ave. How can you go wrong with that name? The decor is adorably sake-bar, with karaoke on the menu. Men and women are welcome.

LOUNGES La Mer (923-2311; halekulani.com), Halekūlani, 2199 Kalia Rd. Even if dinner at Hawai'i's most exclusive restaurant is out of your budget, the bar may still be open for negotiation. Serene sumptuousness in caramel lighting and the most highbrow of libations await. High-level dress code in effect.

Lewers Lounge (923-2311; haleku lani.com), Halekūlani, 2199 Kalia Rd. Also at the Halekulani, this luxuriant and design-award-winning bar for the sophisticated set comes in first place for quality cocktails and Rat-Pack-style live music. Add the final touch to the evening with caviar or choco-late fondue.

Nobu Bar & Lounge (237-6999; noburestaurants.com), Waikīkī Parc Hotel, 2233 Helumoa Rd. Deliciously upscale in dark, trendy decor, the bar also serves a full menu from the adja-cent restaurant. A sleek and hip escape.

✪ **RumFire** (922-4222; rumfirewai kiki.com), Sheraton Waikīkī, 2255 Kalākaua Ave. Part of the Sheraton's hip new look, RumFire has an out-standing location right on the water and more than 100 rum-based drinks to choose from. Unique patio fire pits are cutting-edge cool.

PUBS The Yard House (923-9273; yardhouse.com), Waikīkī Beach Walk, 226 Lewers St. Not so much a tradi-tional pub as a Mainland chain restaurant and sports bar, the Yard House still makes our list because of its incredible selections of beer.

SUNSET PATIOS ✪ **Beach Bar** (921-4600; moana-surfrider.com), Moana Surfrider, 2365 Kalākaua Ave. Service and drink quality are heavily trumped by location. Your evening will unfold in a romantic, oceanfront courtyard beneath a sprawling banyan tree more than a century old. Live performances of dreamy Hawaiian songs begin at 6 PM each evening and will transport you back in time.

Duke's Waikīkī/Barefoot Bar (922-2268; dukeswaikiki.com), Outrigger Waikīkī, 2335 Kalākaua Ave. You've probably already heard about it—and yes, real beach boys do in fact some-times hang out here. Crowds are a guarantee, as well as touristy schlock and questionable quality, but it's still a good time. Request to be seated on the sand-level terrace. Live perform-ances start at 4 PM nightly, often by well-known Hawai'i musicians.

✪ **House Without a Key** (923-2311; whalekulani.com), Halekūlani, 2199 Kalia Rd. Our favorite destination has attracted residents and visitors since the 1930s with a picture-perfect oceanfront and Diamond Head view. Add timeless Hawaiian music per-formed by an accomplished trio—and accompanied most evenings by former Miss Hawai'i Kanoe Miller, an out-standing hula dancer—your cocktail hour will likely be fabulously soothing. Arrive before sunset and stay for the light dinner fare if you can't tear your-self away. Music begins at 5:30 PM.

Mai Tai Bar (931-4600; royal -hawaiian.com), The Royal Hawaiian, 2259 Kalākaua Ave. Rumor has it that this is where the mai tai drink came of age. The setting is as close to the sand and sunset as you can get, and live music begins at 6 PM, except on Monday. A colorful, so-chic-under-the-umbrella kind of experience.

✳ Selective Shopping

ALOHAWEAR It's true that in Hawai'i we're happiest in aloha shirts, shorts, bathing suits, and slippers. Men, pick up a quality, authentic aloha shirt while you're here. You can wear it every day to every activity and almost every restaurant. Ladies, we're sad to report that the days of mu'umu'u are dying out (Hawai'i's missionaries created the first mu'umu'u—it's a twist on the Mother Hubbard, designed to fit the larger Hawaiian frame), but we're giving you directions to the best sources on the island.

Moonbow Tropics (924-1496), Outrigger Reef, 2169 Kalia Rd. Better-quality men's aloha shirts from name brands, as well as attractive tropical resort wear and accessories for women.

Pineapple County (926-8245; pineapplecounty.com), 342 Lewers St. Mostly a cutesy store catering to Japanese visitors, for years they've also featured a rack on the sidewalk with excellent-quality used aloha shirts at a reasonable price.

Tori Richard (924-1811; toririchard .com), Hyatt Regency, 2424 Kalākaua Ave. In business for about 50 years, as well as local and family run, Tori Richard designs and creates high-end, original, internationally styled Island clothing for men and women. Also in Waikīkī at (943-9472) Hilton Hawaiian Village, 2005 Kalia Rd., and (921-

2702) The Royal Hawaiian, 2259 Kalākaua Ave.

ANTIQUES & COLLECTIBLES
Gallery Tokusa (926-1766), Halekūlani, 2199 Kalia Rd. Located in the Halekūlani hotel, this petite shop carries necklaces and antique Japanese netsuke, or obi fasteners.

ART & CRAFTWORK Artists have always been attracted to the natural beauty of Hawai'i. And like countless scenic and heavily visited regions of the world, Hawai'i now has galleries swollen with watercolor paintings of abandoned coastlines, lone cabins in misty glens, leaping dolphin sculptures, and the like—especially in Waikīkī and Hale'iwa. Wyland Galleries Hawai'i, Galerie Lassen, and Tabora Gallery, all found along

TORI RICHARD

Waikīkī's main drags, specialize in these themes.

To purchase paintings directly from the artists themselves, visit Waikīkī's **Art on the Zoo Fence** (artonthezoo fence.com), held along the east fence of the Honolulu Zoo weekends 9–4. For decades, bands of artists have set up lawn chairs here and hung up their works; some have made a name for themselves over time. The **Waikīkī Artfest** (696-6717) is presented by the Handcrafters and Artisans Alliance and features a broader collection of arts and crafts. It's held one weekend every month at the west end of Kapiolani Park. For both, expect a variety of quality.

BOOKS & MUSIC Borders Express (922-4154; borders.com), Royal Hawaiian Center, 2250 Kalākaua Ave. The only general bookstore in Waikīkī is open late and also features a small selection of Hawaiian CDs.

BOUTIQUES Cina Cina (926-0444; cinacinahawaii.com), The Royal Hawaiian, 2259 Kalākaua Ave. A unique and artistic store with Asiatic-European clothing, jewelry, and small gifts.

✪ **Noa Noa** (949-8980), Hilton Hawaiian Village, 2005 Kalia Rd. Upscale silken scarves, dresses, and robes feature Polynesian tapa-cloth designs and are hand-printed in Tahiti. Also at Waikīkī Beach Walk (923-6500), 227 Lewers St., and in Greater Honolulu (593-0343), Ward Centre, 1200 Ala Moana Blvd., Kaka'ako.

HAWAIIANA & OTHER HAWAI'I-MADE CRAFTS Check local calendar listings for craft fairs, where many of Hawai'i's best-quality handcrafts are sold at the best prices. Our favorite is the twice-yearly fair at the Mission Houses Museum. The **Pacific Handcrafters Guild** (254-6788; pacifichandcraftersguild.com) periodically holds public shows and sales—a great opportunity to meet the artists and purchase crafts wholesale.

Aloha 'Ukulele (955-5255; aloha ukulele.com), Hilton Hawaiian Village, 2005 Kalia Rd. Bring home a tenor, concert, or soprano ukulele from some of Hawai'i's best makers.

Bob's Ukulele (372-9623; bobsukulele .com), Waikīkī Beach Marriott, 2552 Kalākaua Ave. Bob carries a huge collection of 'ukulele from top brands, as well as private label makers.

Hawaiian Quilt Collection (922-2462; hawaiian-quilts.com), The Royal Hawaiian, 2259 Kalākaua Ave. The unique styles and philosophy of Hawaiian quilting began with the introduction of the art by missionaries, and carefully crafted quilt works still carry great prestige and value. Also at the Hyatt Regency Waikīkī (926-5272), 2424 Kalākaua Ave.

Little Hawaiian Craft Shop (926-2662), Royal Hawaiian Center, 2201 Kalākaua Ave. In business since 1968, this special store features quality work from more than 100 local artists. It emphasizes traditional crafts such as koa bowls, classic Hawaiian-style feather hatbands, and delicate shell necklaces, plus carries a few trinkets.

Mana Hawai'i (923-2220), Waikīkī Beach Walk, 226 Lewers St. Half studio space and half shop, Mana is a cooperative by Hawaiian practitioners and craft workers.

Martin & MacArthur (792-1140; martinandmacarthur.com), Hilton Hawaiian Village, 2005 Kalia Rd. If you want exclusive, handcrafted native koa products such as a rocking chair, hand mirror, bowl, or jewelry box, this is your store. They also carry locally made jewelry and other smaller items. Also at (941-0074) Ala Moana Center, Greater Honolulu.

✪ **Nohea Gallery** (923-6644; noheagallery.com), Moana Surfrider, 2365 Kalākaua Ave. Another local gallery known for quality Hawaiiana and other arts and crafts. They represent more than 450 artists, most whom live and work in Hawaiʻi. Choose from handcrafted koa boxes, ceramic pieces, paintings, jewelry, and more.

KID STUFF Kids deserve fun souvenirs from Hawaiʻi, too. Consider gifts such as surfwear, Hawaiian-print baby clothing, creative plush toys, Hawaiʻi-themed storybooks, or locally made jewelry.

✍ **Natural Selection Gift Shop** (923-9741; waquarium.org), Waikīkī Aquarium, 2777 Kalākaua Ave. Books on Hawaiian marine life, kid-sized

T-shirts, cuddly plush ocean critters, and more.

✍ **Today's Little People** (922-1772; alohakids.com), Outrigger Waikīkī, 2335 Kalākaua Ave. A locally founded shop carrying handmade Island clothing, books, games, collector's dolls, and educational toys, some found nowhere else.

✍ **Tropical Outpost** (971-7171; honoluluzoo.org), Honolulu Zoo, 151 Kapahulu Ave. Creative, zoo-inspired kids' (and adults') gifts like animal masks, educational toys, plush critters, and T-shirts.

SHOPPING CENTERS DFS Galleria Hawaiʻi (931-2700; dfsgalleria .com/en/Hawaii), 330 Royal Hawaiian Ave. A recent total overhaul turned trinketville into designerville, mostly still catering to Japanese visitors. Find Marc by Marc Jacobs, Coach, Chloé, Ralph Lauren and more. Wind your way to the back for Island gifts and an excellent "hideaway" patio Starbucks.

THE HONOLULU ZOO'S TROPICAL OUTPOST

International Market Place (971-2080; internationalmarketplace.com), 2330 Kalākaua Ave. The year 1955 calls—as do millions of chotchkies from around the world posing as Hawai'i-made gifts. A surreal experience worth seeing.

Royal Hawaiian Center (922-0588; shopwaikiki.com), 2201/2233/2301 Kalākaua Ave. With more than 100 shops, the Royal Hawaiian Center stretches for three blocks and up several floors. A recent $84 million renovation really upgraded the look.

Most of the streetfront shops are big designers like Hermès, Kate Spade, Cartier, and Salvatore Ferragamo. Other stores include Ferrari, the Apple Store, Borders Express, Lush, Little Hawaiian Craft Shop, Princess Tam-Tam Lingerie, Royal Hawaiian Golf Shop, Allure Swimwear, and

L'Occitane, plus dining options like the popular Cheesecake Factory. Validated parking available.

Waikīkī Beach Walk (931-3953; waikikibeachwalk.com), 226/227 Lewers St. Hawai'i's newest shopping destination opened in 2007 after several blocks of aging buildings were swept out of the way. Special stores include Noa Noa, Oasis, Mana Hawai'i, Quiksilver, and Malibu Shirts. Eateries include Yard House, Ruth's Chris, and the excellent Roy's Waikīkī. Validated parking available at Embassy Suites or Wyndham.

Waikīkī Shopping Plaza (923-1191; waikikishoppingplaza.com), 2250 Kalākaua Ave. A middle-road, five-floor mall with a few good choices such as Guess, Le Sportsac, Ukulele House, Tanaka of Tokyo, and new-wing retailer Sephora. The Visitor

WAIKĪKĪ BEACH WALK

Aloha Society/Travelers Aid of Honolulu is also here.

SURF & OTHER SPORTING GEAR

Buy top-name surfboards, board shorts, bikinis, and other cool surf and beachwear at one of our many surf shops. They're on every corner, so we'll just list a few of the biggest and best.

Billabong (923-4491; billabong.com), Hyatt Regency, 2424 Kalākaua Ave. One of the biggest names in the sport, with hot clothing designs that reflect the spirit of the Aussie Billabong's pro surfer team.

Local Motion (924-4406; localmotionhawaii.com), Sheraton Waikīkī, 2255 Kalākaua Ave. Local Motion is a "for real" surf shop, and boards are their true calling. But they've also made a name for trendy, good-looking surf clothing and accessories.

Quiksilver (921-2793; quiksilver.com), Waikīkī Beach Walk, 270 Lewers St. The name Quiksilver is legendary in the surfing world. This 6,200-square-foot signature shop is loaded with surfboards and surfing gear, plus clothing for kids, women, and men. Also pick up wetsuits, skateboarding equipment, and surf DVDs.

South Seas Aquatics (922-0852), Kalākaua Business Center, 2155 Kalākaua Ave. This small shop has some of the best prices on the island for quality fins, masks, wet suits, rash guards, and scuba gear.

SWIMWEAR

Allure Swimwear (926-1174; allure-hawaii.com), Royal Hawaiian Center, 2201 Kalākaua Ave. One of the best swimwear collections for teen girls and women on the island. Styles are hot and trendy, and selection is copious. Allure has a second location in Waikīkī (949-6651), Hilton Hawaiian Village, 2005 Kalia Rd.

Loco Boutique (922-7160; locoboutique.com), Pacific Beach Hotel, 2490 Kalākaua Ave. These "bad girl" bikinis are unique and playful, with a touch of urban sass. They also have a second Waikīkī location (926-7131), Waikīkī Outrigger Malia, 358 Royal Hawaiian Ave.

Macy's (926-5217; macys.com), 2314 Kalākaua Ave. The Waikīkī Macy's overflows with great bathing suits for everyone in all shapes, sizes, and styles.

Greater Honolulu 2

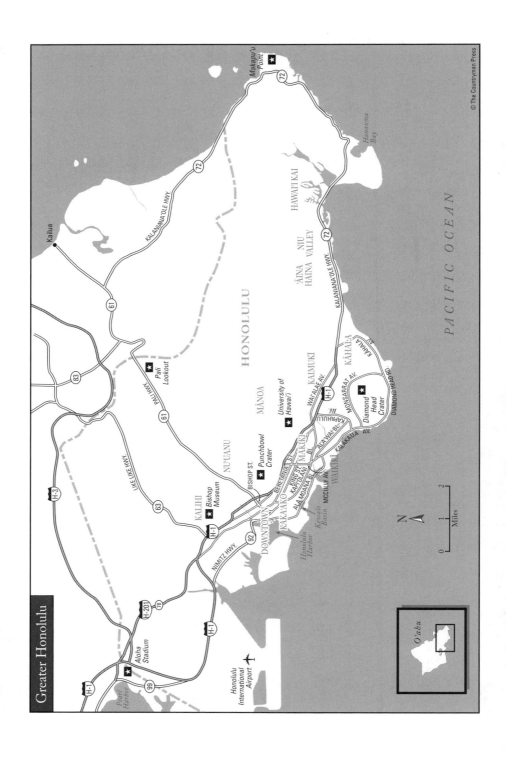

Greater Honolulu

© The Countryman Press

PACIFIC OCEAN

HONOLULU

Makapu'u Point

Hanauma Bay

HAWAI'I KAI

'ĀINA HAINA

NIU VALLEY

KALANIANA'OLE HWY.

KAHALA

KAHALA AV.

WAI'ALAE AV.

KAIMUKI

MONSARRAT AV.

DIAMOND HEAD RD.

Diamond Head Crater

Kailua

KALANIANA'OLE HWY.

PALI HWY.

Pali Lookout

MĀNOA

University of Hawai'i

Punchbowl Crater

NU'UANU

LIKE LIKE HWY.

BISHOP ST.

BERETANIA ST.

KING ST.

KAPI'OLANI BL.

MAKIKI

ALA MOANA BL.

ALA WAI AV.

MCCULLY AV.

KAPAHULU AV.

KALĀKAUA AV.

WAIKIKI

KAKA'AKO

Kewalo Basin

DOWNTOWN

KALIHI

Bishop Museum

Honolulu Harbor

NIMITZ HWY.

H-3

Aloha Stadium

Pearl Harbor

Honolulu International Airport

O'ahu

N

Miles

0   1   2

GREATER HONOLULU

The City and County of Honolulu includes the entire island, but the boundaries of the city of Honolulu stretch 18 miles from eastern Pearl Harbor to Makapuʻu Point, and to the high mountain crests deep behind the city. Often referred to on Oʻahu simply as "town," Honolulu is the only full urban experience in the entire state and home to more than a third of Hawaiʻi's 1.3 million residents.

Within Honolulu's great expanse you'll find every kind of resident, from Micronesian immigrants working three jobs to Hollywood celebrities with three estates. Prized residential suburbs include the venerable and grand neighborhoods of Mānoa and Nuʻuanu, and the glamorous Kāhala, Portlock, Diamond Head, and Hawaiʻi Loa Ridge. Kāhala Avenue still reigns as our most prominent address.

The greater downtown Honolulu area is the heartbeat of the state. Here you'll find the Merchant Street Historic District, Capital Historic District, Chinatown Historic District, and historic shipping waterfront, as well as the financial district.

HOSPITALS Kaiser Permanente Medical Center & Clinic (432-0000), 3288 Moanalua Rd., Moanalua.

Kapiʻolani Medical Center for Women & Children (983-6000), 1319 Punahou St., Punahou.

The Queen's Medical Center (538-9011), 1301 Punchbowl St., downtown.

Straub Clinic & Hospital (522-4000), 888 King St., Makiki.

✳ Neighborhoods

Chinatown Historic District. On the western edge of downtown, Chinatown is one of Hawaiʻi's most colorful districts. It developed in the late 1800s, shop by shop, through the hard work of Chinese immigrants who'd left local plantations to establish better lives for themselves. Encompassing the area within Nimitz Highway, Bethel Street, School Street, and River Street, Chinatown is still an

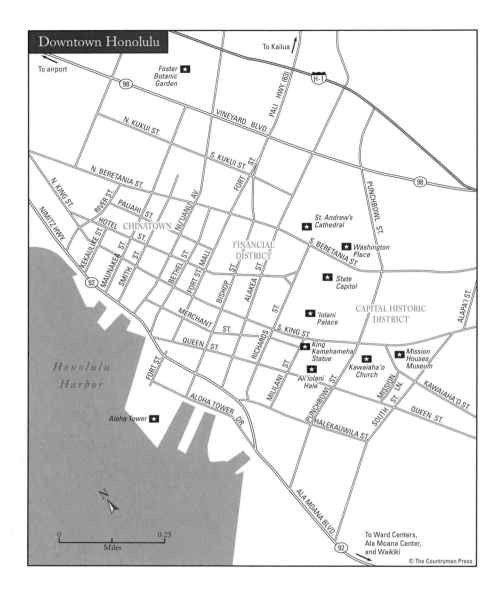

Downtown Honolulu

To Kailua

To airport

Foster Botanic Garden

PALI HWY. (63)

H-1

98

VINEYARD BLVD.

N. KUKUI ST.

S. KUKUI ST.

FORT ST.

PUNCHBOWL ST.

98

N. BERETANIA ST.

N. KING ST.

RIVER ST.

PAUAHI ST.

HOTEL ST.

NU'UANU AV.

St. Andrew's Cathedral

NIMITZ HWY.

KEKAULIKE ST.

MAUNAKEA ST.

SMITH ST.

CHINATOWN

BETHEL ST.

FORT ST. MALL

FINANCIAL DISTRICT

S. BERETANIA ST.

Washington Place

92

BISHOP ST.

ALAKEA ST.

State Capitol

ALAPA'I ST.

MERCHANT ST.

'Iolani Palace

CAPITAL HISTORIC DISTRICT

Honolulu Harbor

QUEEN ST.

RICHARDS ST.

S. KING ST.

King Kamehameha Statue

Mission Houses Museum

FORT ST.

MILILANI ST.

Ali'iolani Hale

Kawaiaha'o Church

MISSION ST. LN.

KAWAIAHA'O ST.

Aloha Tower

ALOHA TOWER DR.

PUNCHBOWL ST.

HALEKAUWILA ST.

SOUTH ST.

QUEEN ST.

N

ALA MOANA BLVD.

0   0.25
Miles

To Ward Centers, Ala Moana Center, and Waikīkī

92

© The Countryman Press

authentic, working neighborhood, although many of its occupants nowadays are immigrants from Southeast Asia and Micronesia instead of China.

Most of Chinatown's buildings date from the early 1900s. It was ravaged by fire twice—in 1886, and again in 1900, during which 38 blocks were destroyed in an attempt to eradicate bubonic plague. In World War II the downtown area was the undisputed heart of the city, and Chinatown's bars overflowed with servicemen eager to enjoy legal prostitution. When Japan attacked Pearl Harbor in

1941, stray anti-aircraft bombs crashed down on Chinatown's northern boundary, killing 12 area residents.

From the 1950s until the late 1990s, Chinatown degenerated into little more than skid row. By day working-class Asian families still ran the old fruit and fish markets, the herbal and flower shops. By night Hotel Street emptied, leaving only the most down-and-out prostitutes and the hopelessly addicted on the streets. Hotel Street was your last stop when you'd used up all your chances everywhere else. *Hawai'i Five-0* busts always seemed to climax in Chinatown.

There's more to the neighborhood these days, with slow gentrification working its way inward toward the core at King and Kekaulike. It still bustles with Asian markets, and the day starts early. Along Nu'uanu, Smith, and Bethel, small art galleries, hip bars, and trendy cafés radiate around the restored Hawai'i Theatre, the center of the "revived" Chinatown and its catalyst for change. A few World War II good-time hot spots remain, like Smith's Union Bar, worn down like an old army boot for the vagabond and hard-edged. And skid row it still is, although safer than it once was.

There's plenty to see in Chinatown if you're up for grit and local color. Leave the kids behind and wear jeans and a T-shirt instead of shorts and bright resortwear. Get lost on your own by day (we've included a basic map of the downtown area), or take a guided history or culinary tour (see listings later in this chapter). At night, be alert and have your destination mapped out.

On your own: Park at the Chinatown Municipal Lot on Beretania St., just past Nu'uanu Avenue. Exit the garage onto Pauahi Street and walk west. Check out Pacific Traditions Gallery, HASR, Grand Café & Bakery, Little Village Noodle House, Mei Sum, and Char Hung Sut, as well as the Ramsey Museum and One Night Stand. Turn left onto Maunakea. Enter Maunakea Marketplace, passing through food stalls to the fish market and exiting on Hotel Street. Cut through the pedestrian mall markets to King Street for the 100-year-old O'ahu Market and other shops. Head east on King and turn up Nu'uanu, where Tea at 1024, Louis Pohl Gallery, Lai Fong, and Indigo are

HONOLULU'S HISTORIC CHINATOWN

located. Turn right onto Hotel and left at Bethel for the Hawai'i Theatre, Du Vin, Soul de Cuba, and J. J. Dolan's. Return by turning west onto Pauahi to see the Bethel Street Gallery, ARTS at Marks Garage, Art Treasures Gallery, Peggy Chun Gallery, Chinatown Boardroom, and Pegge Hopper Gallery.

✪ **Hawai'i Capital Historic District**. Waikīkī may appear to visitors to be the center of Honolulu, but most residents would agree that downtown is still the heart of the island. Downtown's most important subdistrict is the Capital Historic District, bordered approximately by Ala Moana Boulevard, South Street, Vineyard Boulevard, and Richards Street. It houses many of Hawai'i's most famous historic sites, covered in this chapter. Beautiful, wide lawns and mature monkeypod, banyan, and shower trees surround many of the older buildings, making it one of Hawai'i's most lovely and interesting walks, despite heavy traffic running through it.

In the holiday season the neighborhood explodes with Honolulu City Lights, an illumination of buildings and heavy decoration aimed at pleasing the kids. The viewing frenzy increases as the big day approaches, with late-night auto gridlock Christmas Eve.

As an aside, local government officials seem to disagree on whether this is the "Capitol" district or the "Capital" district. We vote for the former, but go with the latter according to prevailing custom.

Park at Ali'i Hale, on Alakea and Hotel, and head east. Turn left onto Richards, walk east on Beretania, down Punchbowl, and west on King back to Richards. This takes you along the Hawai'i State Art Museum, St. Andrew's Cathedral, Washington Place, the State Capitol, Honolulu Hale, Kawaiaha'o Church, the Mission Houses Museum, the Hawai'i State Library, Ali'iolani Hale, the King Kamehameha Statue, and 'Iolani Palace, as well as other notable historic buildings like the Territorial Building and the YWCA. St. Damien's Cathedral of Our Lady of Peace is two blocks farther west. If you have time, tour the museums and the palace. The best area lunch is at the Hawai'i State Art Museum (weekday service; reservations recommended).

Merchant Street Historic District. One of the most charming streets on the entire island is the narrow and very brief Merchant Street, between Bishop and Nu'uanu in downtown's financial district area. Once the core of Honolulu trading and business, it's still home to law offices and other companies nestled in rows of vintage buildings spanning 150 years of history.

Begin on the corner of Richards and Merchant at the 1922 Old Federal Building, now a post office. Head west on Merchant, taking a quick detour left onto Alakea Street then right onto Bishop Street to see the beautiful arches of the 1929 Dillingham Transportation Building and the imposing Alexander & Baldwin Building. Its facade is loaded with symbolic designs, such as the water buffalo, which was used to pull sugarcane carts in the early years of the industry.

On weekdays, look up Bishop to see Hawai'i's prime business crowd in action, then continue west on Merchant. Pass the American Institute of Architects (AIA) at the 1901 Stangenwald Building, the 1902 Star-Bulletin Building, the

1896 Bishop Estate Building, the 1878 Bishop Bank, the 1854 Melchers Building, the 1898 Judd Building, the 1891 T. R. Foster Building, the 1906 McCandless Building, the 1871 Kamehameha V Post Office, the 1931 Honolulu Police Station, and the 1909 Yokohama Specie Bank, among others.

At the end of the street, grab a pint in Murphy's Bar & Grill. It occupies the old Royal Saloon, which opened in 1890. Its front sidewalk is made from blocks of granite used to ballast ships en route to the Islands from China, and a bar reportedly existed on the same site for at least 40 years prior to the saloon. The old post office you passed once featured separate service windows for ladies, as well as for Hawaiian, Japanese, and Portuguese customers. It now houses the theatrical playhouse Kumu Kahua, which specializes in productions that emphasize Hawaiian/local Hawai'i culture.

MODERN-DAY MERCHANT STREET

As a side run, step down Fort Street Mall along the way to see the 1930 C. Brewer Building, plus a small park with a historic gate and cannon. Straight ahead of you on the waterfront is Aloha Tower, erected in 1926. Get a free 360-degree view of downtown from the top.

✳ To See

ARCHAEOLOGICAL AND SACRED SITES ✪ Nu'uanu Pali Lookout,
Nu'uanu Pali State Wayside Park, off Hwy. 61. While not an archaeological site per se, the Nu'uanu Pali (cliffs of Nu'uanu) is a historic and culturally significant site for more than its panoramic view of Windward O'ahu. At this approximate location in 1795, Kamehameha I backed hundreds, or even thousands, of Hawaiians off its precipice in a decisive battle for control of O'ahu's kingdom. During the construction of the Old Pali Road in 1897 (you'll see remnants of it to the right of the lookout), workers along the base of the cliffs discovered an estimated 800 skulls and other bones, further proof of the great battle.

From Pali Hwy. (61) headed toward Kailua, take the Nu'uanu Pali Lookout exit, just before the tunnels. From Kailua, the exit is just after the tunnels. The lookout is open daily, with a small parking fee. Prepare for possible high winds, mist, or rain.

DIGGING UP THE PAST

Sometimes you can learn as much about a town from its departed as you can from living residents. **Oʻahu Cemetery** (538-1538; oahucemetery.org), 2162 Nuʻuanu Ave., Nuʻuanu, is Hawaiʻi's oldest public cemetery, founded in 1844. About 30,000 men, women, and children are buried here, many in graves and crypts with extraordinary funerary art. Some of its inhabitants played significant roles in Hawaiʻi's history, such as Lorrin Thurston, who led the overthrow of the Hawaiian monarchy. Others contributed to our knowledge of pre-contact Hawaiʻi, such as Hawaiian historian Samuel Kamakau and noted modern anthropologist Kenneth Emory. Internationally recognized individuals such as mythologist Joseph Campbell and the "father" of American baseball, Alexander Cartwright, are also here.

A Japanese cemetery, called Honolulu Memorial Park, was built next door in 1958. It houses **Kyoto Gardens**, which consists of two remarkable and historic columbarium: Kinkaku-Ji memorial and Sanju Pagoda. Neither has been properly maintained due to funding disputes, but they merit a glimpse from a safe distance.

HISTORIC SITES Read about the Mission Houses in *Museums & Galleries*.

Aliʻiolani Hale/King Kamehameha Statue/Judiciary History Center (539-4999; jchawaii.net), 417 S. King St., downtown. Open Mon.–Fri. 9–4. Free. Both the building and the statue are listed on the National Register of Historic Places. Gift shop. The trilogy of Aliʻiolani Hale, the famed King Kamehameha Statue, and the King Kamehameha V Judiciary History Center are rolled into one tidy location in the Capital Historic District. Learn more about the Judiciary History Center in the *Museums & Galleries* section of this chapter.

The Neoclassical Aliʻiolani Hale (also known as the Judiciary Building) was originally created to serve as the royal palace for King Kamehameha V but never fulfilled its destiny; instead the architectural plans were transformed into the Kingdom of Hawaiʻi's first and much-needed government building. When it finally opened in 1874 during the reign of King Kalākaua, it housed the legislature, treasury, boards of health and education, and state supreme court. A time capsule containing pictures of the royal family, stamps and coins of the kingdom, a newspaper, and other items was buried by Kamehameha V during the construction of the building and still lies beneath its walls. On its steps in 1893, American annexationists announced their overthrow of the Hawaiian kingdom. Today the building houses the Hawaiʻi State Supreme Court, court administration offices, a law library, and the Judiciary History Center.

Fronting Aliʻiolani Hale is a gold-leaf statue of Hawaiʻi's most celebrated king, Kamehameha I, commissioned by the Hawaiian monarchy in 1878. Designed by a Boston sculptor, it was bronze-cast in Italy and shipped to Hawaiʻi from Germany, only to be lost at sea when the vessel sank near the Falkland Islands. The statue you see is a

Established in 1823, the **Mission Cemetery**, Kawaiahaʻo Church, 957 Punchbowl St., downtown, is the oldest Western-style graveyard in Hawaiʻi. Buried behind the church are the original missionary settlers and their descendants, many of whom became prominent and powerful citizens. The Victorian-era **Kawaiahaʻo Cemetery** on the south side of the church contains the remains of many Hawaiians and other residents, some still unidentified.

The **National Memorial Cemetery of the Pacific** (532-3720), 2177 Puowaina Dr., Punchbowl, also known as Punchbowl Cemetery, is the most celebrated graveyard in the Islands and dedicated to those who served in the US armed forces. Learn more about it under *Historic Sites*.

Native Hawaiian burials exist across Oʻahu, from remote sand dunes to the Walmart foundation near Ala Moana Center. When discovered, local burial councils work to assess, guard, and repatriate them as best possible, and construction halts until archaeological excavations and proper care have been taken. Make your final stop at the circular grave site on the corner of Kalākaua and Kapahulu Avenues, next to the Honolulu Zoo. Here lie unidentified Hawaiian remains unearthed during the construction of modern Waikīkī.

duplicate cast from the same mold, dedicated in 1883 as part of King Kalākaua's coronation ceremony. The first statue was later recovered by fishermen and now rests in the birthplace of the king, on the island of Hawaiʻi; as predicted by numerous Hawaiians before the original statue had even left Europe, it would never stand anywhere but at Kohala. The 2008 Hawaiʻi state quarter features this statue. A triplet stands in Washington, DC's Emancipation Hall.

KING KAMEHAMEHA STATUE, DRAPED WITH LEI

Every June 11 King Kamehameha is celebrated with a series of events and an elaborate parade. The draping of his statue with strands of ʻilima and plumeria lei is one of the highlights.

Aloha Tower (528-5700; alohatower .com), 1 Aloha Tower Dr., downtown. Open daily 9:30–5. Free. An official National Historic Landmark on the old harbor front near downtown's Capital Historic District, Aloha Tower rivals Diamond Head and Waikīkī Beach as an internationally recognized Hawaiʻi icon.

Built in a mix of art deco and late Gothic Revival styles in 1926, this 10-story tower was the tallest building in the state for decades. One of the most endearing symbols of Hawai'i's welcome to the world, it's enthusiastically emblazoned with ALOHA in letters large enough that visitors arriving by ship could see them long before they reached the shore. The tower itself is visible from 15 miles out at sea, and in earlier days was a navigational landmark. During World War II it was painted in camouflage and served as a command and control center. Today it still serves as the harbormaster's control tower.

A vintage elevator takes you to the observation lookout at the top for a great view in all directions.

Cathedral of Our Lady of Peace (536-7036; cathedralofourladyofpeace.com), 1184 Bishop St., downtown. Open daily; call for hours. Free. On the National Register of Historic Places. Gift shop. The first Catholic missionaries arrived in Hawai'i from France in 1827. Congregationalist missionaries had already been working their magic in the Islands for nearly a decade by that time, so when the Catholics arrived, the royal family expelled them. In 1839 the king issued an edict of toleration for other religions, which attracted the Catholic missionaries back to Honolulu. They soon set about constructing Our Lady of Peace. In fact, King Kamehameha III donated the land to enable them to erect it.

Built using coral slabs and completed in 1843, the charmingly petite and simple Romanesque Revival cathedral is reputedly the oldest Catholic church in continuous use in the United States. It has served as the site of significant events, such as dignitary funerals, and was where Father Damien, sainted in 2009, was ordained in 1864. The tower has been rebuilt several times, most recently in 1917, and formerly held two French-made bells. The pipe organ inside the cathedral dates from 1934. The front doors are often locked; if so, enter through side doors. The gift shop almost exclusively carries St. Damien articles, and shop hours are limited.

Diamond Head Lighthouse, 3399 Diamond Head Rd., Diamond Head. On the National Register of Historic Places. Not open to the public. In 1878 a simple lookout was built at a rocky outcropping below Diamond Head crater, where Swedish-born "Diamond Head Charlie" was to keep an eye out for approaching ships. The first actual lighthouse on the spot was erected near his lookout in 1899 and featured a lens imported from France. When cracks were later found in its base, a new lighthouse was built at the same site in 1918. It is one of the best-known lighthouses in the world.

The Diamond Head Lighthouse stands nearly 57 feet high, provides 7,300 candlepower that can be seen from a distance of 18 miles at sea, and still contains the original 109-year-old lantern and watch room ironwork. Now fully automated and under the jurisdiction of the US Coast Guard, it continues to guide today's vessels as they maneuver off the coast of Honolulu. A keeper's bungalow built in 1921 sits adjacent to the tower.

Although there's no place to pull over next to the lighthouse, Diamond Head Road has several lookout points popular for parking. From the lookouts you'll get three sights for the price of one: the lighthouse tower, a famous windsurfing spot offshore, and the spectacular coastline.

Hawai'i State Capitol (586-0178; capitol.hawaii.gov), 415 S. Beretania St., downtown. The building courtyard and grounds are always open. Free. On the National Register of Historic Places. Opened in 1969, only 10 years after Hawai'i became a state, our colossal state capitol building emphasizes the modern while paying homage to Hawai'i's heritage and environment. Surrounded by nearly 2 acres of reflecting pools fed by artesian wells, the building represents an island in the Pacific—in fact a volcanic island, with a central 100-foot ceiling that opens to the sky and cone-shaped legislative chambers on either side. At nearly 360 feet long and 270 feet wide, the building's eaves are supported by 60-foot columns on four sides, which represent palm trunks. In the central courtyard, the 600,000-piece mosaic *Aquarius* glimmers like a pond. Within the House of Representatives and Senate halls, each paned by strips of glass for easy viewing, chandeliers made from hundreds of nautilus shells suspend from above. Fifteen-foot state seals weighing more than 7,000 pounds hang on two sides of the building.

A statue of St. Damien stands at the northern entrance in honor of his dedication to the people of Kalaupapa; the liberty bell near it was a gift of the federal government while Hawai'i was still a territory. At the southern entrance, a humanistic statue of Queen Lili'uokalani, the last royal monarch of the Islands, is always draped with fresh flowers. Also on the property is a memorial to veterans of the Vietnam and Korean Wars.

The capitol's entirely open-air design was intended to signify a government and people that are open and welcoming. It makes a statement at a glance: strong, united, and unique. Inside, the action begins in late January with the opening of Hawai'i's legislature, which lets out in late April/early May.

Hawai'i Theatre (528-0506; hawaii theatre.com), 1130 Bethel St., Chinatown. Guided tours available Tue. at 11 AM. Call for reservations. Admission $5. On the National Register of Historic Places. The downtown area's only surviving theater opened in 1922 and featured popular entertainment, theater productions, and films. As the years passed, along with the district's heyday, the need for the theater waned; it shuttered in 1984. Citizens and local organizations rallied to save the "Pride of the Pacific" from demolition; in 1996, following an outstanding and national-award-winning renovation of its art deco, Greek, and Roman elements, it reopened to much

HAWAI'I THEATRE

Courtesy David Franzen

fanfare. More than 100,000 residents and visitors now crowd into its halls each year for performances ranging from Chinese acrobatics to Russian ballet and cultural films.

The exterior design embellishments of the theater are minimal. A docent-guided tour of the interior, however, yields gold-leaf artistry, allegorical murals, split mohair seating, a mosaic dome, and a wonderful Robert Morgan orchestral theater pipe organ, in residence at the theater since 1936.

Honolulu Hale (768-4385), 530 S. King St., downtown. Open Mon.–Fri. 8–4:30. Free. On the National Register of Historic Places. Honolulu Hale serves as city hall and houses numerous municipal government offices, the most notable of which is that of the mayor. You'll see his parking stall out front. As you enter the building, note the 1,500-pound bronze front doors and 4,500-pound chandeliers.

This 1928 architectural gem reflects the Mediterranean Mission style design popular in Hawai'i at the time, with an interior courtyard, stairways, a speaker's balcony, and ceiling details modeled after the Bargello, a 13th-century palace in Florence. Designed by a team that included renowned island architect Charles Dickey, it was the first government building in Hawai'i to also incorporate Hawaiian motifs. Stonework by Italian sculptor Mario Valdastri and frescoes by Einar Peterson complement the beautiful inner courtyard, which has a ceiling that can be opened to the elements.

Thematic works of local artists or historic tributes are always on display in the courtyard. Portraits of Honolulu mayors line the hall behind it. In the small front garden, a traditional Japanese stone lantern memorial marks 100 years of Japanese immigration to Hawai'i, and an eternal flame burns in honor of September 11, 2001, bombing victims.

During the Christmas season, Honolulu Hale is the center of the city's popular Honolulu City Lights celebration.

✪ **'Iolani Palace State Monument** (522-0832; iolanipalace.org), 364 S. King St., downtown. Open Tue.–Sat. Call for hours and to reserve a tour. $12–$20 adults, $5 ages 5–12. Children under 5 not permitted. National Historic Landmark. Gift shop. If you choose to visit only one Hawaiian heritage historic site while in Hawai'i, this should be it. A Victorian-era palace built for King Kalākaua, 'Iolani Palace follows a long line of powerful and spiritually significant structures that have rested on the same site. Over the years it has served the people of Hawai'i as an official royal residence, republic and territory headquarters, American military headquarters, state government capitol, monument, and inspiration.

In ancient times a Hawaiian heiau, or temple, stood on these grounds; all that remains is the memory of its existence and its name, Ka'ahaimauli. Homes of several pre- and post-contact Hawaiian chiefs were also located here, as well as the crypts of post-contact royalty. In the mid-1800s a single-story, coral-block home on the site, belonging to an O'ahu chief, was transformed into the first royal palace; it served during the reign of several kings until the aging structure needed to be torn down.

When 'Iolani Palace was built in 1882, critics fumbled to explain its unique mix of mostly Italianate Renaissance architectural styles. Imposing and regal on the exterior, its interior was lushly decorated and absolutely state of the art. Featuring elevators, full-plumbing bathrooms, telephones, and electric lighting, it was more modern than the White House, which, at that time, had yet to install electric lighting and extensive plumbing. Crowned heads from around the world came to meet the king and marvel at his palace's illuminated beauty.

Despite its opulence, 'Iolani Palace has seen tragedy as much as gaiety. Its most notorious role was as a prison for Hawai'i's last queen. The popular Kalākaua had died unexpectedly in 1891 while in San Francisco, and his sister, Lili'uokalani, ascended to the throne. In an effort to thwart her plan to restore Hawaiian rights stripped from Kalākaua by force, a group of American-oriented businessmen initiated a coup d'état, claiming Hawai'i for the United States and holding the queen hostage.

Once the monarchy was disbanded, palace furniture and other effects were auctioned off. The Friends of 'Iolani Palace, an organization that today manages the estate, has succeeded in locating approximately 4,000 of the estimated 10,000 artifacts dispersed worldwide and placing them in their original positions within the palace walls.

The lovely grounds of the palace also include the old 'Iolani Barracks, a bandstand dating from 1883, traces of burials, and a banyan tree reportedly planted in the 1880s by Queen Kapi'olani.

'IOLANI PALACE, DRESSED IN HONOR OF KING KALĀKAUA

For residents, 'Iolani Palace is a poignant reminder of Hawai'i's history. Hawaiian rights activists and other groups often use the grassy acreage fronting the palace for protests and important commemorations.

✪ Kawaiaha'o Church/Lunalilo Mausoleum/Kawaiaha'o Cemetery (469-3000; kawaiahao.org), 957 Punchbowl St., downtown. Open Mon.–Fri. 8–4:30. Services Sun. at 9 AM (8:30 AM selected Sundays). Free (donations welcome). The church is a National Historic Landmark and is on the National Register of Historic Places. The first permanent Christian church to be built in the Islands, Kawaiaha'o Church is a technological marvel and one of the most important buildings in the state, where royal coronations were once held and historic events continue to take place. Before it was built, a series of thatched, Hawaiian-style houses served on the same site as places of worship; as the congregation grew, Island missionaries were forced to build even larger structures. The final thatched house could hold 4,500 people seated cross-legged on the ground and standing on the sides.

Completed in the New England style of architecture in 1842, the 144-by-78-foot-long Congregational church was built by hand by Hawaiian worshippers over the course of five years, using 14,000 coral slabs chiseled from underwater reefs. Each block of coral weighed more than 1,000 pounds and was ferried to shore by canoe or raft. Some of the wooden beams used in construction were carried by hand over steep mountain passes to Honolulu. The church once had a wooden steeple, but it was damaged during a storm in 1885 and never replaced.

KAWAIAHA'O CHURCH

The interior of Kawaiaha'o is modest, the most notable characteristic being portraits of the royal family and chiefs lining its upper walls. The name Kawaiaha'o is from a nearby spring, Ka Wai a Ha'o—the water of Ha'o—once frequented by a high chiefess.

To the right of the church entrance you'll see a Victorian mausoleum housing the body of King Lunalilo, Hawai'i's first elected monarch, who passed away in 1874 after only one year on the throne. Rather than be buried at the Royal Mausoleum in Nu'uanu Valley, he asked to be placed at the church "to be entombed among his people, rather than the kings and chiefs." Entrance is not permitted.

Behind the church is an old cemetery, consecrated in 1823, containing the remains of the founding missionaries and hundreds of their congregation members, many of whom now rest in unmarked graves or multiple burial sites. For those with tombstones, you'll find surnames that echo across Hawai'i's oldest buildings, corporations, and trusts. Descendants of the original missionaries can still be buried here. You're welcome to enter and respectfully view the grave sites.

Just beyond it is the Adobe Schoolhouse, which, at the time of its creation in 1835, was called "the most beautiful room in Honolulu." There the missionaries taught high-status Hawaiian children the "three R's." Today it serves as a school once again and is not open to the public.

National Memorial Cemetery of the Pacific (532-3720; cem.va.gov/CEMs /nchp/nmcp.asp), 2177 Pūowaina Dr., Punchbowl. Open 8–5:30 or 6:30 daily (seasonal). Free. On the National Register of Historic Places. Known to most as Punchbowl Cemetery and a significant site for millions, the National Memorial Cemetery is the "Arlington of the Pacific." It is where nearly 47,000 men and women who served in the US armed forces during World War I, World War II, the Korean War, the Vietnam War, and other conflicts are buried.

Punchbowl itself is actually a volcano crater once called Pu'uowaina by Hawaiians, or "hill of sacrifice." Near its base stood as many as four luakini heiau, sacrificial temples, where offenders such as those who broke the strict taboo system met their fate, and high chiefs were secretly buried.

The crater's gently sloping, 116-acre interior features manicured lawns; banyan, monkeypod, shower, and plumeria trees; and flat, uniform, marble gravestones in careful rows. Symbols on the stones signify religious beliefs. Because of Punchbowl's semi-lush, midvalley location, rainbows often arch above the treetops.

On the left flank, halfway between the park entrance and the colossal Memorial Building war monument, a paved walkway leads to a spectacular lookout at the crest of the crater. At the Memorial Building, a chapel and mosaic gallery outlining the Pacific's role in World War II and the Korean War are well worth viewing. A small visitors center at the entrance is a moving tribute to the individuals interred.

Punchbowl's history, purpose, and natural beauty stir the emotions of many who enter it. Sit under one of the park's many sprawling trees to listen to the wind as it sweeps across the crater.

Queen Emma Summer Palace (595-6291; daughtersofhawaii.com/summer palace), 2913 Pali Hwy., Nu'uanu. Open daily 9–4. $6 adults, $1 youths under 18. On the National Register of Historic Places. Gift shop. Built in 1848 by part-Hawaiian businessman John Lewis, this beautiful Nu'uanu Valley home was called Hānaiakamalama—Foster Child of the Moon. It was given to Queen Emma by her uncle, John Young II, in 1857. She and King Kamehameha IV, along with their adored young son Prince Albert, frequently retreated to this home from glamorous 'Iolani Palace for more "personal living."

Although bestowed with extreme grace, intelligence, education, and power, the royal couple was destined to encounter a series of tragedies overcome only by the enduring determination and faith of Queen Emma. Their story is told in this house and visible in its cherished possessions, lovingly restored to their original state by the nonprofit Daughters of Hawai'i organization.

Docents from the organization will walk you through the home's several rooms, sharing information about its history and artifacts. If you know how to play the piano, you may be invited to do so on one of two that once belonged to the queen. The tour groups tend to be very small, which makes visiting an especially delightful, intimate, and educational experience. The gift shop has a charming selection of handcrafted Hawai'i items and books.

✪ **Shangri La Islamic Art Museum** (532-3853; 866-385-3853; shangrilahawaii .org), 900 S. Beretania St. (Honolulu Academy of Arts meeting point), Makiki. Tours available Wed.–Sat. 8:30–1:30. Admission $25. Children under 12 are not permitted. Advance reservations required.

Shangri La, the former estate of American tobacco heiress Doris Duke, opened to the public in 2002, nearly 10 years after her death. During an around-the-world honeymoon tour in 1935, this fascinating woman developed a deep love of Islamic art and artifacts, which she collected over her lifetime. Duke's home is a breathtaking and unique testament to her interest. Not only is it filled with authentic treasures, but the home itself has also been designed to replicate elements of Moroccan, Turkish, Spanish, Syrian, Egyptian, and Indian architecture. Rooms glisten with thousands of mosaic tiles, and fountains trickle amid a stunning, tropical oceanfront setting.

SHANGRI LA
Courtesy Doris Duke Charitable Foundation Archives, Duke Farms, Hillsborough, NJ

Tours of the estate are offered only through the Honolulu Academy of Arts, which provides your round-trip transportation between the museum and the Kāhala neighborhood site. Docents take you through public rooms in the main house and through portions of its 5-acre grounds. Your Shangri La ticket also permits you to tour the Academy, so be sure to plan for both on the same day. Book in advance.

St. Andrew's Cathedral (524-2822; saintandrewscathedral.net), 229 Queen Emma Square, downtown. Open Mon.–Fri. 7–6, Sat.–Sun. 8–4. Free. On the National Register of Historic Places. During a visit with Queen Victoria in 1861, King Kamehameha IV and Queen Emma were greatly impressed by the Church of England; upon their return to Hawai'i, they began commissioning for an Anglican church to be built in Honolulu.

At their request, in 1862 Bishop Thomas Staley and two priests arrived in Honolulu from London to help develop the Episcopal Church in Hawai'i, then known locally as the Hawaiian Reformed Catholic Church. When the king passed away in 1863 on St. Andrew's Day, his brother and successor chose to name the church after that day. By 1867 the cornerstone for the dramatic, Gothic Revival St. Andrew's Cathedral was laid on land bestowed to the Episcopalians in downtown Honolulu. The cathedral was assembled piece by piece throughout the years, the last of it set in place in 1958, nearly 100 years after it was begun. The cathedral is the centerpiece of St. Andrew's Priory, a private girls' school also founded in 1867.

Washington Place (586-0248; washingtonplacefoundation.org—for the foundation), 320 S. Beretania St., downtown. Open Mon.–Fri., by appointment only. Free. On the National Register of Historic Places. In 1842 wealthy American sea captain John Dominis constructed what was to be one of the grandest residences in the entire Hawaiian kingdom—an impressive Colonial Greek Revival home built from coral block. Ironically, on the long journey to China to purchase furnishings for his family's new home, he was lost at sea.

The captain's son eventually married a young Hawaiian noblewoman. In 1891 she was crowned Queen Lili'uokalani and ruler of Hawai'i, and moved from Washington Place to 'Iolani Palace, across the street. Deposed only two years later during a coup coordinated by American businessmen, Lili'uokalani was eventually arrested and imprisoned within the palace. After her release, she lived out her years at Washington Place.

Upon her death in 1917, Washington Place became the residence of all governors of the territory—and later the state—until 1999. The current governor now resides in a new mansion just behind the property so that special dignitary events may be hosted here and that the public may view the historic home's exquisite interior year-round. In December, Washington Place is beautifully decorated and opened to the public for one subtly glamorous evening that recaptures the glory of its past.

HISTORIC WALKING TOURS Nothing beats the personal experience of walking a historic area, especially with a knowledgeable guide. We list several great contacts for you here. Also see the descriptions and maps of Honolulu's Chinatown Historic District, Hawai'i Capital Historic District, and Merchant Street Historic District under *Neighborhoods*, earlier in this chapter.

AIA Architectural Walking Tour (545-4242; aiahonolulu.org), 119 Merchant St., Suite 402, downtown. This wonderful tour is offered by the Honolulu chapter of the American Institute of Architects, so you know it'll be good. Led by well-known local architects, you'll spend about two and a half hours exploring downtown Honolulu's historic and modern buildings and learning about the culture and history. Reserve well in advance; tours take place Sat. at 9 AM if enough participants sign up. $10.

Chinatown Historical and Cultural Walking Tour (521-2749). Sponsored by the Chinese Heritage Center. You'll get the inside scoop on the real workings of Chinatown as you spend about two hours poking through its herbal shops, markets, acupuncture shops, and other specialty stores. Reserve in advance; tours take place Wed. and Fri. at 9:30 AM if enough participants sign up. $10.

Hawai'i Geographic Society Tours (538-3952; 800-538-3950). This local organization leads unique cultural tours to Hawaiian petroglyphs and natural sites, downtown temples and historic sites, and more. The tours are arranged by appointment only and require at least two people. For more information, e-mail hawaiigeographicsociety@gmail.com.

O'ahu Ghost Tours (524-4944; 877-597-7325; oahughosttours.com). "Honolulu City Haunts" is the only tour we know of that operates at night, guiding you for about two and a half hours on foot around some of downtown Honolulu's supernatural sites. Thu. and Sat. at about 7 PM. $29 adults, $22 children.

MUSEUMS & GALLERIES ✎ ✪ **Bishop Museum** (847-3511; bishopmuseum .org), 1525 Bernice St., Kalihi. Open Wed.–Mon. 9–5. $17.95 adults, $14.95 seniors and children under 13; free for children under 4. Selected buildings are on the National Register of Historic Places. Café and gift shop.

Hawai'i's largest museum contains one of the most expansive natural history and specimen collections anywhere in the world. Its more than 1.3 million Hawaiian and Pacific cultural artifacts indeed make up the biggest collection in the world, earning this nearly 120-year-old institution recognition for unique research and discovery.

The center of the campus is the Victorian-era Hawaiian Hall, which completed a three-year renovation in 2009. The room itself is a magnificent masterpiece of architecture. The first floor reveals the world of pre-contact Hawai'i; the second, Hawaiian daily life and cultural traditions; and the third, the realm of Hawaiian gods. Other highlights of the hall include a rebuilt grass home and a suspended sperm whale skeleton that has been the museum's trademark icon for decades.

Another must-see is Polynesian Hall, a gallery of two floors representing Pacific Island cultures from Polynesia, Melanesia, and Micronesia. In the same building you'll find the Kāhili Room, with royal portraits, priceless feather kāhili, and other traditional court effects; and the Picture Gallery, which houses extraordinary oil paintings and rare books on a rotating basis.

The newest building in the museum is the Science Adventure Center—a state-of-the-art, interactive presentation of island geology, geography, oceanography, and biodiversity, oriented toward children. The highlight is a 26-foot-high reimagining of a Hawaiian volcano that belches steam and bubbles with simulated lava. Other notable aspects of the museum include a planetarium, the Hawai'i Sports Hall of Fame, natural history artifacts, and touring exhibits.

The collection of books available in the gift shop is excellent; a modest and inexpensive café is on the premises as well, enabling you to take your time and enjoy the collections. In summer several concerts by some of Hawai'i's best Hawaiian

Courtesy Linny Morris/Bishop Museum

THE NEWLY RESTORED HAWAIIAN HALL AT BISHOP MUSEUM

music performers take place under the stars on the Great Lawn. Tours, demonstrations, and special exhibits are ongoing.

The Contemporary Museum (526-0232; tcmhi.org), 2411 Makiki Heights Dr., Makiki Heights. Open Tue.–Sat. 10–4, Sun. noon–4. Closed Mon. $8 adults, $6 seniors and children 13 and over; free for those under 13. Free every third Thu. of the month. On the National Register of Historic Places. Café and gift shop. This exquisite 3.5-acre estate was designed in 1925 by renowned local architect Hart Wood for the Cookes, one of Hawai'i's most prestigious kama'āina families. It was converted into a museum in 1988. The gorgeous hilly gardens offer a moderate view of Honolulu and Diamond Head, and the grounds house a smart little café and gift shop, making it destination enough. But happily, the museum's rotating, 2,500-strong permanent collection and temporary exhibits also tend to be inspiring, controversial, and fresh for those who appreciate modern art. The collection covers all media, spanning from 1940 to the present time.

TCM offers gallery talks, workshops, and other educational and fun opportunities to visitors of all ages. The museum is also planning to expand onto historic properties nearby, which will certainly mean more excellent presentations in the future.

East–West Center Gallery (944-7177), University of Hawai'i at Mānoa, John A. Burns Hall, 1601 East–West Rd., Mānoa. Open Mon.–Fri. 8–5, Sunday noon–4. Located on the University of Hawai'i at Mānoa campus, the internationally renowned East–West Center was established by the US Congress to promote good relations between the United States and the Asia/Pacific region. Its educational gallery presents several exhibitions per year on traditional and contemporary arts of the Pacific, with themes such as Toys Across Asia, Japanese Temple Architecture in Hawai'i, and Quiet Splendor: Yupik Eskimo Culture. While there, be sure to step into the nearby Japanese Garden, donated by Japanese businessmen, and also see the Thai Pavilion, a gift from the king of Thailand.

❧ **Hawai'i State Art Museum** (586-0900; hawaii.gov/sfca), 250 S. Hotel St., downtown. Open Tue.–Sat. 10–4. Free. On the National Register of Historic Places. Café. One of Hawai'i's newer museums has long been in the making. Although opened in 2002, its history can be traced to 1965, when the State Foundation on Culture and the Arts was founded by the Hawai'i State Legislature to promote, perpetuate, preserve, and encourage the arts as a fundamental aspect of Hawai'i's quality of life. In 1967 Hawai'i was the first state in the US to pass a law requiring 1 percent of the cost of every state building to be used for the acquiring or commissioning of visual art to beautify the environment. Since that time, the state has amassed approximately 5,000 works of art by 1,400 island artists, and the museum houses selected works from this collection of unique sculptures, paintings, photography, and other pieces.

The building's striking Spanish Mission style features Italianate scrollwork and other architectural details inspired by Florence's Davanzatti Palace. Constructed in 1928 as the Armed Services YMCA, it rests on the site of the "first" Royal Hawaiian Hotel, built in 1872 by King Kamehameha V.

The downstairs café, Downtown @ the HiSam, is one of the best lunch eateries in Honolulu (weekday service; reservations recommended). The adjacent gift shop, Showcase Hawai'i, carries exquisite and artistic gifts made by local artists. On the first Friday of each month, the museum stays open into the evening to coincide with the Chinatown gallery walk, First Friday.

✎ ✪ **Honolulu Academy of Arts** (532-8700; honoluluacademy.org), 900 S. Beretania St., Makiki. Open Tue.–Sat. 10–4:30, Sun. 1–5. $10 adults, $5 seniors and children over 12. Free first Wed. and third Sun. of the month. Guided tours available. On the National Register of Historic Places. Café and gift shop. Even if you only visit the Honolulu Academy of Arts museum for its outstanding gift shop and fabulous Pavilion Café, one of the best lunch spots on the island (reservations recommended), you'll have the benefits of passing through this poetic building and glimpsing its displays on the way. However, if you appreciate beautiful traditional and contemporary fine arts and crafts, or quiver when you hear names such as Picasso, do not miss the chance to visit the galleries by purchasing a ticket. The collection will surprise you not only in content, but also in artful presentation. Galleries are open for self-guided walks, audio tours, or docent-led tours.

The museum was founded in 1927 by the Cooke family, who donated their former home as well as countless pieces of their private art collection. It now includes nearly 40,000 items ranging from Southeast Asian headdresses to oil portraits of Hawaiian royalty and French impressionist master works. Rotating exhibits are generally impressive. Despite being a small museum, the Academy has hosted rare international exhibits like the Xian terra-cotta warriors. As the hub of Hawai'i's fine-arts scene, its openings are big events packed with residents.

Courtesy HTJ

HONOLULU ACADEMY OF ARTS

The Doris Duke Theatre features documentaries, independent films, and foreign films, as well as exotic music and dance concerts and educational lectures. On the last Friday of every month, ARTafterDARK in the museum courtyards is a decadently hip event.

Also worth the extra money is a tour organized by the museum that takes visitors to Shangri La, tobacco-heiress Doris Duke's extravagant, Turkish-style mosaic palace on a 5-acre beachfront estate near Diamond Head (see *Historic Sites*).

Honolulu Police Department Law Enforcement Museum (529-3551; honolulu pd.org/info/index.htm), Main Police Station, 801 S. Beretania St., Makiki. Open Mon.–Fri. 9–3:30. Guided tours available with advance notice. Free. HPD officer Eddie Croom has spent 20 years collecting local artifacts that range from exotic weapons to cockfighting equipment, and they're all here in this quirky and amazing little museum. Learn about the Honolulu Police Department's royal beginnings and the story behind the legendary fictional character Charlie Chan, who was based on real-life Honolulu tough guy Charlie Apana.

Japanese Cultural Center of Hawai'i (945-7633; jcch.com/gallery.asp), 2454 S. Beretania St., Mō'ili'ili. Open Tue.–Sat. 10–4. $7 adults, $5 seniors and children 6 and over. Free every second Sat. of the month. Gift shop. Japanese cultural influence in Hawai'i cannot be overstated. Immigration from Japan during plantation years was enormous—at one time nearly 40 percent of the entire state's population was Japanese. Today many thousands of their descendants still live here, and a high visitor count from Japan ensures that the Islands always look to the East. At the Japanese Cultural Center, learn more about the deep relationship between Japan and Hawai'i and the contributions and sacrifices Japanese Americans have made here through its historical gallery. Also enjoy rotating artwork on Japanese themes in the community gallery. The gift shop is awesome, with both new and used Japanese wares for sale.

John Young Museum of Art (956-3634; outreach.hawaii.edu/JYMuseum), University of Hawai'i at Mānoa, Krauss Hall, 2500 Dole St., Mānoa. Open Wed. 11–2, Sun. 1–4. Free. Local painter John Young (1909–1997) spent a lifetime creating and collecting eclectic pieces of art in hopes that one day the university would establish its first museum for the betterment of students and the general public. Shortly after his death, that vision was realized. The growing collection presented here emphasizes Asia and the Pacific in particular, with many noteworthy items originating from ancient China. Early Buddhist figurines from Korea and Khmer ceramics are among the museum's highlights. The building itself dates to 1931.

Judiciary History Center (539-4999; jchawaii.net), Ali'iolani Hale, 417 S. King St., downtown. Open Mon.–Fri. 9–4. Guided tours available with advance notice. Free. Inside Ali'iolani Hale you'll find a charming and free little museum worth your while: the King Kamehameha V Judiciary History Center. It includes several brief movies on land-use rights and water privatization; an antique courtroom; and galleries filled with information on the evolution of the Hawaiian legal system, martial law in Hawai'i, and the trial of Queen Lili'uokalani. Also interesting is a detailed model of Honolulu in the 1850s.

✎ **Mission Houses Museum** (531-0481; missionhouses.org), 553 S. King St., downtown. Open Tue.–Sat. 10–4. Guided tours are available. National Historic Landmark. Café and gift shop. After months of traveling across the Pacific, the first missionaries of any kind arrived in Hawai'i from New England, ready to spread the Congregationalist word. The year was 1820; King Kamehameha had just passed away, ending the old Hawaiian system of religious beliefs. Although the Hawaiians were suspicious of their intentions, this small group of young, newly wed, well-educated men and women was permitted to stay—as long as they settled far enough from the busy and boisterous port. The missionaries were moved into thatched housing along a dusty strip until the arrival of their prefabricated wooden homes.

Within these walls several missionary families cared for the sick, translated the oral Hawaiian language into written form, and taught reading and writing, along with religious beliefs. They eventually produced literally millions of pages of text in both English and Hawaiian with the first printing press in Hawai'i.

The mission houses in the Capital District are the oldest wood-framed buildings still standing in Hawai'i and consist of the Frame House, Chamberlain House, and Printing Office. They sit exactly where they were erected in the 1820s, now among yawning trees and lush grass, and can be explored via guided tour—a great way to understand the depth of the missionaries' influence on the kingdom.

Ramsay Museum (537-2787; ramseymuseum.org), 1128 Smith St., Chinatown.

Open Tue.–Sat. 10–5. Free. This small museum is more like a gallery showcasing the fascinatingly detailed pen-and-ink architectural works of Ramsay Goldstein, recognized as a "Living Treasure of Hawai'i for Outstanding Achievement" by the City of Honolulu. Ramsay has also been instrumental in promoting Hawai'i artists, hosting nearly 200 solo shows over the last 30 years.

University of Hawai'i Art Gallery (956-6888;.hawaii.edu/artgallery), University of Hawai'i at Mānoa, Art Bldg., 2444 Dole St., Mānoa. Open Mon.–Fri. 10:30–5, Sun. noon–5. Closed in summer and between shows. Free. Greek and Russian Icons, International Shoebox Sculpture Exhibition, and The Art of Asian Costume are several interesting shows recently presented at this visual-arts forum. Its smaller Commons Gallery showcases student work as well as that of visiting artists. Check the Web site above or call to confirm that a show is on.

MISSION HOUSES MUSEUM

✳ To Do

CANOEING & KAYAKING Go Bananas Kayaks (737-9514; gobananaskayaks .com), 799 Kapahulu Ave., Kapahulu. Rent a single, double, or child-sized kayak from this company located right up the street from Waikīkī. Rates are reasonable, and rental periods run from a day to a week. Choose from touring kayaks to surf kayaks—as the largest dealer in the state, Go Bananas carries more than 30 different types. Everything is included in the rental price—racks for your car, paddles, life jackets, and more; drag them where you will.

FISHING Inter-Island Sportfishing (591-8888; 877-806-3474; maggiejoe .com). These folks have been operating in Hawai'i since 1950 and have several boats to choose from, as well as either private or shared charters. Trips leave from Kewalo Basin, between Waikīkī and downtown, for big-game fish like Pacific blue marlin, mahimahi, and 'ahi.

GARDENS & PARKS ✐ **Ala Moana Regional Park**, 1201 Ala Moana Blvd., Ala Moana. This enormous and popular city park is idyllic yet bustling, with tennis courts, food concessions, event pavilions, a yacht harbor, picnickers, joggers, stand-up paddlers, surfers, and a beautiful, shallow-water beach running its entire length. Ala Moana Park is the heartbeat of outdoors Honolulu, where you'll see Island life in full color. It's just across from Ala Moana Center.

The Contemporary Museum Gardens (526-1322; tcmhi.org), 2411 Makiki Heights Dr., Makiki Heights. The artistically designed, 3.5-acre, 75-year-old botanical gardens at this modern art museum are a peaceful, hilly retreat with glimpses of the city below. Works of art from the museum's collection dot the landscape. Both the museum and gardens are open Tue.–Sat. 10–4 and Sun. noon–4, and its café serves a wonderful lunch you can enjoy on the lawn. There is a museum admission fee to visit the gardens.

Foster Botanical Garden (522-7065), 50 N. Vineyard Blvd., Chinatown. Created in 1853, the 13.5-acre city-run garden is an urban oasis of exotic foliage and on the National Register of Historic Places. Special collections include its Orchid Gardens, Prehistoric Glen, Exceptional Trees, and Palm Collection. Kuan Yin Temple, on park grounds since 1880, is dedicated to the Chinese goddess of mercy. The park's summertime twilight concerts are especially charming. Open daily 9–4; guided tours are available Mon.–Sat. at 1 PM. Small fee to enter.

✪ **Harold L. Lyon Arboretum** (988-0456; hawaii.edu/lyonarboretum), 3860 Mānoa Rd., Mānoa. Enough cannot be said about this exquisitely beautiful and quiet Mānoa Valley garden, established in 1918 as a forest restoration project and now a research facility of the University of Hawai'i. Nearly 200 acres of trees and plants—many of gargantuan proportions—live in this rich, wilderness-like setting, and myriad forest birds peek from its many nooks and crannies. Tours,

THE CONTEMPORARY MUSEUM'S UPPER GARDEN

demonstrations, workshops, lectures, and other programs are available. Wear plenty of mosquito repellent, and dress for nature trails and rain sprinkles. Visiting is permitted Mon.–Fri. 9–4, Sat. 9–3. Closed holidays. Sign in at the welcome center first. Donations are appreciated.

GOLF Ala Wai Golf Course (733-7387; co.honolulu.hi.us/des/golf/alawai.htm), 404 Kapahulu Ave., Kapahulu. This city-run, 18-hole, par-72 golf course is reputedly the busiest in the entire world, with more than 500 rounds per day. Built in 1931, it's the oldest course on the island; located on the edge of Waikīkī, it's also the only public golf course in town. Consider yourself lucky to get a tee time. Green fees start at $45.

Hawai'i Kai Golf Course (395-2358; hawaiikaigolf.com), 8902 Kalaniana'ole Hwy., Honolulu. The popular Hawai'i Kai Golf Course features a par-72, 123-slope championship course designed by William Bell in 1973, and a par-54 executive course with no slope designed by Robert Trent Jones Sr. in 1962. The distant ocean views and just-beyond-town location make for a spectacular setting. Wear a hat—it's hot and dry. The driving range is popular with visitors and residents. Green fees start at $70, including a cart.

HIKING Diamond Head Crater Trail (stateparks.org), Diamond Head/Kāhala. This trail was established by the American military in 1908 to provide access to observation stations along the volcano crater's rim. It's now within our state park system and more of an urban walk than hike, with handrailed walkways, stairs, and a man-made tunnel. We've seen Japanese tourists manage it in high heels. At the top you'll have fantastic 360-degree summit views of Honolulu, the mountains, and the ocean.

Many visitors arrive as early as 6 AM, as the crater really heats up by midday and crowds can be nose-to-buttocks by late morning. Bring plenty of water with you. Parking is available inside the crater (for a nominal fee), near restrooms and the trailhead.

The trail itself is an upward climb that takes 45 minutes or so, although it's less than a mile. Anyone who's claustrophobic or unable to climb through a few smaller spaces might want to reconsider the trip.

To get there: Take Monserrat Ave. (or Diamond Head Rd., which together form a loop) to the crater entrance driveway, near 18th Ave.

✈ **Judd Trail**, Nu'uanu/Makiki. A 0.75-mile, family-friendly loop hike through bamboo forest to a freshwater stream swimming hole called Jackass Ginger, which is usually swarmed with local kids and mosquitoes but still charming. Other foliage along the way includes eucalyptus and Norfolk pine.

The Judd Trail is just one of perhaps 20 or more Makiki Forest Recreation Area trails in the hills behind urban Honolulu. More advanced hikers can connect from Judd (and other trails) to longer and steeper pathways, such as the Nu'uanu Trail. Bring a more detailed map or guide with you if you do—side trails get confusing and aren't always marked.

To get there: Take Pali Hwy. (61) to Nu'uanu Pali Dr. Follow it to a small concrete bridge at a bend in the road; parking and the trailhead are across from it. The trail begins across the little brook below.

The spectacular and underutilized **Lyon Arboretum** (988-0456; hawaii.edu /lyonarboretum), 3860 Mānoa Rd., Mānoa, has a network of short, easy-to-moderate mountain trails for guided or independent hikes/walks. Wear plenty of mosquito repellent here, and prepare for possible rain showers. Open Mon.–Sat.

♪ **Makapu'u Point Lighthouse Trail**, Hawai'i Kai/Waimānalo. If you're visiting between December and April and want to see whales from shore, this might be your chance. The walk takes about an hour each way, winding up a paved coastal path to about 600 feet. At the top, a lookout above the still-operational 1909 Makapu'u Lighthouse offers spectacular view of the Windward Coast and offshore islets. Frigate birds and other seabirds are commonly seen as well.

A recent explosion of visitors to the trail has warranted the construction of extensive parking. Go early on a weekday morning or in late afternoon to avoid crowds and the dry heat of a more parched landscape. No restrooms are available.

To get there: From town, travel east on Kalaniana'ole Hwy. until you pass the Hawai'i Kai Golf Course. Look for the parking entrance just beyond it, on the right.

♪ ✪ **Mānoa Falls Trail**, Mānoa. Of all O'ahu trails, this is "the" trail; everyone knows it, and every guidebook written in the last 10 years sends you there. Why? It's the perfect family hike—easy, short, near Waikīkī, and full of all those tropical pleasures you came to find. You'll encounter many visitors along the path; go early on a weekday if you'd prefer it quieter. Either way, douse yourself with repellent first.

Parking has been relocated to a monitored lot (small fee) farther from the trail due to recent overcrowding and theft. The adventure begins as you leave the parking lot; the walk to the trailhead is thick with towering tropical foliage that continues along much of the 1-mile trail itself, which borders a streambed. It can be very muddy along the way. At the end of the trail, if it has rained recently, a narrow waterfall slides down the rock face into a green pool.

The 'Aihualama-'Ōhi'a Trail branches off from the Mānoa Valley Trail near the waterfall; this is a long and complex trail that branches into more trails, so only use it if you're armed with time, water, and more detailed information.

To get there: In Mānoa, take Mānoa Rd. to its very end, in the back of the valley. You'll see the parking lot on the right.

SALONS & SPAS Keep a smile on your face with a massage, nail treatment, or hair trim. Our biggest hotels each have a spa, with special services that often incorporate Island-style treatments. Try a traditional Hawaiian lomilomi massage, which involves long, rhythmic strokes that release tension and free energy.

Aveda Lifestyle Salon & Spa (947-6141; aveda.com), Ala Moana Center, 1450 Ala Moana Blvd., Ala Moana. The best thing to do after a day of shopping is to get a massage and be pampered with delicious organic products—without even leaving the mall.

Kāhala Spa (739-8938; kahalaresort.com), The Kāhala Hotel & Resort, 5000 Kāhala Ave. Each 550-square-foot private spa suite is pure luxury. Services include Hawaiian scalp massages, firming and lifting facials, "golfer's tonic" massages, and volcanic mud envelopments. Shuttle service can bring you from Waikīkī directly to the hotel for your appointment.

TENNIS Ala Moana Regional Park (983-3713), 1201 Ala Moana Blvd., is a very popular public tennis area with 10 lit, open-air playing courts. It's easy to pick up a game if you hang around with your racket.

✳ Beaches

Waikīkī Beach may be Honolulu's most famous stretch of sand, but we have other notable town beaches as well. Except for Hanauma Bay, which is almost exclusively filled with tourists, our town beaches primarily attract residents, giving you the chance to experience authentic Island life.

✎ **Ala Moana Regional Park**, 1201 Ala Moana Blvd., Kakaʻako. This gargantuan beach park is a second home to residents and is growing in popularity with visitors. The long, sandy beach is protected by a low reef, making it safe for small children, lap swimmers, and stand-up paddlers. Some days, internationally renowned beach boy and surf contest organizer China Ueymura sits under a tent near the western-end snack bar, ready to offer stand-up paddle lessons for free. If you're lucky enough to receive one from this legend, do all you can to show your gratitude. Magic Island, the peninsula on the eastern edge of the park, offers a nice view of Waikīkī and the harbor. The park is located across the street from Ala Moana Center, just west of Waikīkī.

✎ ✪ **Hanauma Bay Nature Preserve** (396-4229), 100 Hanauma Bay Rd., Hawaiʻi Kai. Hanauma Bay offers one of Oʻahu's most incredible ocean experiences. You'll swim in a seawater-inundated volcanic crater, now a protected marine life conservation district. Feeding or otherwise disturbing its 400-plus species of marine life is strictly prohibited, as is walking on its delicate coral reefs. Hanauma is also the first public beach in the nation to ban smoking.

KĀHALA SPA

Courtesy The Kāhala Hotel & Resort

Don't let these rules, the nominal entrance fee, lines of people, or mandatory viewing of a brief educational video discourage you from visiting—they're for the protection and management of an astounding natural site that has been far over-taxed in every way for many years. In the 1980s as many as 10,000 people tromped through its waters each day; the park has now shaved it down to about 3,000 per day. Remember, this is a nature preserve, not a beer-and-volleyball pic-nic destination—please treat it with the utmost care and respect.

Hanauma's turquoise waters are shallow and very safe inside the reef and rougher outside it, where the very occasional ray or shark might also roam. In the visitors center you'll find tons of information on the creatures of the bay and a history of the crater itself. Even if you choose not to descend to the beach, the view from above is a very worthwhile stop and requires only a $1 parking charge. At times, schools of fish can even be seen from the cliffs.

Do not sign up with a company touting trips to Hanauma Bay. Instead, take TheBus or drive yourself and rent a snorkel, mask, fins, and even a locker down on the beach. Early morning is best, when the crater fills with soft light. By mid-morning the parking lot fills and sometimes closes, and the beach can be very hot. If the steep road down to the beach is daunting, a wheelchair-accessible tram can shuttle you back and forth for a small fee. The park is open from 6 AM to about sunset and closes on Tue. for a rest. On Thu. evenings the theater above the beach is open for educational films and lectures.

To get to Hanauma Bay from Waikīkī, travel east on Kalaniana'ole Hwy. past the

HANAUMA BAY

community of Hawai'i Kai; at the crest of the hill, you'll see the entrance on the right.

Kāhala Beach, Kāhala Ave., Kāhala. We suggest you park at Wai'alae Beach Park, at the easternmost end of Kāhala Ave. Although the beach fronting the park is rubbly and the water brackish, walk west along the sand to find a bit of paradise. Multi-million-dollar mansions line the beach, and sandy pockets in the reef are perfect for dips. During high tide, sections of the beach virtually disappear. Strong winds can be a problem. Note: Neighborhood residents covet this enclave away from Waikīkī and

A LITTLE BIT OF PARADISE AT A HONOLULU BEACH

value its peace and privacy. Please keep your visit low-key.

From Waikīkī, head west over Diamond Head Rd.—it changes names to Kāhala Ave. past the crater. The park will be on your right-hand side just past the only stop sign and before the golf course.

Sandy Beach, 8899 Kalaniana'ole Hwy., Hawai'i Kai. Hard to reach until 1931 when a coastal road was built, this local favorite is what Californian dudes in the 1980s would have called "totally gnarly." Sandy's is one of the best bodyboarding sites in the state—and the second most dangerous. The crushing waves at this beach are powerful, and have been known to break necks and backs. Needless to say, stay out of the water and simply enjoy the heavy atmosphere of salt spray, competition bikinis, and local partying.

From Waikīkī, take Kalaniana'ole Hwy. east past the community of Hawai'i Kai. Follow the winding coastal road until it descends to the beachfront.

✳ Lodging

Aston at the Executive Centre Hotel (539-3000; 877-997-6667; aston hotels.com), 1088 Bishop St., downtown. Moderate. Perhaps you're not the Waikīkī type and have no interest in the visitor scene—or you're a business traveler with a tight schedule. The Executive Centre in downtown's financial district will put you right in the middle of real Honolulu business life. This hotel has an elegant marble-and-glass lobby and sharp-looking rooms with jet spas, and you can even

get accommodations with kitchen facilities, a washer and dryer, or a wet bar. Free high-speed Internet access is available, as well as a business center, complimentary breakfast, and a swimming pool.

Note that during the week downtown is filled with bustle; on weekends, however, it becomes a ghost town.

✪ **The Kāhala Hotel & Resort** (739-8888; 800-367-2525; kahalaresort .com), 5000 Kāhala Ave., Kāhala. Very expensive. The Kāhala boasts a pedigreed past that rivals the best. It sits on a secluded beachfront several miles from Waikīkī, surrounded on all sides by a prestigious private golf course and exclusive suburbs. Because of its high level of privacy, security, and opulence, nearly every American president has stayed here over the last 40 years, as have royalty, countless celebrities, and tycoons. It caters to an upmarket Japanese clientele as well.

Formerly a Hilton and then a Mandarin-Oriental property, The Kāhala has been an independent hotel for several years and is a member of the Leading Hotels of the World. The atmosphere is serenely opulent, with dolphins lolling in the suite-side lagoon and wind tinkling through beach-glass chandeliers in the open-air lobby. Recent renovation has produced timeless contemporary decor in its 338 spacious guest rooms and

suites, and a lap-of-luxury spa. Hoku's is an excellent restaurant, and it would be hard to beat the settings of the Veranda or Plumeria Beach House (see *Where to Eat* for all three). The hotel-front pool can get a little bit too busy and loud.

Creative guest activities include canoe paddling, surfing lessons, Pilates, dolphin encounters, bicycles, and even light-tackle fishing. A complimentary shuttle provides transportation to and from Waikīkī, Ala Moana Center, and Kāhala Mall.

✳ Where to Eat

DINING OUT 12th Avenue Grill (732-9469; 12thavegrill.com), 1145C 12th Ave., Kaimukī. Open Mon.–Sat. for dinner. Moderate–expensive. Reservations recommended. A casually upscale, cosmopolitan, award-

THE KĀHALA HOTEL & RESORT

Courtesy The Kāhala Hotel & Resort

winning retro-American bistro in the snug neighborhood of Kaimukī, 12th Avenue Grill may be just what you're looking for. This little place doesn't cater to tourists—it caters to resident foodies. Leave beachwear behind and bring an appetite for seasonal dishes and specials, such as bacon-wrapped roasted Asian pear salad, baked macaroni and cheese, fresh fish of the day, signature pork chops, "Yankee" pot roast, and double chocolate buttermilk cake, plus a great wine selection. Most produce is locally grown and organic whenever possible. Service is warm and efficient, and the atmosphere is lively and sometimes incredibly loud. Two-hour parking is available at the surrounding public lot, although competitive to score. The Grill can give you change for the meters. This is a popular place, so expect crowds.

Alan Wong's Restaurant (949-2526; alanwongs.com), 1857 S. King St., Makiki. Open daily for dinner. Expensive–very expensive. Reservations recommended. If you have a deep appreciation for top-of-the-line cuisine and want a truly authentic Honolulu dining experience, make reservations at Alan Wong's immediately. Let's look at a few of the facts: It has been named by *Gourmet* magazine as one of the "Top 50 Restaurants in the US" (Wong's came in 8th); it has been designated by *Food & Wine* magazine as one of the hottest restaurants in the world; and it gets voted locally as Hawai'i's best restaurant year after year.

Alan Wong himself was one of the pioneers of Hawai'i Regional Cuisine and has a world-class reputation as a chef and restaurateur. He is one of only a handful in Hawai'i to earn the

highest culinary accolade, a James Beard Award. Wong is always combing for the freshest ingredients and new presentations, so the menu changes all the time. Some star dishes he's showcased include fork-tender oil-poached lamb rib-eye with three sauces, beet and tomato salad with shiso buds and li hing mui-ume vinaigrette, ginger crusted onaga, macadamia nut coconut crusted lamb chops with Asian ratatouille, and Hawaiian vanilla mascarpone cheesecake. The restaurant also offers five- and seven-course menu tastings, paired with or without wines.

Alan Wong's is so prestigious that you might expect to feel intimidated. On the contrary—this is a local-style, upscale-casual dining environment where you can relax and have a great time. Valet parking is available.

✪ **Café Sistina** (596-0061; cafesistina .com), 1314 King St., Makiki. Open for lunch Mon.–Fri; daily for dinner. Moderate. Reservations recommended. We didn't include Café Sistina in our last edition of the book. Stupid us! We'd heard good things, but had never been. Since then we've eaten here a bunch, and the hubby now insists on Sistina's homemade lamb-sausage gnocchi for his birthday meal.

Chef and owner Sergio Mittroti is originally from Torino, Italy, and in addition to loving to cook, he loves to paint. This will be evident to you upon entering: He has coated the entire airy interior of the restaurant with murals copied straight from the Sistine Chapel. The extensive menu is categorized by recipes from his grandmother's kitchen, recipes from his mother's kitchen, and recipes that are all his own. You'll find all the classics, like linguine carbonara and eggplant parmigiana, as well as the more unusual boar sausage gnocchi and venison ragu pappardelle. Everything we've tasted has been good to very good, and the tiramisú is excellent. Service is warm and friendly.

Another reason we like Sistina is the atmosphere. It draws that unusual mix of everyone, from local business people to baby-birthday gatherings to gay couples, although it can get very loud. Parking is available in the building or on the street.

Chef Mavro (944-4714; chefmavro .com), 1969 S. King St., Makiki. Open Tue.–Sat. for dinner. Very expensive. Reservations recommended. Serious diners, prepare: George Mavrothalassitis is a prestigious James Beard Foundation Award recipient and a founding member of the Hawai'i Regional Cuisine movement. In 2009 his restaurant earned the only AAA Five-Diamond rating in Hawai'i. The Provence-born chef owns restaurants in France as well as in Honolulu, although this has been his home for many years.

The restaurant presents a food-and-wine pair experience, instead of separate wine lists, so dinner is a prix fixe affair. A sampling of the winter menu at the time of writing includes the three-course menu of maitake mushroom Indochine paired with Jermann 2007 Pinot Grigio, Venezia Giulia; Colorado lamb paired with Tinto Pesquera, 2006 Criana Ribera del Douro; and marinated date tarte paired with Olivares, 2006 Dulce Monastrell, Jumilla. A vegetarian menu is also available. No view or trendy locale here, but the food is worth it.

Chai's Island Bistro (585-0011; chais islandbistro.com), Aloha Tower Marketplace, 1 Aloha Tower Dr., downtown. Open for lunch Tue.–Fri.; daily

CAFÉ SISTINA

Courtesy Sergio Mittroti

for dinner. Moderate–expensive. Reservations recommended. Winner of *Gourmet* magazine's America's Top Table Award and frequently voted into Oʻahu's top 10 restaurants, Chai's is a Honolulu tradition. Owner and chef Chai Chaowasaree also owns Singha in Waikīkī, but this is his masterpiece, a regional-cuisine bistro with influences from his native Thailand. Dishes such as Japanese eggplant and zucchini soufflé, organic Waimānalo baby greens salad, fresh ʻahi katsu, seafood risotto with Hāmākua mushrooms, fresh mahimahi with Thai red curry sauce, beef tenderloin, and white chocolate amore truffle should soothe you into the comfort zone. The setting is Island-contemporary, and Hawaiʻi's best-loved big-name performers perform nightly (sit on the patio if you prefer a quieter evening). That itself makes the evening worthwhile.

Go to Chai's Web site to print an exceptional-value coupon, saving you at least $25 on selected nights. Valet parking is available at Aloha Tower Marketplace.

✪ Downtown @ the HiSAM (536-5900), Hawaiʻi State Art Museum, 250 Hotel St., downtown. Open for lunch weekdays; closed Sun., and offering limited service Sat. Inexpensive–moderate. Reservations recommended. Oh boy—how many faves are we allowed to have? Local chef and restaurateur Ed Kenney, who also owns the popular Town restaurant in Kaimukī, is at the helm of this new café at the Hawaiʻi State Art Museum. His motto is local first, organic whenever possible, and with aloha always. The restaurant setting is chic and artsy, as it should be, and bustling

with the downtown business crowd almost before the doors open. On Saturday service is limited to the take-out counter.

The menu changes every day, with dishes like seared ʻahi, chorizo quiche, butternut squash soup, panini with olive tapenade, sea bass with polenta, shutome, beet salad, and peanut butter and chocolate tart.

No parking is available—best choices are Aliʻi Place, a garage on Alakea St., or the ʻIolani Palace meters. Both are just around the corner. Be sure to tour the excellent (and free) art museum upstairs if you dine here.

✪ Grand Café & Bakery (531-0001; grandcafeandbakery.com), 31 N. Pauahi St., Chinatown. Closed Mon., but otherwise open daily for breakfast and lunch; for dinner Fri.–Sat.; brunch is served Sat.–Sun. Moderate. Reservations are recommended for lunch. Grand Café is nestled within one of Chinatown's oldest buildings, but you'll feel more like you're in Santa Barbara in its indoor dining room or alfresco courtyard patio. And although it only opened in the last several years, its history harks back to 1923, when executive chef Anthony Vierra's great-grandfather founded the original Grand Café & Bakery. Many of the recipes are the same—and they're delicious. You'll likely meet one or more of the family during your meal, and service is always warm, courteous, professional, and even stylish, while at the same time humbly gracious. This is one of our favorite destinations, and we're not alone in that sentiment.

Chef Vierra is especially fond of eggs Benedict, so if you come for breakfast, be sure to try any variation on the

GRAND CAFÉ & BAKERY

theme he has cooking. Another original breakfast winner is the bananas Foster French toast. At lunchtime house favorites include traditional meatloaf, quiche, chicken potpie, and the extra-outstanding cola-braised short ribs. All the pastries in the cupboard are homemade and tasty, so no reason to hold back.

Closest parking is at the Chinatown Municipal Parking garage on Beretania St., just past Nuʻuanu St. (pop out of the elevator onto Pauahi, right across from the restaurant).

Hale Vietnam (735-7581), 1140 12th Ave., Kaimukī. Open daily for lunch and dinner. Moderate. Reservations are accepted for four or more people only. Many of Honolulu's best neighborhood restaurants are now found in the homey community of Kaimukī, which is gradually turning upper-middle-class boutique. Here you'll

find Hale Vietnam, probably the city's favorite Vietnamese restaurant, though perhaps not quite as authentic as it once was. Some rave about Hale Vietnam, and some find it very overrated. On weekend nights in particular it's packed with all kinds of folks, and although more of a trendy spot than family diner, kids are welcome. Dishes are served family-style, to be shared. Classic Vietnamese menu items such as green papaya salad, phô, and summer rolls are consistently decent to good, and the eggplant dishes are delicious. Parking is available (although competitive) in an adjacent metered lot.

Hoku's (739-8888; kahalaresort.com), The Kāhala Hotel & Resort, 5000 Kāhala Ave., Kāhala. Open daily for dinner; Sun. brunch. Expensive–very expensive. Reservations recommended. This is yet another award-winning restaurant, and located in the exclusive Kāhala Hotel & Resort. We've had overall excellent dining experiences here. Executive chef Wayne Hirabayashi blends the freshest Pacific ingredients into perfect harmony, making Hoku's extremely popular with residents as well as visitors-in-the-know. A night at Hoku's is about feasting and celebrating life. The ambience is congenial and festive, and dress is casual upscale, with collared shirts for men.

The restaurant was relatively recently redesigned into a gracious, warm-wood-tone, contemporary dining room, complemented by fine touches such as Christofle silver and Italian bone china. Arrive before sunset, if possible, for views directly onto tranquil ocean and leaning coconut trees.

The food is delicious, with selections

that vary from Chinese-style whole fish (a marvel to witness) to pancetta-crusted onaga, pan-seared island moi, salt-crusted rack of Wisconsin lamb, and mango tarte tatin. They also have a kids' menu, and the wine list is excellent. Sunday brunch is seafood-and-champagne focused.

Indigo Eurasian Cuisine (521-2900; indigo-hawaii.com), 1121 Nuʻuanu Ave., Chinatown. Open for lunch Tue.–Fri.; for dinner Tue.–Sat. Moderate–expensive. Reservations are recommended. Since opening in 1994, Indigo has garnered numerous local awards and recognition from national publications such as *Bon Appétit*, *Gourmet*, and *Condé Nast Traveler*. Its deliciously atmospheric indoor–outdoor decor recalls an exotic Hong Kong hideaway or old New Orleans jazz bar. Hip and moody, Indigo manages to draw both the gentler folk for pre-theater dining as well as the clubby set, who ease into the restaurant's Green Room or Opium Den & Champagne Bar later in the evening.

Lunch is served both à la carte and all-you-can-eat buffet. Drop your car off at the valet in front for dinner, then prepare to savor goat cheese wontons, tempura ʻahi roll, Hanoi shrimp summer rolls, Singapore laksa seafood soup, beef rendang coconut curry, or Mongolian grilled Australian lamb chops with tangerine sauce. A large wine selection offers more than 30 wines by the glass.

✪ **Le Bistro** (373-7990), 5730 Kalanianaʻole Hwy., Niu Valley Shopping Center, Niu Valley. Open daily (except Tue.) for dinner. Expensive. Reservations recommended. It takes something extra these days to convince this author's mother that good food is worth paying good money for—especially if it's French—but Le Bistro did it. The restaurant, located in a no-man's-land shopping center (with plenty of parking!), surprises you with a buttery dining room, charming lighting, flowers, and a festive, subtly elegant attitude that will envelop you before you even taste the delicious dishes and wines to come. Everything's fantastic—the escargots

HOKU'S

Courtesy The Kāhala Hotel & Resort

de Bourgogne, foie gras with red currants and quince, New Orleans scallops, filet mignon, and incredible desserts, as well as the service. The restaurant offers nightly specials and a selection of "petite" entrées as well. We almost want to keep this outstanding, off-the-tourist-path gem to ourselves, but we know you'll help keep our secret.

🦐 ✎ ✪ **Little Village Noodle House** (545-3008; littlevillagehawaii.com), 1113 Smith St., Chinatown. Open daily for lunch and dinner. Inexpensive–moderate. Reservations recommended. This wonderfully simple Chinese restaurant in the depths of Chinatown bustles with local families, office co-workers, a smattering of visitors, and everyone else. The owners grew up in Hong Kong and know food—and Little Village has picked up big local awards to prove it. Family-sized dishes are fresh, savory, and non-greasy. This author's friend labeled the pecan spinach salad "the best salad ever," and our Euro in-laws barely wanted to eat anywhere else after trying it.

The extensive non-MSG menu features all the classics, plus specials. The dried green beans, orange chicken, garlic spinach, and pan-fried beef with chili and garlic are standouts. Decor is tasteful and even fanciful, and the restaurant is tidy and well lit. On weekends, expect a wait. Customer parking is located in a lot just past the restaurant, but tight and limited.

Mariposa (951-3420; neimanmarcus .com), Neiman Marcus, Ala Moana Center, 1450 Ala Moana Blvd., Ala Moana. Open daily for lunch and dinner. Moderate–expensive. Reserva-

tions recommended. We're happy to say that the service and food quality at Neiman Marcus's signature restaurant seems to have markedly improved since our last edition to consistently good or very good, meriting the awards it wins. The setting is Island-style glamour, as perfect for upscale business luncheons as for bridal showers and couples. Most days you'll see models working the floor in the latest fashions.

The free, fresh popovers are fantastic—encourage staff to indulge you with as many as possible. A petite cup of consommé joins popover delivery. Menu choices include applewood-roasted salmon salad, fennel-crusted 'ahi, seared breast of chicken, garlic-roasted tiger prawns, and scallops, and the desserts are positively sinful (try the warm lilikoi-pudding cake). If you don't mind traffic noise, request to sit on the open-air patio for views of Ala Moana Park, rows of coconut trees, and the wide, blue ocean. They also offer afternoon tea service on Sundays.

🦐 **Marketplace Cafe** (953-6110; nordstrom.com), Nordstrom, Ala Moana Center, 1450 Ala Moana Blvd., Ala Moana. Open daily for lunch and dinner; lunch only on Sun. Inexpensive–moderate. A great new choice at the mall, with contemporary, fresh, and extra-delicious dishes such as panko-crusted chicken salad (author favorite), roast chicken, tomato-basil soup, pizzas to order, and red velvet cake. Cafeteria-style ordering with light table service keeps prices reasonable.

Mediterraneo (593-1466), 1279 S. King St. Open daily (except Sun.) for dinner. Moderate. Reservations are accepted only for large groups. There are several really wonderful and popular Italian trattorias in Honolulu, but in our opinion Mediterraneo wins for charm. Opened nearly 25 years ago by Fabrizio Favale, who grew up in Rome, Mediterraneo features freshly house-made sauces, pastas, and ravioli; and flavorful dishes like insalata di mare, veal Piccata, carbonara, and tiramisú.

Although located on bland business avenue away from the happenings, it feels neighborhoody inside, and it's quiet and romantic. The interior glows as if a fireplace is roaring, and colorful ceramic and tile artifacts decorate walls. We've experienced service ranging from enthusiastic to sleepy, although it has always been friendly. Limited parking is available behind the restaurant, or you can park on the street.

Panya Bistro & Bar (946-6388; panyabakery.com), Ala Moana Center, 1450 Ala Moana Blvd., Ala Moana. Open daily for all three meals. Inexpensive–moderate. Reservations recommended. We keep returning to Ala Moana Center's Panya ("the bread house" in Japanese), despite the fact that several of its youthful servers seem slightly indifferent to our presence. It never stops us from enjoying this unique, fun, simple, and tasty dining spot started by a couple of gals from Hong Kong.

An extensive predominantly Asian fusion menu features items like laksa noodles, Russian-style borscht, shrimp scampi, and bread pudding. Its atmosphere of vaguely clubby music, mirrored walls complete with dangling strands of silver disks, and a blue-tinted bar area serving lychee martinis belies the fact that patrons are mostly area professionals and mall shoppers, not Japanese pop musicians. The front area of the restaurant features a small Japanese-Euro bakery, and its Hokkaido-style cakes and buns are very popular.

✪ **The Pavilion Café** (532-8734; honoluluacademy.org), 900 S. Beretania St., Makiki. Open for lunch Tue.–Sat. Moderate. Reservations recommended. At the Honolulu Academy of Art's Pavilion Café, the understated, natural elegance of teak furniture, ceramic Japanese sculptures along a waterfall, and a monkeypod-tree-shaded terrace remind you you're at an art museum. The crowd is predominantly casually chic residents enjoying business lunches or discussing their next exotic vacation.

Fresh local ingredients and elevated simple dishes leave you feeling nourished but not overwhelmed. Dishes include items like Niçoise salad, Portuguese bean soup, grilled long egg-

THE PAVILION CAFÉ

Courtesy Honolulu Academy of Arts

plant, filet mignon sandwich, and chocolate pot de crème. Try their house-made ginger lemonade. Wines are available by the bottle or the glass.

Don't skip the opportunity to buy an entrance ticket to the excellent museum itself and browse its memorable grounds, collections, and gift shop. Validated parking is available kitty-corner to the museum at the Academy Art Center at Linekona, on the corner of Beretania and Victoria.

Phuket Thai (942-8194; phuketthai hawaii.com), McCully Shopping Center, 1960 Kapi'olani Blvd., McCully. Open daily for lunch and dinner. Inexpensive–moderate. Reservations are recommended for dinner. If you've never been to Thailand, you might not know that this regional name is pronounced approximately *poo-KET*. That issue aside, this is a delicious, tasteful, contemporary destination just across the border from Waikīkī. Over the years it's grown in popularity as a reliable neighborhood spot and has started to attract a number of outside visitors as well. It serves standard family-sized dishes of mee krob, crab legs, sweet-and-sour fish, shrimp rolls, tom yum gai, rice noodles, and paht Thai. Curries can be ordered mild on up. They also serve nice little desserts, such as Thai sticky rice with coconut milk and ice cream. Park in the shopping center lot.

The Pineapple Room by Alan Wong (945-6573; alanwongs.com), Macy's, Ala Moana Center, 1450 Ala Moana Blvd., Ala Moana. Open for breakfast on weekends; serving lunch daily, dinner Mon.–Sat. Moderate–expensive. Reservations recommended. The Pineapple Room is so *not* beach blankets and tropical cocktails. And don't be discouraged when you hear it's located in Macy's and has a parking-lot view. This is a first-class bistro owned by international culinary genius and founder of Hawai'i Regional Cuisine Alan Wong, and it exhibits all the style and flavor you'd expect and hope for.

Recently fully renovated, the tone is set by an extremely spacious, contemporary, and warm interior illuminated with sleek woods and diffused light, plus casually elegant furnishings and professional service. The lava-rock, wood-burning oven in its exhibition kitchen is of special note. Taste creations like crispy calamari somen salad, kiawe-grilled kalbi short ribs, 'ahi poke, pan-roasted onaga, filet mignon, and housemade ice cream.

Plumeria Beach House (739-8760; kahalaresort.com), Kāhala Hotel & Resort, 5000 Kāhala Ave., Kāhala. Open daily for all three meals. Moderate–expensive. Reservations recommended. Although not an award-winning restaurant like its upstairs sister, Hoku's, Plumeria Beach House serves pretty good food nevertheless—and sometimes very good food, with the extremely awesome bonus of a dreamy, elegant, grassy beachfront setting. Removed from the clutter of Waikīkī Beach, this restaurant is truly a peaceful retreat and has recently been nicely redecorated. Sit on the patio for full enjoyment.

The Sunday brunch used to be the crown jewel, but now it's off the menu; still, it's a great spot for breakfast. Lunch and dinner service has been updated to more moderately priced prix fixe and à la carte selections, with choices such as gazpacho, grilled lobster salad, escargots, rosemary and Hawaiian salt-roasted half chicken, homestyle potpie, and filet mignon. Clam bake and grilled seafood buffets appear selected days as specials.

Soul de Cuba Café (545-2822; souldecuba.com), 1121 Bethel St., Chinatown. Open daily (except Sun.) for lunch and dinner. Moderate. Reservations recommended. Tiny, busy, hip, loud, and downtown/Chinatown makes it better for friends than family dining. This is the second restaurant for Jesus Puerto and his cofounders, the first being in New Haven, and the casual, folksy, homestyle Cuban sabor and smart interior hit it big in Honolulu from day one—without even advertising. The walls are lined with old family portraits, images of Cuban life, and colorful prints.

The food is absolutely delicious, with recipes from Puerto's father, aunt, and grandmother. Items range from black bean soup, catfish sandwich (our favorite), and pan-fried ʻōpakapaka to sautéed shrimp and the classic Cuban dish ropa vieja. Live evening performances and a small bar set you up for the evening.

❧ **Tanaka of Tokyo West** (945-3443; tanakaoftokyo.com), Ala Moana Center, 1450 Ala Moana Blvd., Ala Moana. Open daily for lunch and dinner. Moderate–expensive. Reservations recommended. Tanaka's has been in Hawaiʻi for decades and has received plenty of positive recognition, including "Best Japanese Restaurant in Hawaiʻi" by *Honolulu Magazine* and "Best Teppan Room Anywhere" by *Zagat*. If you've been to Benihana, you know the teppanyaki

drill—chairs in a semicircle around a chef, who cooks your food at the table with entertaining flair. Families, coworkers, and friends love it.

The food is actually good, too. The menu centers around certified Black Angus sirloin steaks, imported lobster tails, shrimp, scallops, and melt-in-your-mouth filet mignon. Your entrée selection automatically comes with a series of other dishes, such as tossed salad, miso soup, rice, and dessert, which makes the overall cost per person very reasonable.

In addition to the above Tanaka of Tokyo location, there are two others in Waikīkī, serving dinner only: **Tanaka of Tokyo Central** (922-4702), Waikīkī Shopping Plaza, 2250 Kalākaua Ave.; and **Tanaka of Tokyo East** (922-4233), King's Village, 131 Kaʻiulani Ave.

Tango Contemporary Café (593-7288; tangocafehawaii.com), 1288 Ala Moana Boulevard, Kakaʻako. Open daily for all three meals. Moderate. Reservations recommended. Relative newcomer Tango appealed to us even before first bite, as we settled into the perfectly paired urban-patio-style interior and Euro-ambient music. Finnish chef and owner Goren Streng seems to have woven the feel of his homeland into the landscape, and yet it feels right in Honolulu.

Dishes incorporate these two influences with a sense of fresh, healthful, artful cooking. Breakfast selections include items such as gravlax Benedict, Swedish-style hash, and sweet bread French toast. Lunch and dinner introduce dishes like roasted beet salad, Hāmākua mushroom risotto with asparagus, roasted garlic clams, crispy tempura seafood, sautéed duck breast, and dessert crêpes.

Although the café's address is Ala Moana Blvd., it actually sits just off it, on Auahi St.

Town (735-5900; townkaimuki.com), 3435 Wai'alae Ave., Kaimukī. Open daily (except Sun.) for continental breakfast, lunch, and dinner. Moderate. Reservations recommended. Chef Ed Kenney had already built a reputation in Honolulu for culinary excellence—and then he opened Town, which instantly became one of Kaimukī's hottest and most eclectic restaurants. The modern, minimalist interior of dark woods against soft green and oranges is comforting and unpretentious. When the bistro fills with people, especially the dinner crowd, you'll feel it and hear it.

Kenney's philosophy is simple and appealing: Local first, organic whenever possible, with aloha always. The kitchen is always experimenting and changing the menu, but emphasizes Mediterranean flavors, slow-roasted meats, fresh herbs, and quality. Dishes served have included tomato-ginger soup, tomato tart, salt cod fritters, crispy fried green beans with rémoulade, braised lamb, and crêpe cake. Service is sometimes spotty and dishes range from outstanding to off-base, but that hasn't curbed its popularity.

✪ **Wai'oli Tea Room** (988-5800; the waiolitearoom.net), 2950 Mānoa Rd., Mānoa. Open for breakfast weekends; daily for lunch. Inexpensive–moderate. Reservations recommended. We'd be crazy to not share this historic spot with you, even though the food ranks only as "pretty good" most of the time. There are few dining experiences like this on O'ahu anymore. Opened by the Salvation Army in 1922 to teach girls the art of cooking

WAI'OLI TEA ROOM

and "gracious living," Wai'oli has served the public as a bakery and restaurant for decades, consistently attracting residents who cherish its old-time peaceful setting and atmosphere. Nestled in a plantation-style cottage on 8 acres of tropical jungle, and with an antique car parked in the garage, this is authentic old Hawai'i.

The menu offers items such as guava and berry French toast, roast beef sandwich, corned beef sandwich, and homemade soup, and on weekends a Hawaiian guitarist often performs. House-made teas add extra charm—in fact, they also offer full afternoon tea service, but you must reserve a day in advance. The building is on the National Register of Historic Places.

✪ **Yanagi Sushi** (597-1525; yanagi sushi-hawaii.com), 762 Kapi'olani Blvd. Open daily for lunch and dinner. Moderate–expensive. Reservations recommended. Open since 1978, this Japanese restaurant is a local institution with nearly every type and style of Japanese food, including one-pot stewed nabe dishes, teishoku, and shabu shabu. Judging by the outside—and even the brightly lit warren of nooks inside—you might think mediocre goods are coming your way. Nope. Their sushi is legendary, and two sushi bars work full time to deliver to mostly local crowds and more than a few celebs. We once sat next to a regular who insisted on loading us up with all his favorites, including yellowtail tuna belly that blew our minds. Complete dinners are a worthwhile splurge, and private tatami rooms are available for those who want the full experience. Open until 2 AM (except Sun.).

Bogart's Café & Espresso Bar (739-0999), 3045 Monsarrat Ave., Diamond Head. A favorite haunt of the neighborhood, Bogart's serves "coffee house chow" like fully loaded bagels and egg dishes. Morning service can be slow and lines long, so prepare for a wait.

❧ **Boston's North End Pizza Bakery** (988-1055; bostonspizzahawaii.com), 2740 E. Mānoa Rd., Mānoa. Probably O'ahu's most popular pizza stop, you'll get zero ambience along with a delicious slice of pizza a quarter-pie in size. A good option after hiking Mānoa Falls.

❀ **The Contemporary Café** (523-3362; tcmhi.org), The Contemporary Museum, 2411 Makiki Heights Dr., Makiki. Open for lunch daily except Mon. Reservations recommended. The petite Contemporary Café, tucked into a grassy corner of the lovely Contemporary Museum, is a destination unto itself. This getaway is a secret favorite of many residents and a peaceful, artistic retreat for anyone. The current menu features fresh and simple Americanesque classics such as deviled eggs, crostini, grilled vegetable sandwich, Waldorf salad, grilled cheese sandwich, and cheesecake created by Otto, a local cheesecake specialist. One caveat: We've had some shockingly slow and lackluster service here in the past.

Consider their awesome new "Lauhala and Lunch," which includes a choice of sandwich or salad, dessert bars, and drinks for two packed in a little picnic basket so you can eat on the parkland grounds of the museum.

Diamond Head Market & Grill (732-0077), 3158 Monsarrat Ave., Diamond Head. At the "Market" side, pre-wrapped and high-end little dishes are ready to go. At "the Grill" next door, it's plate-lunch deluxe, made with quality ingredients. A good grab if you're headed east for the day.

Haili's Hawaiian Foods (728-8079; http://mybackyardluau.ning.com), across from Ward Theatres, 1050 Ala Moana Blvd., Kaka'ako. This parked step van serves up really good traditional Hawaiian food. They've also opened up a restaurant proper at 760 Palani Ave., on the corner of Kapahulu Ave., and have been around for decades in other locations.

India Café (737-4600; indiacafe hawaii.com), Kilohana Square, 1016 Kapahulu Ave., Kapahulu. Open for lunch Fri.–Sun.; daily for dinner. Inexpensive–moderate. Reservations are recommended for dinner. A friendly, family-run café with dishes based on Grandma's recipes; tastes are southern Indian/Malaysian and the setting earthy and easygoing. India Café just might serve the best Indian food on the island, and residents have voted them so several times. An extensive menu includes samosas, several types of chutneys and dosai, lamb

masala, fish curry, cauliflower kari, and coconut cabbage. They specialize in curries, breads, and dosai, so be sure to include one or more in your order. Parking within the wee Kilohana Square can fill quickly—if it fails, street parking's a backup.

Kaka'ako Kitchen (596-7488), Ward Centre, 1200 Ala Moana Blvd., Kaka'ako. Pick up an upscale plate lunch (as well as breakfast or dinner) and enjoy the patio seating. This is a local favorite, run by one of Hawai'i's respected chefs.

Kua'Āina (591-9133), Ward Centre, 1200 Ala Moana Blvd., Kaka'ako. Also at Ward Centre, this is another burger shop residents love, local-style and fresh.

Le Crepe Café (372-3989; lecrepecafe .com; 2740 E. Mānoa Rd., Mānoa). On your way to Mānoa Falls, or back from it, grab a traditional French crêpe. The location is teeny tiny, but adorable.

Murphy's Bar and Grill (531-0422), 2 Merchant St., downtown. Someone's sure to give us heat for not listing Murphy's in the *Dining Out* section, but it's more of a bar to us than a restaurant. For good (and slightly pricy) pub food and to eaves-drop on local journalists' conversations, this is the place.

Nico's at Pier 38 (540-1377; nicos pier38.com), Pier 38, 1133 N. Nimitz Hwy., 'Iwilei. This is the spot down-towners drive to when they want affordable seafood. It's right next door to the early-morning fish auctions, and closed Sun.

☙ **Olive Tree Café** (737-0303), 4614 Kilauea Ave., Kāhala. Our top pick for inexpensive Greek-Mediterranean eats in the Kāhala area, perfect after a day at Hanauma Bay. Buy a bottle of wine at the store next door and enjoy it on the café's open-air patio. Waits can be long, and they serve dinner only.

Ono Hawaiian Food (737-2275), 726 Kapahulu Ave., Kapahulu. The best-loved traditional Hawaiian eatery in town and a true hole-in-the-wall, Ono's is under attack from overexpo-sure. Do it a favor and grab food to go—we do—to avoid overcrowding.

Pa'ina Café (356-2829), Ward Ware-house, 1050 Ala Moana Blvd., Kaka'ako. In the Ward shopping com-plex, this is a best bet. Fresh, original little dishes with local touches are delicious.

Rainbow Drive-In (737-0177), 3308 Kana'ina Ave., Kapahulu. It couldn't look grimier—but it's a favorite local stop offering up a hard-core plate lunch (served all day and evening). The teriyaki beef plate and beef stew plate are the best. You'll want to take the food to go, despite the availability of tables.

AFTERNOON TEA The Veranda (739-8760; kahalaresort.com), The Kāhala Hotel & Resort, 5000 Kāhala Ave., Kāhala. A gracious ambience and serene service make afternoon tea sheer delight. Dress the part.

Wai'oli Tea Room (988-5800; http:// thewaiolitearoom.net), 2950 Mānoa Rd., Mānoa. Enjoy daily afternoon tea in a tropical Hawaiian-plantation set-ting. Reservations must be made at least a day in advance.

SWEETS & TREATS ☙ **Bubbies Homemade Ice Cream & Desserts** (396-8722), Koko Marina Shopping Center, 7192 Kalaniana'ole Hwy., Hawai'i Kai. Try unique-to-Hawai'i ice cream flavors like mochi, or "naughty" flavors such as Keep It Up All Night. Bubbies made it onto Oprah's *O Magazine* "O List."

LE CREPE CAFÉ

Char Hung Sut (538-3335), 64 N. Pauahi St., Chinatown. An authentic Chinatown bakery with some of the best manapua on the island. Get there early.

✿ **Dave's Ice Cream** (944-9663), Ala Moana Center, 1450 Ala Moana Blvd., Ala Moana. Located on the ground floor of Sears, Dave's locally made ice cream includes surprising flavors like haupia and Okinawan sweet potato.

✿ ✪ **Leonard's Bakery** (737-5591; leonardshawaii.com), 933 Kapahulu Ave., Kapahulu. Open since 1952. There's one reason tourists and locals line up here: the malasadas. They're simply the best. Try the "original" style first, and eat them while they're piping hot. Good packaged sweet bread, too.

✿ **Liliha Bakery** (531-1651; liliha bakeryhawaii.com), 515 N. Kuakini St., Liliha. Way off the beaten tourist path, 60-year-old Liliha is open 24 hours a day (closed Mon.) for baked goods and counter dining. But it's most famous for its coco puffs, choco-late-filled delights with chantilly topping.

✿ **Waiola Bakery & Shave Ice** (735-8886), 3113 Mokihana St., Kapahulu. A real local-style shop down the street from Leonard's, Waiola's nearly 70 years old and the winner for shave ice in Honolulu. Choose from 40 different flavors.

TEA & COFFEE The Pacific Place Tea Garden (944-2004; pacific-place .com), Ala Moana Center, 1450 Ala Moana Blvd., Ala Moana. For quality teas, an open-air setting at the shopping center, and baked goodies.

WINE BARS ✪ **Brasserie du Vin** (545-1115; brasserieduvin.com), 1115 Bethel St., Chinatown. One of the freshest ambiences in Honolulu, transporting you to a brick-cobbled European side street. Trendy and cozy at the same time. Dishes are French-oriented, such as escargots and baked Brie.

Formaggio Wine Bar (739-7719; formaggi0808.com), Market City Shopping Center, 2919 Kapi'olani

BRASSERIE DU VIN

Courtesy Brasserie du Vin

Blvd., Kaimukī. Tucked away next to Fujioka's Wine Times, Formaggio offers an aficionado's selection of wines, premium vodkas, gins, liqueurs and bourbons, plus petite dishes like caprese and Kobe beef panini.

Vino Italian Tapas & Wine Bar (524-8466; vinohawaii.com), Restaurant Row, 500 Ala Moana Blvd., Kaka'ako. A must for hard-core wine lovers, Vino features one of the best wine selections in the state, presided over by master sommelier and part owner Chuck Furuya. It has even been named one of "America's 50 Most Amazing Wine Experiences" by *Food & Wine* magazine. Closed Sun.–Tue.

✱ Nightlife

DANCE CLUBS **Pearl Ultralounge** (944-8000; pearlhawaii.com), Ala Moana Center, 1450 Ala Moana Blvd., Ala Moana. More upscale nightclub than ultralounge, Pearl attracts business-trendy Generation X, Generation Y, and Boomers. The appetizer selection is notable.

LOUNGES **Green Room/Opium Den & Champagne Bar** (521-2900; indigo-hawaii.com), Indigo, 1121 Nu'uanu Ave., Chinatown. In separate nooks within the atmospheric Indigo restaurant, bohemian young professionals savor sake martinis and Mandarin cosmos mixed with jazz, reggae, dance-hall, hip-hop, electro, and drum and bass music.

The Veranda (739-8888), The Kāhala Hotel & Resort, 5000 Kāhala Ave., Kāhala. Casually swanky and soft edged, the Kāhala's Veranda draws a mellow older crowd for cocktails and jazzy classics.

PUBS **Kona Brewing Co. & Brew Pub** (394-5662; konabrewingco.com), Koko Marina Center, 7192 Kalaniana'ole Hwy., Hawai'i Kai. This hot weekend gathering place looks onto killer marina and mountain views, a tasty pairing with its Big-Island-brewed beers and live entertainment.

Murphy's Bar & Grill (531-0422; gomurphys.com), 2 Merchant St., Chinatown. This is Honolulu's best-loved pub, located in a historic saloon building once frequented by waterfront merchants, ship captains, and even Hawaiian royalty. Get your fish-and-chips and Guinness here.

SUNSET PATIOS ✪ **La Mariana Sailing Club** (848-2800), 50 Sand Island Access Rd., Sand Island. Looking for that tiki bar from yesteryear? Then set sail for the 50-year-old harbor-front La Mariana, home of netted glass balls, tiki columns, balloon fish lanterns, and a few sea captains. We recommend you order the li hing margarita. Food's plentiful but not the big draw. All service ends about 9 PM, but arrive before sundown because finding the place will test your salt. (Tip: Several blocks down Sand Island Access Rd., look for a hand-painted sign pointing the way.)

✱ Entertainment

MOVIE HOUSES ✪ **The Doris Duke Theatre** (532-8768; honoluluacademy.org), 900 S. Beretania St., Makiki, at the Honolulu Academy of Arts features a variety of excellent documentaries, foreign films, and alternative productions, in addition to lectures and performances.

For a less staid environment, try the homegrown and funky ✿ **Movie**

Museum (735-8771), 3566 Harding Ave. Suite 4, Kaimukī. With a handful of Barcalounger-style seats and a bring-your-own-grub policy, this one-man-band operated by a true film buff will treat you to vintage and cult classics as well as new goodies. Call ahead for showings and arrive early to scout for public metered parking.

The most agreeable locations for big-time movies in town are **Consolidated Theatres Kāhala Theatre** (733-6235), Kāhala Mall, 4211 Wai'alae Ave., Kāhala; ✪ **Consolidated Theatres Ward Stadium** (594-7045), Ward Entertainment Center, 1044 Auahi St., Kaka'ako; and **Signature Theatres Dole Cannery** (526-3456), 735B 'Iwilei Rd., 'Iwilei, which also includes an IMAX theater. All feature first runs. The Ward theaters are very busy on weekends, making parking a challenge.

PERFORMING ARTS Doris Duke Theatre (532-8700; honoluluacademy.org), 900 S. Beretania St., Makiki. Year-round. Ticket prices vary according to type of production. Eclectic and academic presentations, films, and performances from the Chamber Music Hawai'i quintet to Chinese calligraphy lectures to the punk-rock extravaganza *Hedwig and the Angry Inch*. All part of the extraordinary Honolulu Academy of Arts programming.

✪ **Diamond Head Theatre** (733-0274; diamondheadtheatre.com), 520 Makapu'u Ave., Kaimukī. Sept.–July. Tickets $12–42. The third oldest continually operating community theater company in the United States, Diamond Head Theatre has been in operation since 1915, when it was founded as The Footlights by some of Honolulu's most prominent women, who also starred in early productions. During World War II they entertained thousands of troops throughout the Pacific. Popular, innovative, fun, and cozily stylish, productions usually feature guest stars in the main roles. Book in advance, as seats fill quickly. Past shows have included *The Sound of Music*, *The Full Monty*, and *The Joy Luck Club*.

Hawai'i Opera Theatre (596-7372; hawaiiopera.org), 848 S. Beretania, Suite 301, Kaka'ako. Jan., Feb., July. Tickets $29–120. Hawaiian Opera Theatre, or HOT, productions are highly anticipated and feature international operatic stars in lead roles. A sophisticated, well-dressed crowd attends three operas in spring and one operetta each summer; if you can get tickets to opening night, you'll experience the entire audience rising before the curtain opens to sing Hawai'i's former national anthem—now the state anthem—"Hawai'i Pono'i." Sets and costumes are always magnificent, especially considering the moderate stage size at the Blaisdell Concert Hall.

Hawai'i Theatre (528-0506; hawaiitheatre.com), 1130 Bethel St., Chinatown. Year-round. Ticket prices vary according to type of production. Read more about this extraordinary theatrical venue in our *Historic Sites* segment.

Honolulu Theatre for Youth (839-9885; htyweb.org), Tenney Theatre, 229 Queen Emma Square, downtown. Sept.–May. Tickets $6–20. Founded in 1955, this exceptional nonprofit theater group presents professional one-hour weekend productions for the young, such as *Tales of Old Hawai'i*, at Tenney Theatre at downtown's historic St. Andrew's Cathedral. *Christmas Talk Story*, a local-style production performed each year, is especially popular. Other lovely productions have included *Snow White* and *A Thousand Cranes*.

Kennedy Theatre (956-7655; hawaii .edu/kennedy), University of Hawai'i, 1770 East–West Rd., Mānoa. Sept.– Apr. Tickets $12–15. The University of Hawai'i at Mānoa's Kennedy Theatre presents a wide range of productions, such as *As You Like It* and the more unique *Kyōgen*, a program of four traditional plays featuring this medieval Japanese farcical form. Shows are student performed and held on the campus, giving you a chance for insight into the daily workings of the local university.

Kumu Kahua Theatre (536-4441; kumukahua.org), 46 Merchant St., downtown. Aug.–Apr. Tickets $10–16. Kumu Kahua is affiliated with the University of Hawai'i at Mānoa and features well-written, locally created productions, such as *Folks You Meet at Longs*, *Aging Is Not for Sissies*, and *Who the Fil-Am I?*. This is a special opportunity for a glimpse at authentic Island life. Be prepared for liberal language choices in some performances, ranging from cursing to thick "pidgin."

Mānoa Valley Theatre (988-6131; manoavalleytheatre.com), 2833 E. Mānoa Rd., Mānoa. Sept.–July. Tickets $20–35. Mānoa Valley Theatre (MVT) has had an enthusiastic following since opening in 1969. Located in the verdant and cozy neighborhood of Mānoa, the theater is on the site of a 19th-century chapel and surrounded by an old Hawaiian graveyard. Productions tend toward edgier classics and soft experimentals like *The Graduate*, David Sedaris's *Santaland Diaries*, and the controversial and celebrated *M. Butterfly*.

✳ Selective Shopping

ALOHAWEAR **Bailey's Antiques & Aloha Shirts** (734-7628), 517 Kapahulu Ave., Kapahulu. Aged and musty stuff overflows here, but it's well known to those wanting used and vintage aloha shirts at a few bucks on up. They have more than 10,000 to choose from.

🍃 **Kāhala** (524-4252; kahala.com), Ala Moana Center, 1450 Ala Moana Blvd., Ala Moana. Local, family owned, and more than 70 years old, the Kāhala brand is a standard classic. They also carry a good selection of board shorts.

Macy's (941-2345; macys.com), Ala Moana Center, 1450 Ala Moana Blvd., Ala Moana. You've hit the mother lode of excellent aloha shirts, with a selection of the best designers including Reyn's, Tori Richard, Kāhala, Ono, and more. They also sell mu'umu'u ranging from hokey to quality.

Mamo Howell (591-2002; mamo howell.com), Ward Warehouse, 1050 Ala Moana Blvd., Kaka'ako. Over the years former fashion model and hula dancer Mamo has become well known for her beautiful mu'umu'u designs, as well as her alohawear for men and children.

Reyn's (949-5929; reyns.com), Ala Moana Center, 1450 Ala Moana Blvd., Ala Moana. Reyn's didn't invent aloha shirts, but they might as well have. Their reverse-print styles have become the definitive word in what an aloha shirt should look and feel like. Each year they come out with a new Christmas shirt that is a must-have for many of Honolulu's executives. This location is their flagship store.

Reyn's Rack (524-1885; .reyns.com), 125 Merchant St., downtown. Want a Reyn's aloha shirt but not the price? Head to the Rack for an oldie but goodie. A secret gem coveted by residents.

Sears (947-0399; sears.com), Ala Moana Center, 1450 Ala Moana Blvd., Ala Moana. Yes, Sears. We were stunned to discover a relatively large goldmine of decent to excellent aloha shirts here at good prices, including several notable brands. Steer clear of the mu'umu'u.

Tori Richard (949-5858; toririchard .com), Ala Moana Center, 1450 Ala Moana Blvd., Ala Moana. In business for about 50 years, as well as local and family run, Tori Richard designs and creates high-end, original, internationally styled Island clothing for men and women.

ANTIQUES & COLLECTIBLES In addition to the shops below, head to **Kilohana Square** (737-2547; 1016 Kapahulu Ave., Kapahulu) just outside Waikīkī to explore the small but interesting Asian collections at **Shangri-La Asia** (737-3600) and **T-Fujii** (732-7860; tfujiiantiques.com).

Art Treasures Gallery, 1136 Nu'uanu Ave., Chinatown. A neighborhood fixture for more than 25 years, the shop carries jewelry, textiles, and other antiques and collectibles that owner Phuong Tran has collected traveling

in Southeast Asia. Prices are very reasonable, and everything's artfully presented.

✪ **Antique Alley** (941-8551; hawaiian collectibles.com), 1347 Kapi'olani Blvd., Ala Moana. Antique Alley is dusty, jumbled, crowded, and surreal—just the way a good antiques and collectibles store should be. Fascinating items from old and new Hawai'i and elsewhere, plus estate jewelry, ivory, prints, bottles, cameras, and more. The owners are just as fascinating, and used to be buddies with President Obama's father—stories abound.

Lai Fong (537-3497), 1118 Nu'uanu Ave., Chinatown. Lai Fong was a picture bride who arrived in Hawai'i from Canton; she opened the store approximately 70 years ago, and it's become a landmark. Still family owned, it carries Chinese antiques and other curios from Pan Am flight bags to jade sculptures. Call first—they keep really odd hours.

Peggy's Picks (737-3297), 732 Kapahulu Ave., Kapahulu. Peggy's is funky fun—a jumble of old and not-so-old Island finds like canoe oars, furniture, jewelry, prints, lamps, and hula girl statues.

Robyn Buntin of Honolulu (523-5913; robynbuntin.com), 848 S. Beretania St., Makiki. A spacious interior displays quality ivory carvings, Chinese paintings, Buddhist artwork, textiles, and more from past and present Asia and the Pacific; specialized staff can help you discover just the right piece.

BOOKS & MUSIC Also see *Bookstores*, under "What's Where," for suggestions on museum shops with a large selection of books.

Moana Blvd., Kaka'ako. A 30,000-square-foot store with the requisite café and late hours, you'll have access to many Hawai'i-related books and CDs, as well as material on all other subjects.

☼ Native Books/Nā Mea Hawai'i (596-8885; nativebookshawaii.com), Ward Warehouse, 1050 Ala Moana Blvd., Kaka'ako. A locally owned shop with an excellent selection of Hawaiiana books, Hawaiian music CDs, and other authentic Hawaiiana.

Sam Goody (945-9027; fye.com), Ala Moana Center, 1450 Ala Moana Blvd., Ala Moana. This national music store chain carries modern and classic music, plus a large a Hawaiian collection.

BOUTIQUES Anne Namba (589-1135; 877-578-0001), 324 Kamani St., Kaka'ako. For those with sophisticated tastes and an appreciation for fine textiles and art, this small shop is a must-visit. Vintage kimono, obi, and silk fuse with updated Hawaiian classics for one-of-a-kind pieces, and the wedding dresses are gorgeous. Namba frequently creates the costumes for Hawai'i's operas, where both patrons and performers appear in her designs.

Cinnamon Girl (947-4332; cinnamongirl.com), Ala Moana Center, 1450 Ala Moana Blvd., Ala Moana. Cinnamon Girl boutiques carry women's clothing ranging from sweet to sexy, and their styles are fun and playful for any age. They also specialize in cool matching mom–daughter sets. The shops are locally owned and the designs locally created. Also at Ward Warehouse (591-6532), 1050 Ala Moana Blvd., Kaka'ako.

☼ Shanghai Tang (942-9800; shanghaitang.com), Ala Moana Center, 1450

LAI FONG

☼ The Academy Shop (532-8703; honoluluacademy.org), Honolulu Academy of Arts, 900 S. Beretania St., Makiki. The Honolulu Academy of Art's elegant store features 1,500 square feet of art books, textiles, handcrafted Hawaiian-wood bowls and glassware, locally made jewelry, posters, stationery, and more.

Barnes & Noble (949-7307; barnesandnoble.com), Ala Moana Center, 1450 Ala Moana Blvd., Ala Moana. This is the only bookstore at Ala Moana, and it has all the features you've come to expect from the chain—including endless magazines, books, bargain tables, and a café. They have a strong Hawaiiana book and CD selection.

Borders Books & Music (591-8995; borders.com), Ward Centre, 1200 Ala

FLOWER POWER

Residents give lei to honor almost any special occasion, such as a birthday, graduation, retirement, or even to welcome a keynote speaker or friend from the Mainland. Our favorite place to buy lei is in Chinatown, and the grande dame of Chinatown lei shops is the family-owned **Cindy's Lei & Flower Shoppe** (536-6538; cindysleishoppe.com), 1034 Maunakea St. Ask to peek in the back to see their lei makers at work.

You'll pay anywhere from a few dollars to more than $50 for a lei, depending on the rarity of the flower, complexity of design, and season. Some have no fragrance, such as the basic purple dendrobium orchid lei visitors often receive at lū'au, while ginger, tuberose, pikake, and many others illuminate a room with their perfume. Many people choose based on personal preference, but selecting a lei can also be an art, as some flowers and lei types carry cultural connotations.

Treat lei with grace and respect, as you would a Christmas tree or beautiful bouquet. A lei should never dangle from your neck like a cowbell; instead, adjust it so about a third falls gently over your back. If it has a ribbon bow, rotate the lei until the bow rests about where brooches are pinned. If you are giving a lei to someone else, follow the local custom of placing it over the recipient's shoulders so it lies in the correct position and follow it with a hug and perhaps even a peck on the cheek.

OLD-TIME LEI SELLERS IN HONOLULU

Courtesy the Hawai'i State Archives

Ala Moana Blvd., Ala Moana. Exotic Chinese-inspired, ready-to-wear dresses, coats, and other high-end apparel perfect for your next cocktail party. Stores are found exclusively in Asia, New York, Paris, Zurich, London, and Honolulu.

COMMERCIAL ART GALLERIES

If you enjoy poking through galleries, snacking, and socializing, we hope you're in town the first Friday of the month. At ❀ **First Friday** (739-9797; firstfridayhawaii.com), thousands of visitors and residents flit like trick-or-treaters among Chinatown galleries 5–9 PM. Pick up a gallery map at The ARTS at Marks Garage (below). Dress up, dress down—it doesn't matter. You'll see punks and heiresses alike, all out for some simple fun and to be seen. The nearby Hawai'i State Art Museum also holds free Hawaiian music concerts and other events on its front lawn those nights.

The hippest art event in town is undoubtedly the Honolulu Academy of Art's ✪ **ARTafterDARK** (532-6099; artafterdark.org), held on the last Friday of each month. Each features a wildly different theme, which might include performance art, trance music, ethnic foods, costuming, and other creative presentations.

✪ **The ARTS at Marks Garage** (521-2903; artsatmarks.com), 1159 Nu'uanu Ave., Chinatown). Marks Garage is one of Honolulu's finest and most eclectic collaborative art galleries, as well as a performance and office space for businesses and non-profits. Shows rotate frequently; you might see a Hawai'i Watercolor Society exhibit one week and an Indonesian cultural event the next. It's also the hub for the popular Chinatown art walk event, First Friday.

Bethel Street Gallery (524-3552), 1140 Bethel St., Chinatown. Striking oil paintings with an emphasis on modern figures, large ceramic works, and glass are some of the finds at this local-artist-owned and -operated gallery.

✪ **The Gallery at Ward Centre** (597-8034), Ward Centre, 1200 Ala Moana Blvd., Kaka'ako. A cooperative of well-known O'ahu artists, this small gallery has fine works in paper, clay, scratchboard, oils, watercolors, collages, woodblocks, lithographs, glass, jewelry, and more. The artists themselves tend the gallery in rotating shifts.

Louis Pohl Gallery (521-1812), 1111 Nu'uanu Ave., Chinatown. Dedicated to the spirit of Hawai'i painter Louis Pohl, the gallery carries paintings and fine-art prints by a collection of resident artists and other Hawai'i artists.

The Pegge Hopper Gallery (524-1160), 1164 Nu'uanu Ave., Chinatown.

FIRST FRIDAY, A DOWNTOWN GALLERY-WALK SOCIAL

Hopper's works are internationally recognized and found in both private collections and museums. Her signature paintings feature sumptuous Hawaiian women in bold graphic shapes and pastel colors. The gallery often rotates works of other artists as well, and it's a major draw during First Friday events.

FARMERS' MARKETS are growing in popularity in Hawai'i, and KCC is one of the best.

✪ **KCC Farmers' Market** (391-3804; hfbf.org), Kapi'olani Community College, 4303 Diamond Head Rd., Kaimukī. A market and casually upscale Saturday scene both, with live music. Get there early (it opens at 7:30), eat your way through, and score locally made jams and other great food-based souvenirs.

United Fishing Agency's Honolulu Fish Auction (536-2148), Pier 38, 1131 N. Nimitz Hwy. Most of O'ahu's local seafood is caught offshore and sold to restaurants at this 50-year-old, Japanese-style fish auction. Get to Pier 38 as early as dawn to see the best of it. This is the real deal, so dress warm and wear shoes that can get dirty. Closed Sun.

HAWAIIANA & OTHER HAWAI'I-MADE CRAFTS ✪ **The Academy Shop** (532-8703; honoluluacademy .org), Honolulu Academy of Arts, 900 S. Beretania St., Makiki. The Honolulu Academy of Art's elegant store features 1,500 square feet of art books, textiles, handcrafted Hawaiian-wood bowls and glassware, locally made jewelry, posters, stationery, and more.

Jeff Chang Pottery & Fine Crafts (591-1440), Ward Centre, 1200 Ala Moana Blvd., Kaka'ako. Local artist Jeff Chang contributes his own pieces to the gallery, but also carries a wide

THE ACADEMY SHOP

Honolulu Academy of Arts

selection of interesting, intricate, and mostly Hawaii-made arts and crafts.

The Museum Shop (523-3447; tcmhi.org), The Contemporary Museum, 2411 Makiki Heights Dr., Makiki Heights. For a more progressive take on locally made crafts, from hand-decorated Chinese soup spoons to jewelry.

✪ **Native Books/Nā Mea Hawaiʻi** (596-8885; nativebookshawaii.com), Ward Warehouse, 1050 Ala Moana Blvd., Kakaʻako. An outstanding selection of Hawaiʻi-related books and CDs, as well as a wide variety of higher-end, artisan-made crafts ranging from handmade sachets to Niʻihau shell necklaces.

Shop Pacifica (848-4158; bishop museum.org), Bishop Museum, 1525 Bernice St., Kalihi. Count on this museum shop to provide quality Hawaiian crafts from Niʻihau shell necklaces to model canoes, plus posters and an excellent selection of books.

HOME DECOR While you may not be ready to shop for a four-poster bed while on vacation, surf for Asiatic furniture hard to find in your hometown, strikingly different tabletop decor, and creative accent pieces. All of the stores can ship items to the Mainland for you.

✪ **Baik Designs** (524-2290; baik designs.com), Gentry Pacific Design Center, 560 N. Nimitz Hwy., Suite 108B, ʻIwilei. Indonesian furnishings ranging from antique hand-painted Balinese bed frames to basketry. All pieces are hand selected overseas by the owners and exhibit quality craftsmanship as well as unique design. Mahalo, Baik—we love our new desk.

Bali Aga Furniture (593-9030; bali -aga.com), 307D Kamani St., Kakaʻako. A favorite of local decorators and furnishings addicts, Bali Aga imports unusual and exciting wood pieces from Indonesia, China, and Thailand.

C. S. Wo & Sons (545-5966; cswo .com), 702 S. Beretania St. A landmark Honolulu store dating back several generations, with a huge and high-end collection of classic Asiatic and tropical-inspired furniture.

Fishcake (593-1231; fishcake.com), 307C Kamani St., Kakaʻako. An artful, eclectic, international collection that blends clean lines with exotic influences.

Indich Collection (524-7769), Gentry Pacific Design Center, 560 N. Nimitz Hwy., Suite 101, ʻIwilei. Indich has been around for years and specializes in handwoven Oriental carpets. They also carry unique Hawaiian-style rugs designed locally and woven in Nepal, China, and India.

KOA, MANGO, NORFOLK PINE, AND OTHER HANDMADE WOODEN BOWLS

Courtesy OVB

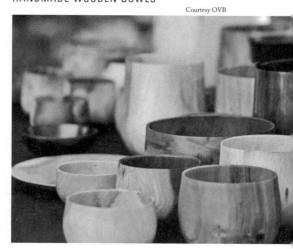

Pacific Home (596-9338; pacific -home.com), 420 Ward Ave., Kaka'ako. Hawai'i meets the tailored crispness of Cape Cod with bold, clean pieces and soft palettes. Eclectic, upscale, and tasteful.

Pacific Orient Traders (531-3774; pacificorienttraders.com), Gentry Pacific Design Center, 560 N. Nimitz Hwy., Suite 123, 'Iwilei. Many of the shop's antique Chinese furnishings date back between 100 and 300 years, and each original piece is hand selected and refinished by craftspeople in China.

Martin & MacArthur (791-6595), Ward Centre, 1200 Ala Moana Blvd., Kaka'ako. Upscale handcrafted koa-wood furniture and tabletop decor. Also at Ala Moana Center.

Mesh by Shari Saiki (536-6374; sharisaiki.com/mesh), 650 'Iwilei Rd., Suite 110, 'Iwilei. Local interior designer Shari Saiki has assembled a large Pacific-Asiatic home collection that is hip, sophisticated, and contemporary.

Red Bamboo (548-0001; redbamboo hawaii.com), Aloha Tower Marketplace, 1 Aloha Tower Dr., downtown. A fresh mix of Island-inspired, beach-themed home decor and Balinese furnishings.

KID STUFF *Animation Magic* (949-2525), Ala Moana Center, 1450 Ala Moana Blvd., Ala Moana. Browse this popular, locally owned shop filled with everything from Power Rangers to Betty Boop novelty items.

Cupcake Boutique (597-8305; cupcake-boutique.com), Ward Centre, 1200 Ala Moana Blvd., Kaka'ako. Hip and hot mamas with babies will enjoy this little fashion boutique, which carries unique gear and clothing for both of you.

The Growing Nest (591-2881; the-growingnest.com), Ward Warehouse, 1050 Ala Moana Blvd., Kaka'ako. Hawai'i's biggest upscale maternity and baby boutique, with baby-friendly events always under way.

Sanrio (949-2990; sanrio.com), Ala Moana Center, 1450 Ala Moana Blvd., Ala Moana. This is the ultimate "Hello Kitty" store. Merchandise ranges from gum to television sets, and selected items are Hawai'i themed. The characters sometimes stop in for photo ops.

Thinker Toys (946-3378; thinker-toyshawaii.biz), Ala Moana Center, 1450 Ala Moana Blvd., Ala Moana. Pick up interesting educational toys, puzzles, and games here. Thinker Tots is for the infant set and just a few yards away in the mall.

Up and Riding (955-7433; upand riding.com), Ala Moana Center, 1450 Ala Moana Blvd., Ala Moana. Score top-end surf clothing for toddlers and older kids. A Hawai'i-founded shop.

SHOPPING CENTERS O'ahu's most exciting shopping centers are in Honolulu, with Ala Moana Center certainly the grande dame for the entire state.

Ala Moana Center (955-9517; alamoanacenter.com), 1450 Ala Moana Blvd., Ala Moana. Welcome to one of the world's largest open-air shopping centers, with more than 320 restaurants, shops, and other businesses. Stores are mostly national and international, such as Chanel, Jimmy Choo, Sephora, Neiman Marcus, Williams-Sonoma, Diesel, Bebe, Banana Republic, J. Crew, Nordstrom,

Macy's, Victoria's Secret, and the Apple Store.

Other great stores include Artlines, Reyn's, Up and Riding, Cinnamon Girl, Tapestries by Hau'oli, Kāhala, Hawaiian Island Creations, Sanrio, Splash, Shirokiya, Martin & MacArthur, and Shanghai Tang. Dining options within the mall are plentiful, as is parking. Best lunch bets: Marketplace Cafe, Mariposa, and Panya.

Ward Centers (591-8411; victoria ward.com). Loosely connected across several square blocks, the cornerstones of Ward Centers are **Ward Warehouse**, 1050 Ala Moana Blvd., Kaka'ako; **Ward Centre**, 1200 Ala Moana Blvd., Kaka'ako; and **Ward Entertainment Center**, 310 Kamake'e St., Kaka'ako. Ward Warehouse and Ward Centre house some of our best locally owned boutiques, like Cupcake, Cinnamon Girl, Mamo Howell, Nohea Gallery, Noa Noa, Kicks/HI, Native Books/Nā Mea Hawai'i, The Wedding Café, Martin & MacArthur, and Hawaiian Moon, plus Paul Brown Salon & Day Spa, Kaka'ako Kitchen, Kua 'Āina, and Pa'ina Café.

The Entertainment Center features a 16-theatre movie house. In and around it you'll also find Roxy, Hurley, Dave & Buster's, Nordstrom Rack, Sports Authority, and Pier 1. Parking is free but tight on weekends.

SURF & OTHER SPORTING GEAR Buy top-name surfboards, board shorts, bikinis, and other cool surf and beachwear at one of our many surf and sport shops.

Blue Planet Surf (922-5444; blue planetsurf.com), 813 Kapahulu Ave., Kapahulu. Purchase longboards,

stand-up paddleboards, surfwear, and other quality ocean gear, just up the road from Waikīkī.

✪ **Hawaiian Island Creations** (973-6780; hicsurf.com), Ala Moana Center, 1450 Ala Moana Blvd., Ala Moana. This is Hawai'i's largest locally owned surf shop and it sells tons of surf clothing, as well as surfboards and accessories. Their board shorts for guys and bikinis for girls are extra cool, and a signature tee is a great souvenir.

Sports Authority (596-0166; sports authority.com), 333 Ward Ave., Kaka'ako. The recently expanded national store now houses even more tents, fishing rods, bodyboards, sleeping bags, tennis shoes, golf clubs, and other sports equipment.

Town & Country Surf Design (973-5199; tcsurf.com), Ala Moana Center, 1450 Ala Moana Blvd., Ala Moana. Another respected surf shop is Town & Country, which carries popular brands of surf clothing like Quiksilver and Hurley as well as top-quality surfboards and accessories.

SWIMWEAR Macy's (941-2345; macys.com), Ala Moana Center, 1450 Ala Moana Blvd., Ala Moana. Pick through a mountain of great styles at Macy's main store location, perhaps the largest collection of women's and men's suits on the island. They have something for everyone.

Splash! Hawai'i (942-1010; splash hawaii.com), Ala Moana Center, 1450 Ala Moana Blvd., Ala Moana. One of the hottest places on the island to purchase a bikini; enter only when your tan and physique are already paid for. They also have a shop next door for young girls.

Windward Oʻahu   3

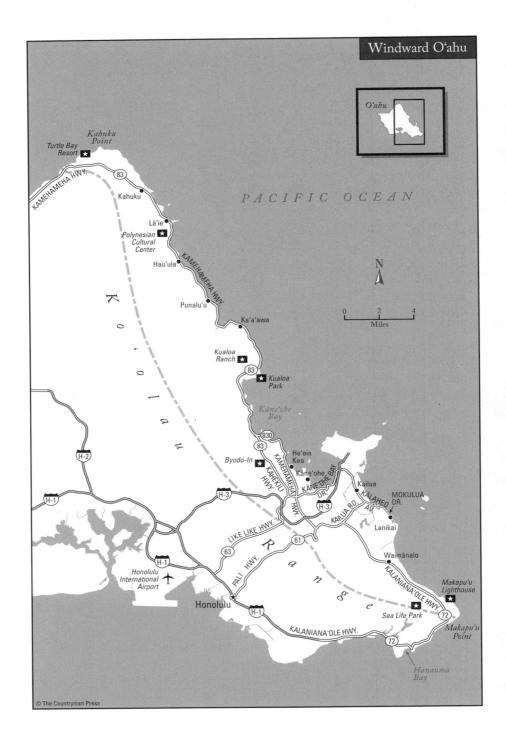

Windward O'ahu

O'ahu

PACIFIC OCEAN

N

0   2   4
Miles

Kahuku Point

Turtle Bay Resort ★

KAMEHAMEHA HWY.

83

Kahuku

Lā'ie

Polynesian Cultural Center ★

Hau'ula

KAMEHAMEHA HWY.

Punalu'u

Ka'a'awa

Kualoa Ranch ★

83

★ Kualoa Park

K   o   '   o   l   a   u

Kāne'ohe Bay

830

83

Byodo-In ★

He'eia Kea

KARREKILI HWY.

KAMEHAMEHA HWY.

Kāne'ohe

KĀNE'OHE BAY DR.

H-3

Kailua

MOKULUA DR.

KALAHEO AVE.

KAILUA RD.

H-3

Lanikai

H-2

H-1

H-3

LIKE LIKE HWY.

63

61

R   a   n   g   e

PALI HWY.

Honolulu International Airport

H-1

Waimānalo

KALANIANA'OLE HWY.

Makapu'u Lighthouse ★

Honolulu

H-1

Sea Life Park ★

72

KALANIANA'OLE HWY.

72

Makapu'u Point

Hanauma Bay

© The Countryman Press

WINDWARD OʻAHU

The windward side of the island is also called Windward Oʻahu, or the Windward Coast. It includes all land east of the Koʻolau Range crestline, from Makapuʻu Point to Kahuku Point. The area is characterized by temperamental weather, dramatic and lush mountain scenery, and unique cultural flavors.

On the southern end, very "local" Waimānalo is a cowboy and Native Hawaiian homestead town flanked by a curtain of ridged mountains and amazingly long, windswept beaches.

Heading northward, you'll find the bedroom communities of Lanikai, an exclusive enclave along the beach, and Kailua, a mix of middle class homes and beachfront estates. Kailua has become a beacon for both visitors and Mainlanders moving to Hawaiʻi, and its wide sandy beach is now a major Island attraction. The town itself features boutiques and quality eateries. The nearby marine base also brings a strong military presence to Kailua.

Suburban Kāneʻohe is the gateway to Hawaiʻi's more rustic country life in the tiny coastal towns of Kaʻaʻawa, Punaluʻu, Hauʻula, Lāʻie, and Kahuku. Here houses progressively become more salt bitten, the vegetation more overgrown, the pace slower, the beaches less crowded. Hauʻula and Lāʻie are Mormon strongholds.

HOSPITALS Castle Medical Center (263-5500), 640 ʻUlukahiki St., Kailua. **Kahuku Hospital** (293-9221), 56-117 Pualalea St., Kahuku.

MEDICAL TREATMENT CENTERS Braun Urgent Care (261-4411), 130 Kailua Rd., Kailua. Daily 8–8.

✱ To See

ARCHAEOLOGICAL & SACRED SITES Ulupō Heiau, behind the Windward YMCA, 1200 Kailua Rd., Kailua. Just outside Kailua is a stone heiau platform 140 feet wide, 180 feet long, and 30 feet in height. Built perhaps as early as AD 900, Ulupō looks out over the former 450-acre Kawainui fishpond, now a marshland. Believed to have originally been an agricultural temple, it may have later

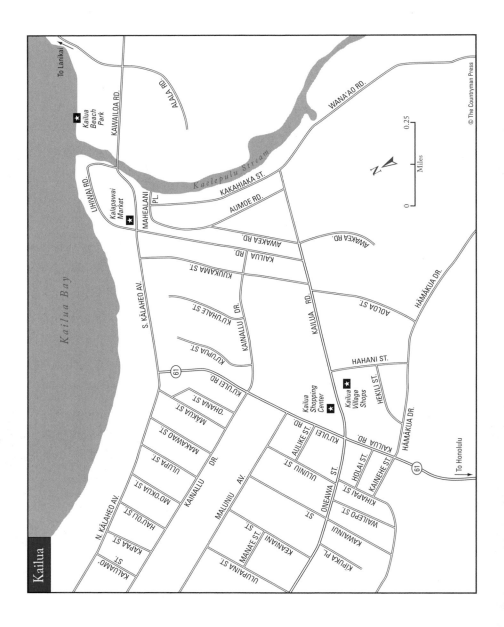

Kailua

become a war temple, at which human sacrifice would have been expected. Learn more at HawaiiStateParks.org.

Just past Castle Hospital headed toward Kailua on Kailua Rd., turn left onto Ulu'oa St. and right onto Manu-Aloha St. Park at the YMCA.

He'eia Fishpond, below He'eia State Park, 46-465 Kamehameha Hwy., Kāne'ohe. This 600-year-old, 88-acre pond was nearly destroyed in the 1980s to make way for a marina; the bluff, once called "the point of shimmering light" and home of the ancient heiau Kalae'ula'ula, was to be converted into a condo development. Thankfully, the bluff instead became a lovely park that looks south onto the enormous fishpond, in use until the mid-1960s when it was severely damaged by flood. Now under the jurisdiction of Kamehameha Schools, the pond is under restoration and has supported several crops of fish and seaweed. Learn more about it and how you can help at Paepaeoheeia.org.

✪ **Mokoli'i Fishpond**, adjacent to Kualoa Park, 49-479 Kamehameha Hwy., Kāne'ohe. At 800 years old, Mokoli'i is in good condition and still filled with fish. Unfortunately, it's located on private land belonging to nearby Kualoa Ranch. The best way to see it is either from the bay itself or by taking one of the ranch's several tours, such as their fishpond and gardens tour.

HISTORIC SITES 🛕 **Byodo-In Temple** (239-9844; byodo-in.com), 47-200 Kahekili Hwy., Kāne'ohe. Open daily 9–5. $3 adults, $1 children. On the National Register of Historic Places. Gift shop. Byodo-In Temple is hidden in the back of a peaceful valley and is a scaled replica of Japan's 11th-century temple at Uji, itself a World Heritage Site.

Byodo-In was built in 1968 to commemorate the centennial of Japanese immigration to Hawai'i. Constructed without the use of any nails, its architectural design is meant to characterize the mythical phoenix. Inside the main hall an 8-foot, gold-leaf lotus Buddha, carved by famed Japanese sculptor Masuzo Inui, sits laced in aromatic incense; remove your shoes before entering. Peacocks meander across the temple's lush, shady gardens. Benches line a 2-acre pond filled with thousands of koi (carp), making it a perfect spot to relax with a book (wear mosquito repellent!). Gently ring the enormous brass bell to experience its calming resonance.

Byodo-In is a house of worship for all denominations. Reach it via the Valley of the Temples Memorial Park, an expansive Shinto, Christian, Buddhist, and pet cemetery in the Windward town of Kāne'ohe.

BYODO-IN TEMPLE

✳ To Do

BICYCLE CRUISING The Bike Shop (261-1553; bikeshophawaii .com), 270 Ku'ulei Rd., Kailua. This well-respected shop rents mountain bikes by the day or the week, including helmets, locks, and repair kits. A car rack is available for an extra fee.

Kailua Sailboards & Kayaks (262-2555; kailuasailboards.com), 130 Kailua Rd., Kailua. Kinda pricey for a bicycle rental, but they got 'em.

BODYBOARDING, STAND-UP PADDLING, & SURFING The very coolest and most authentic place for surfboards on the windward side is **Kimo's Surf Hut** (262-1644; kimossurfhut.com), 776 Kailua Rd., Kailua. For all kinds of equipment and a more touristy scene, visit **Kailua Sailboards & Kayaks** (262-2555; kailuasailboards.com), 130 Kailua Rd., Kailua.

CAMPING Ho'omaluhia Botanical Garden (233-7323), 45-680 Luluku Rd., Kāne'ohe. An underused park of incredible beauty, Ho'omaluhia runs along the base of sheer mountain cliffs and brims with plant and bird life. Bring everything you need for camping, including mosquito repellent, as you won't be able to leave the park at night to forage for food. Note that the park is several miles from the ocean and, though a hidden paradise, it's surrounded by suburban communities. Book camping directly with the park. Learn more about it in *Gardens & Parks*.

Kualoa Regional Park (237-8525), 49-479 Kamehameha Hwy., Ka'a'awa. A more inspiring setting than this county-run park would be hard to find. These sacred Hawaiian grounds are bordered by a peaceful bay and backed by dramatic mountains. The offshore islet Mokoli'i completes the idyllic picture. Campground A is at the very end of the road inward and a bit rugged; Campground B is halfway in, along an open stretch of grassland. Both are waterfront locations. Contact the City and County of Honolulu for a permit.

KUALOA REGIONAL PARK AND MOKOLI'I ISLAND

✪ **Mālaekahana State Recreation Area** (293-1736; malaekahana.net), 56-335 Kamehameha Hwy., Kahuku. This is one of our top recommendations for independent camping. Although a state park, campground management is under the nonprofit Friends of Mālaekahana, so the normal permitting process is different. Mālaekahana itself is an enormous, beautiful, and safe beachfront park that was once a sacred refuge for Hawaiians. Choose from tent sites, old cabins, new yurts, and other types of accommodation, and at reasonable prices. Reservations are accepted up to a year in advance, but they book quickly. Read more about Mālaekahana in *Beaches*.

CANOEING & KAYAKING **Twogood Kayaks Hawai'i** (262-5656; twogood kayaks.com), 345 Hahani St., Kailua. Around since 1982, Twogood offers kayak rentals and adventure tours, as well as lessons led by Bob Twogood, a former national kayak champion and certified instructor. Tours generally head out toward or to the Mokuluas, a pair of seabird sanctuary islets off the Kailua/Lanikai coast. This is a moderately strenuous but exceedingly popular destination, offered by every kayak operation in the area.

FOR FAMILIES For family fun away from the beach, try these well-known O'ahu adventure parks.

✑ **Kualoa Ranch Hawai'i** (237-8515; kualoa.com), 49-560 Kamehameha Hwy., Ka'a'awa. There's no denying the beauty of this 4,000-acre cattle ranch on sacred Hawaiian grounds. Most of their operations these days are tours on the property, which range from horseback riding to catamaran sailing, ATV riding, and its popular movie locations tour (many big-name films were shot here).

We tried several of them and still ended up feeling mixed about the place. About 80 percent of their visitors are Japanese bus tour groups. Each ranch tour offers natural beauty, historical information, and enthusiastic guides, but because they're bunched as packages, they're just too rushed. We wanted more, and more in-depth. Open daily. Full-day admission for adults is $145, $79 ages 3–11.

✑ **Polynesian Cultural Center** (293-3333; 800-367-7060; polynesia.com), 55-370 Kamehameha Hwy., Lā'ie. Open daily, except Sun.; call for hours. Basic admission: $45 adults, $35 ages 5–15. It's touristy, and even kitsch—but if you don't know much about Polynesia (did you know that Hawai'i's in Polynesia?), you might just learn something interesting. A long-running theme park that employs students from neighboring Brigham Young University, the PCC takes its mission of educating and entertaining to heart.

The park showcases traditional cultural aspects of the Marquesas, Tahiti, Hawai'i, Easter Island, Tonga, Samoa, Fiji, and New Zealand. Most of the village performers are actually from the islands they represent, and the new night show, *Hā*, is pretty good, although melodramatic. The trinket shops and lū'au food are very forgettable. General admission includes access to villages, an IMAX theater, and a trolley tour to the Mormon Temple.

✑ **Sea Life Park Hawai'i** (259-2500; 866-365-7446; sealifeparkhawaii.com), 41-202 Kalaniana'ole Hwy., Waimānalo. Owned and operated by a Mainland corporation, this animal entertainment facility offers some unique interactive opportunities such as the Dolphin Royal Swim and Hawaiian Ray Encounter. General admission includes dolphin and sea lion shows, views into a huge aquarium, a seabird refuge, sea turtle feeding, a penguin habitat, and more. We find it a bit sad, but kids seem to like it. Open daily, 9:30–5. Basic admission $29 adults, $19 ages 3–11.

GARDENS & PARKS Ho'omaluhia Botanical Garden (233-7323), 45-680 Luluku Rd., Kāne'ohe. Built by the US Army for flood protection, this is one of O'ahu's most beautiful gardens. Sheer cliffs backdrop 400 acres filled with lush foliage and a variety of birds. Collections include many endangered and rare plants from Malaysia, the Philippines, Hawai'i, Polynesia, Africa, Melanesia, Sri Lanka, India, and the tropical Americas. On weekdays Ho'omaluhia can be virtually uninhabited. The park offers guided walks on selected days, plus camping, fishing, a small visitors center, and an art gallery. Open daily 9–4, except for major holidays.

Senator Fong's Plantation & Gardens (239-6775; fonggarden.net), 47-285 Pūlama Rd., Kāne'ohe. A 700-acre, family-owned tropical garden developed by former US senator Hiram Fong; the land once belonged to King Lunalilo and has changed little since. Although this was formerly a popular attraction, these days you might be one of a handful of visitors. This can be a good thing if you like your gardens peaceful. The gardens can be seen only through guided, 1-mile walking tours. Open daily 10–2. Entry fee.

GOLF Ko'olau Golf Club (247-7088; koolaugolfclub.com), 45-550 Ki'ona'ole Rd., Kāne'ohe. Designed by Dick Nugent and built in 1992, this 18-hole, par-72 course is considered one of the most challenging in the nation, with a slope from the tournament tees at 75/152. Wedged against sheer cliffs and surrounded by lush, tropical foliage, it's a visual delight as well. *Golf Digest* magazine voted it the "number one golf course on O'ahu." Green fees start at $80, including a cart. Call for directions—it can be hard to find the road to the course.

Luana Hills Country Club (262-2139; luanahills.com), 770 Auloa Rd., Kailua. Actually a semi-private country club, this 18-hole, par-72 course opened in 1994 and was designed by golf architect Pete Dye. It sits in ridiculously beautiful surroundings and is a challenge to play. This is a target course, hemmed in by rain forest with a slope of 130 and total yardage of 5,522. Green fees start at $125, including a cart.

'Olomana Golf Links (259-7926; olomanagolflinks.com), 41-1801 Kalaniana'ole Hwy., Waimānalo. Opened in 1967, this 18-hole, par 72, 126-slope golf course designed by Bob Baldock (this author's godfather!) features two distinctly different 9s and gorgeous views of the Ko'olau Range. President Obama played here on one of his visits home. Green fees start at $80, including a cart.

Pali Golf Course (266-7612; co.honolulu.hi.us/des/golf/pali.htm), 45-050 Kamehameha Hwy., Kāne'ohe. This is a beautiful, challenging, and busy 18-hole, par-72 municipal course nestled at the foothills of the Ko'olau Mountains, with a slope of 127. Green fees start at $45.

HANG GLIDING & PARAGLIDING These activities get the wind in your hair without the distraction of roaring engines.

Gravity Hawaiʻi (234-7663; gravityhawaii.com). Tandem paraglide with a US Hang Gliding and Paragliding Association instructor. Pete and Jorge can also give you lessons toward a paragliding pilot license. Jumps take place at the Makapuʻu cliffs in Waimānalo.

Kailua Blue (381-4296). Phil Godwin has been hang gliding for 35 years, 20 as a professional. He'll take you off the Makapuʻu cliffs for half an hour of magic.

HORSEBACK RIDING It's against the law to ride horses on the beach in Hawaiʻi. However, the places that offer horseback riding on Oʻahu walk you through picturesque settings, including alongside the ocean. All use western saddles for the safety of guest riders.

✔ **Kualoa Ranch Hawaiʻi** (237-7321; kualoaranch.com), 49-560 Kamehameha Hwy., Kaʻaʻawa. A working ranch owned by the same family for 150 years, Kualoa branched out a number of decades ago to offer trail rides; it now offers much more as well. We'd recommend the two-hour valley trail ride instead of the one-hour ranch-front trail ride.

✔ **Gunstock Ranch** (341-3995; gunstockranch.com), 56-250 Kamehameha Hwy., Lāʻie. With plenty of acreage to spread out on, they'll take you across wide pastureland on a moonlight ride, advanced trail riding (trotting and cantering permitted), sunset riding, scenic day riding, or three-hour lunch riding. They also offer assisted horse or pony rides for young children. The ranch is closed on Sunday.

SALONS & SPAS Paul Brown Kailua (230-2000), 25 Maluniu Ave., Kailua. Paul Brown's suburban salon offers everything from cutting and styles to microdermabrasion, hair relaxation, waxing, facials, and massages.

✴ Beaches

This beautiful stretch of coastline is a quintessential tropical paradise, and most of its beaches are generally safe for swimming. The weather tends to be stormier, however, even when it's sunny in town, and extensive reef systems can make finding a sandy swimming patch more challenging.

Also, watch out for the Portuguese man-of-war, a passive stinging critter identified by its tiny, cobalt-blue bubble and long blue tentacle. It sometimes floats in the water or washes ashore fully alive. As with bee stings, most people unlucky enough to have bumped into or stepped on one grin and bear the irritation until it passes; rinsing the welt with salt water may help, as well as applying meat tenderizer or soothing heat or cold.

Hukilau Beach Park, Kamehameha Hwy., Lāʻie. Often virtually empty on weekdays and Sunday, this golden-sand beach is an inspiring setting for a thoughtful walk and, on most days, safe for a shoreline dip. There are no lifeguards on duty, so study the water's mood and layout before wading in. There are no toilet facilities. The beach is located in a predominantly Mormon town; community members gathered here for decades to join in traditional fishing net hauls, or hukilau.

To get there, take the H-1 westbound to Like Like Hwy. (63) and follow signs to Lāʻie. Travel north until you're nearly a mile past the Polynesian Cultural Center. The beach park is just beyond the elementary school.

Kailua Beach Park, 526 Kawailoa Rd., Kailua. Kailua Beach is "a little bit country and a little bit rock and roll," and the star attraction of the relatively affluent and bustling beach community of Kailua. With numerous highbrow "best beach" recognition awards under its belt over the last 10-plus years, the wide, 2-mile-long sandy strand has begun filling up with visitors, stirring into existence countless unofficial lodgings within close proximity to its shore.

In addition to brilliantly blue and swimmable water, playful-to-heavy shore breaks, and occasional rip tides, it's the center of Oʻahu's windsurfing culture. Kailua Beach is also one of the takeoff points for kayaking journeys to the Mokulua Islands. The offshore seabird sanctuary Popoiʻa Island (also known as Flat Island) was once graced with a fishing shrine, washed away in the tsunami of 1946.

To get there from Waikīkī, take the H-1 westbound to Pali Hwy. (61), following it over the mountains and on to Kailua. Stick to the same road straight through town until it ends at a T-intersection with S. Kalāheo. Turn right and travel about a mile until you reach the park.

Kualoa Regional Park (237-8525), 49-479 Kamehameha Hwy., Kaʻaʻawa. Coral-strewn bits of beach, a reef-bound shoreline, and frequent strong winds make this beach best for dipping only your toes—but the setting is hard to beat. On the National Register of Historic Places, this is a historically significant Hawaiian heritage site that still earns reverence from many residents. The view toward the mountains of Kāneʻohe is breathtaking, as are the sacred ridges behind the park and the triangular Mokoliʻi Island (also known as Chinaman's Hat) offshore. Do not attempt to wade out to Mokoliʻi Island—currents have swept people away, and coral will be damaged underfoot.

The park has long hosted traditional cultural activities and local family camping. A shallow, more swimmable area and softer sand can be found at the end of the road. Take note that the deeper you go into the park, the more you'll need to wear your "very low-key, respectful visitor" hat.

From Waikīkī, take the H-1 westbound to Like Like Hwy. (63) and follow signs to Kahaluʻu/Lāʻie. As the road becomes coastal, you'll see Mokoliʻi Island in the distance. The park is adjacent to the island, and the entrance is at a sharp curve across from a cow pasture.

Lanikai Beach, Mokulua Dr., Lanikai. Lanikai Beach has earned top accolades from *Condé Nast*, "Dr. Beach," and the Travel Channel for good reason. Powder-soft sands ease into gentle turquoise bathwater, where turtles loll above the reef. Coconut trees arch carelessly in the breeze, and from one of the many multimillion-dollar homes behind you, a parrot squawks. Offshore, two peaked islets stand guard.

Sadly, Lanikai is no longer what it was even a few years ago. This formerly secret jewel has lost some of its glory and peacefulness in the gold rush and, a much more permanent fate, is actually eroding away in many spots as it fights against seawalls constructed by homeowners. Note that there are no public facilities.

To get there from Waikīkī, take the H-1 westbound to Pali Hwy. (61), following it over the mountains and onward to Kailua. Stick to the same road straight through town until it ends at a T-intersection with S. Kalāheo. Turn right and travel about a mile until you pass Kailua Beach Park. Turn left at the intersection and follow the coastal road around the bend. The road becomes one-way and loops back around. Park near any public right-of-way along the loopback and pray for sand.

Makapu'u Beach Park, 41-095 Kalaniana'ole Hwy., Waimānalo. This gorgeous beach has more rescues per year than any other on O'ahu and is a poor choice for families with children. Deceptively mellow, it lacks a protective reef to lessen the strength of waves and the backwash quickly drags waders into its depths. Red warning flags seem to always be up at Makapu'u—and lifeguards will quickly get on their bullhorns to remind you of that so they don't have to save you five minutes later. Enjoy the waves from far up on the beach only, and don't miss the stunning views from the road above.

MAKAPU'U BEACH

From Waikīkī, take Kalanianaʻole Hwy. (72) past the Hawaiʻi Kai Golf Course. The beach will be on your right after you round the sharp, cliffside bend ahead.

Mālaekahana State Recreation Area (293-1736), 56-335 Kamehameha Hwy., Kahuku. An enormous region with a mile-long windswept beach, campgrounds, fancy vacation homes, an ironwood forest, and an offshore seabird sanctuary, Mālaekahana reminds you that you've left town far behind. There are two entrances—one in the town of Lāʻie, the other in Kahuku.

True for all Windward beaches except fun-loving Kailua and chic Lanikai, the atmosphere is mellow and very real, rather than "bikini contest" or "jet ski party." This beach is perfect for daylong picnics. Although daylight-hour visits are permitted on the protected Mokūʻauia (Goat Island), getting there without damaging coral heads or struggling with the tides can be tricky (only cross in very low tide). The coastline can sometimes experience strong, longshore currents that have swept people en route to the island away into deeper waters. As always, and especially since the beach has no lifeguards, use caution and common sense. If you do visit Mokūʻauia, stay on marked paths and leave all birds and nests as you found them.

Traditionally Mālaekahana was a sanctuary of supernatural power for the Hawaiian people, serving as a puʻuhonua (place of refuge) where commoners were allowed to escape punishment for broken laws or find shelter in dangerous times. The area would have once featured a temple, surrounding wall, and perhaps simple residences.

From Waikīkī, take the H-1 westbound to Like Like Hwy. (63) and follow signs to Kahaluʻu/Lāʻie. Once you've traveled through Lāʻie, look for Mālaekahana signage. There are several entrances, near telephone poles 33 and 35.

✍ **Waimānalo Bay State Recreation Area**, 41-1055 Kalanianaʻole Hwy., Waimānalo. A drowsy landscape with an endless powdery white sand beach, whispering ironwood trees, and rumbling waves greets you at Waimānalo Beach. It's a favorite of Windward Coast families and young bodyboarders, so expect a mellow, very local-style day at the beach rather than racy action. Although it can become relatively busy on weekends, weekday mornings often see only a handful of beachcombers. Located in a tight-knit, Hawaiian-oriented community, this is a true Island beach.

From Waikīkī, follow Kalanianaʻole Hwy. (72) past the Hawaiʻi Kai Golf Course to the Windward town of Waimānalo. Watch for park signage across from the polo field.

✴ Lodging

Schrader's Windward Country Inn (239-5711; 800-735-5071; schraders inn.com), 47-039 Lihikai Dr., Kahaluʻu. Inexpensive–moderate. This is the type of place you either completely fall in love with or live to regret. It's a rambling old plantation inn with tropical charm, local touches, and some amazing mountain and bay views from verandas. Perhaps a good place to finish that novel. It's also in a shabby, semi-rural neighborhood that might prefer trading you in for a monster truck. Additionally, you'll be fairly isolated, needing to drive to most attractions. Service can be a tad rough edged, and at the time of writing, a mysterious surcharge, blamed on the economy, is added to your bill.

Schrader's has about 30 thoughtfully decorated rooms, from studios through three-bedrooms with full kitchens or kitchenettes. The hotel also has a pool and several other modest amenities, plus serves complimentary continental breakfasts. Although on a waterfront, there's no beach here; however, staff take guests pontoon-boat cruising for free, plus loan kayaks and other equipment.

✳ Where to Eat

DINING OUT **Baci Bistro** (262-7555; bacibistro.com), 30 Aulike St.,

Kailua. Open for lunch Mon.–Fri., daily for dinner. Moderate. Reservations recommended. An adorable little neighborhood place with Old World as well as Hawai'i charm, Baci Bistro is a second home to local customers for its savory Italian dishes and friendliness. Fresh food is the trademark, and everything is made to order. An extensive wine list emphasizes Italian wines, but also includes many from California and Australia. Choose seating either on an open-air patio, which is especially nice at night, or in the enclosed atrium. Rustic dishes include fresh island moi, homemade ravioli, gnocchi con pesto, bruschetta, prosciutto e melone, tutti mari, and tiramisú. Our Euro in-laws loved this place, and we were all pleased when we began to be treated like old friends whenever we returned for dinner. The owner himself often

SCHRADER'S WINDWARD COUNTRY INN

serves you and welcomes "talk story," neighborhood-style.

♪ **Buzz's Original Steak House** (261-4661; buzzssteakhouse.com), 413 Kawailoa Rd., Lanikai. Open daily for lunch and dinner. Moderate. Reservations recommended. Founded on Windward Oʻahu nearly 50 years ago, family-run Buzz's is a landmark and tradition. It sits nearly on the sand across from Kailua Beach Park and, perhaps needless to say, it's no secret. Even Bill Clinton chowed at Buzz's on one of his presidential visits.

The structure is vintage tropical Hawaiʻi, with an almost Robinson Crusoe interior theme to match. The bar has a hearty sea captain feel, but

HALEʻIWA JOE'S

the food does better than an old ship galley by far, even if the menu appears to hail from days gone by. The small salad bar is fresh and delicious (often with mountains of ripe avocado for the scooping), and the menu's fresh fish, prime rib, rack of lamb, sautéed mushrooms, and salads are really tasty.

Note that they do not accept any credit cards. There's an ATM on the property.

Formaggio Grill (263-2633; formaggi0808.com), 305 Hahani St., Kailua. Open daily for lunch and dinner. Moderate–expensive. No reservations. A big sister location to Honolulu's Formaggio Wine Bar, Formaggio Grill opened in 2007 and was an instant hit. Owners Wes Zane and Almar Arcano each spent more than two decades at the prestigious Hy's Steak House in Waikīkī, so they know meats and wines.

With a Tuscan-inspired decor and an open-air front, the restaurant is lively, festive, and casually upscale. It offers more than 50 international wines by the glass and a Mediterranean-infused menu. Flavorful and robust dishes include items such as Sicilian prime rib panini, oxtail Provençale, sweet potato fries with spicy rémoulade, prosciutto-wrapped jumbo prawns, rack of lamb, and filet mignon.

Haleʻiwa Joe's Seafood Grill (247-6671; haleiwajoes.com), 46-336 Haʻikū Rd., Kāneʻohe. Open daily for dinner; Sun. brunch. Moderate–expensive. No reservations. What's the next best thing to oceanfront dining? A view onto a botanical garden—and that's really the biggest draw of Haleʻiwa Joe's. Below you is the 6-acre Haʻikū Gardens, complete with a lily pond, exotic flowers, and a tiny gazebo. Wait as long as you must for a table next to the windows. The menu offers standard Island dishes like tempura crab roll, Hawaiian premium sashimi, crunchy coconut shrimp, beef satay, filet mignon, and fresh fish. They also have a happy hour every evening. We've found the service friendly, but the food only moderately tasty; in fact, the place is a touch worn. Be sure to walk down to the garden before or after visiting Hale'iwa Joe's—it's open to the public, and free.

Lucy's Grill & Bar (230-8188), 33 Aulike St., Kailua. Open daily for dinner. Moderate–expensive. Reservations recommended. This is considered one of the Kailua area's star restaurants; and although not always entirely up to par, it's a good choice for an evening of casual-upscale neighborhood dining. Walls are artfully lined with surfboards, aquariums, and Hawaiian stone poi pounder displays. The atmosphere is bustling— and sometimes downright loud—with residents who know that the portions will more than satisfy. Sit on the tiki-torch-lit patio and take in the experience. The 'ahi tower, kālua pork tacos, chicken satay with Thai peanut/liliko'i sauce, macadamia nut crusted lamb shank, and chocolate soufflé cake are just a few delicious dishes Lucy's has served. On Wednesday the restaurant offers most of its bottles of wine at half price if you purchase an entrée.

EATING OUT Aloha Salads (262-2016; alohasalads.com), Kailua Shopping Center, 600 Kailua Rd., Kailua. There's only a small seating area, but this is one of the few places you can really make a salad your own way. They also offer subs and soups. The café uses fresh ingredients from local farmers.

🍴 ✎ **Boots & Kimo's Homestyle Kitchen** (263-7929), 151 Hekili St., Kailua. Open daily for breakfast and lunch. Inexpensive. Credit cards are not accepted; nor are reservations. There's at least one reason to get up early in Kailua: pancakes with a special (family secret) macadamia nut sauce on top served at Boots & Kimo's. Until recently a sort of hole-in-the-wall eatery that overflowed with the hungry on weekends, they've now moved into much bigger digs in attempt to accommodate the popularity of their breakfast. Other notable dishes include the fried rice, Hawaiian sausage, pūlehu short ribs, and crab omelet. This is a very kick-back, local-style eatery, a Hawaiian-family-run neighborhood favorite.

✎ **Boston's North End Pizza Bakery** (263-8055; bostonspizzahawaii.com), 31 Ho'olai St., Kailua. Probably O'ahu's most popular pizza place. Slices are a hefty quarter-pie, and terrific.

✎ **California Pizza Kitchen** (263-2480; cpk.com), Kainalu Plaza, 609 Kailua Rd., Kailua. Open daily for lunch and dinner. Moderate. No reservations. For comfortably priced eats that ring a familiar bell, try CPK in Kailua, a very casual sit-down chain eatery serving all their classics: signature pizzas, salads, sandwiches, soups, pastas, and more.

🍴 ✎ **Cinnamon's Restaurant** (261-8724; cinnamonsrestaurant.com), Kailua Square, 315 Uluniu St., Kailua. Open daily for breakfast; Mon.–Sat. for lunch. Inexpensive. Reservations for parties of five or more only. A Windward O'ahu favorite for breakfast since 1985, family-owned Cinnamon's has been locally voted one of Hawai'i's best restaurants several times. A classic '70-style coffee shop inside with airy covered courtyard seating outside, it serves mostly traditional diner fare. With homey touches like great coffee and a newspaper while you wait for a table, plus friendly staff, it's easy to settle into buttermilk pancakes, loco moco omelet, Portuguese sweet bread French toast, and local papaya. Arrive early on weekends to avoid long waits. In our opinion the food and service can be very hit-or-miss, but its neighborhood appeal is undeniable.

Kalapawai Café (262-3354; kalapawai market.com/section/café), 750 Kailua Rd., Kailua. Born from the Kalapawai Market, the café is on Kailua's main drag. It's a popular and upscale stop, with both deli service and seated dining service.

Kalapawai Market (262-4359; kalapawaimarket.com), 306 S. Kalāheo Ave., Kailua. A Kailua landmark open since the 1930s, the market also has a sandwich shop in the back—a perfect grab before the beach.

Ono Loa Hawaiian Foods (239-5117), 48-140 Kamehameha Hwy., Waiāhole. This homespun to-go stop sells traditional Hawaiian food plates out of a vintage roadside poi factory. Owner Maxine farms the taro herself in the valley. At the time of writing, open only Fri. and Sat. for lunch.

🦐 ♻ **Romy's Kahuku Prawns & Shrimp** (232-2202; romyskahuku prawns.org), 56-781 Kamehameha Hwy., Kahuku. The Windward stretch from Punalu'u to Kahuku (and even beyond) has become "shrimp truck country." Romy's is our personal favorite—they harvest from the pond next to the stand, and the native wetland birds at the ponds are beautiful to watch. **Giovanni's** is another classic, located next to the old sugar mill.

✎ **Teddy's Burgers** (262-0820), Kailua Village Shops, 539 Kailua Rd.,

GIOVANNI'S SHRIMP TRUCK

Kailua. A local favorite with quality, mega-juicy burgers made to order and outdoor patio dining.

SWEETS & TREATS Agnes' Portuguese Bake Shop (262-5367; agnesbakeshop.com), 46 Ho'ola'i St., Kailua. On the windward side, this is the place for malasadas. They also serve other baked goods and simple breakfasts.

TEA & COFFEE Morning Brew Coffee Shop and Bistro (262-7770; morningbrewhawaii.com), Kailua Shopping Center, 600 Kailua Rd., Kailua. *The* place in Kailua to grab coffee and read the newspaper.

WINE BARS Formaggio Grill (263-2633; formaggi0808.com), 305 Hahani St., Kailua. More a festive grill atmosphere than a soothing wine bar vibe, the sister location of Honolulu's Formaggio Wine Bar is just as serious about wine as it is about good food and fun.

✷ Entertainment

MOVIE HOUSES Signature Theatres Windward Stadium (234-4006), Windward Mall, 46-056 Kamehameha Hwy., Kāne'ohe, offers first-runs. Trivia: President Obama and family saw *Avatar* here. ♪ **Lā'ie Palms Cinemas** (232-0006), Lā'ie Shopping Center, 55-510 Kamehameha Hwy., Lā'ie, is the only movie house serving the entire northern windward side and North Shore areas. It shows family-oriented, G through PG-13 first-run movies. It's closed Sunday, in keeping with the town's Mormon lifestyle.

PERFORMING ARTS Palikū Theatre (235-7310; windward.hawaii .edu/paliku), Windward Community College, 45-720 Kea'ahala Rd., Kāne'ohe. Spring and fall. Ticket prices vary according to type of production. Folks staying on the windward side of O'ahu should take note that Windward Community College has a beautiful 300-seat theater, eliminating the need to drive into town at night. Productions include concerts, dramas, musicals, dance programs, film festivals, lectures, and Hawaiian music sessions.

SUNSET PATIOS Buzz's Original Steak House (261-4661; buzzssteak house.com), 413 Kawailoa Rd., Lanikai. Get in line for this popular and crowded landmark graced with more than a touch of castaway decor. Just across from Kailua Beach Park, you won't literally get sunset views as you drink, but the atmosphere and booze will leave you thinking you did. Dinner's good, too. Cash only.

✷ Selective Shopping

ALOHAWEAR Manuheali'i (261-9865; manuhealii.com), Kailua Shopping Center, 600 Kailua Rd., Kailua. Manuheali'i features contemporary mu'umu'u and other alohawear inspired by garden florals and Hawaiian quilting. These pieces meld aloha vintage and modern with their large, bold, bright, simple patterns and up-to-date cuts.

ANTIQUES & COLLECTIBLES Ali'i Antiques I and II (261-1705; aliiantiques.com), 21 and 9A Maluniu Ave., Kailua. Lots of stuff here for the curious. Shop I carries mountains of goods such as vintage dishware, knickknacks, jewelry, beads, and dolls. Shop II is stacked with Hawaiiana, including furniture, paintings, poi pounders, and other collectibles.

Antiques & Treasures (263-1177), 315 Uluniu St., Kailua. This charming shop was the longtime dream of owner Mihye Seo Cortese, who emigrated from Korea. She carries a variety of smaller Asiatic, European, and Hawaiian pieces from more than a dozen vendors, and welcomes visitors to enjoy a cup of tea and "talk story."

Heritage Antiques & Gifts (261-8700), 767 Kailua Rd., Kailua. Bury yourself in endless little artifacts from around the world, including carvings, estate jewelry, crystal, rocking chairs, figurines, and snuff bottles.

✪ **Mu'umu'u Heaven** (263-3366; muumuuheaven.com), 767 Kailua Rd., Kailua. Mu'umu'u Heaven made its mark turning old mu'umu'u into awesome new looks. We've listed them here for their new home decor department, which carries beautiful vases and other trinkets that fall somewhere between secondhand and collectible.

The Only Show in Town (293-1295), 56-901 Kamehameha Hwy., Kahuku. Located inside the old Tanaka Plantation Store near Turtle Bay Resort, this collectibles shop overflows with Japanese dolls, glass net fishing floats, license plates, and a host of other appealing nuggets, as well as plenty of atmosphere. Owner Paul is an entertaining host.

BOOKS & MUSIC BookEnds (261-1996), 600 Kailua Rd., Kailua. A cozy bookstore with mostly used volumes

and a large collection of Hawai'i-related books.

Borders Books & Music (235-8803; borders.com), Windward Mall, 46-056 Kamehameha Hwy., Kāne'ohe. Finally expanded to full-store size, and stocking all the subjects you're looking for.

BOUTIQUES Global Village (262-8183), Kailua Village Shops, 539 Kailua Rd., Kailua. Pick up hip apparel with Kailua attitude, plus beads, jewelry, and other tidbits from around the world.

Mu'umu'u Heaven (263-3366; muumuuheaven.com), 767 Kailua Rd., Kailua. Recycled mu'umu'u find new life in one-of-a-kind dresses. President Obama entrusted them with his grandma's favorite mu'umu'u, which they appliquéd onto a dress for wife Michelle.

FARMERS' MARKETS Kailua Farmers' Market (391-3804; hfbf .org), Kailua Town Center Parking Garage, 609 Kailua Rd., Kailua. A short and sweet affair that Kailua residents love—and a good place to get an inexpensive dinner. Thu. 5–7:30 PM.

HAWAIIANA & OTHER HAWAI'I-MADE CRAFTS Island Treasures Art Gallery (261-8131), 602 Kailua Rd., Kailua. Although it contains a few borderline-touristy trinkets, the store also carries a mix of beautiful objects such as Hawaiian quilts, striking pottery, koa-wood crafts, and paintings, all made by Hawai'i artists—including several of local renown.

Lanikai Bath and Body (262-3260; lanikaibathandbody.com), Kailua

HAWAIIAN MUSIC MUST-HAVES

Consider this a Hawaiian music "starter kit" of new and old classics. Also, both of our Hawaiian music radio stations broadcast via their Web sites. Visit hawaiian105.com and am940hawaii.com to hear the best of Hawaiian music. In the car, catch them at FM 105.1 and AM 940.

Amy Gilliom: *Generation Hawai'i*
Brothers Cazimero: *Best of the Brothers Cazimero, Vol. 1*
Cecilio & Kapono: *'Elua*
Dennis Pavao: *All Hawai'i Stand Together*
Eddie Kamae: *Sons of Hawai'i*
Gabby Pahinui: *Best of the Gabby Band 1972–1977*
Hui 'Ohana: *Best of Hui 'Ohana II*
Israel Kamakawiwo'ole: *Facing Future*
Ledward Ka'apana: *Grandmaster Slack Key Guitar*
Mākaha Sons: *Ke Alaula*
Maunalua: *Maunalua*
Nā Palapalai: *Ke 'Ala Beauty*
'Olomana: *Like a Seabird in the Wind*
Raiatea Helm: *Sweet & Lovely*
Slack Key Guitar Vol. 2 (compilation of artists)
Sunday Mānoa: *Guava Jam*

Shopping Center, 600 Kailua Rd., Kailua. An entire store of buttery body products made in Hawai'i from natural, botanical, local ingredients.

Nohea Island Arts (262-2787; noheagallery.com), 767 Kailua Rd., Kailua. Nohea Galleries represents about 450 local artists; their Windward O'ahu shop is tucked away at the entrance to Kailua. Glasswork, ceramics, wooden bowls, and other locally handcrafted pieces are their specialty, and items are truly gorgeous.

Under a Hula Moon (261-4252; hulamoonhawaii.com), Kailua Shopping Center, 600 Kailua Rd., Kailua. A little shop with thoughtful Island items such as woven bags, dried flower wreaths, and small paintings.

HOME DECOR Red Bamboo (263-3174; redbamboohawaii.com), 602 Kailua Rd., Kailua. A fresh mix of Island-inspired, beach-themed home decor and Balinese furnishings.

KID STUFF ✿ Baby Showers Hawai'i (262-8934; baby-showers-hawaii.com), Kailua Shopping Center, 600 Kailua Rd., Kailua. Teensy-weensy shoe sets, simple and earthy dolls, Hawaiian-style baby quilts, clothing, and other items for tiny folks.

✿ Little Sprouts (266-8877; littlesproutshawaii.com), Kailua Shopping Center, 600 Kailua Rd., Kailua. The largest selection of ecofriendly clothes, shoes, toys, and accessories on O'ahu.

SURF & OTHER SPORTING GEAR

Aaron's Dive Shop (262-2333; hawaii-scuba.com), 307 Hahani St., Kailua. With 40 years in business, Aaron's is a Kailua fixture. Their thing is dive tours, but they also sell tons of ocean-related gear for activities such as scuba, snorkeling, and spear diving.

🦐 ✪ **Kimo's Surf Hut** (262-1644; kimossurfhut.com), 776 Kailua Rd., Kailua. Owned by noted Hawaiian activist Kimo Aluli, this is a real surf shack run by a real surfer. Browse through a huge collection of beautiful new and vintage boards and help carry the Island spirit forward.

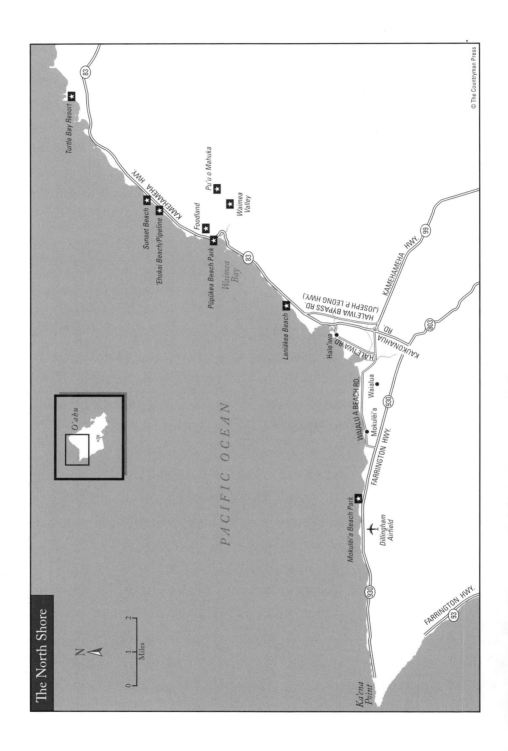

The North Shore

N

0 1 2
Miles

O'ahu

PACIFIC OCEAN

© The Countryman Press

Turtle Bay Resort

KAMEHAMEHA HWY.

Sunset Beach
'Ehukai Beach/Pipeline

Foodland

Pu'u o Mahuka

Waimea
Valley

Pūpūkea Beach Park

Waimea
Bay

Laniākea Beach

HALE'IWA BYPASS RD.
(JOSEPH P. LEONG HWY.)

KAMEHAMEHA HWY.

Hale'iwa

KAUKONAHUA RD.

WAIALUA BEACH RD.

Waialua

Mokulē'ia

FARRINGTON HWY.

Mokulē'ia Beach Park

Dillingham
Airfield

Ka'ena
Point

FARRINGTON HWY.

THE NORTH SHORE

Betwen Kahuku and Hale'iwa, you're in surfer country. This coastal setting of dry pasturelands and chunky hills features an impressive stretch of breathtaking beaches and powerful waves, especially in winter. The renowned surf destinations of Sunset Beach, Waimea, and Banzai Pipeline attract nearly two million annual visitors. When the surf's up, traffic can back up for miles.

The North Shore culture is all its own, shaped by surfing and rural Hawai'i life. It seems few guys think to wear anything but T-shirts and slippers, and few girls anything but bikinis. It's hard to blame them—they're all tan and fit. Everyone knows everyone, evidenced by shakas and shouts from pumped-up trucks piled high with surfboards, friends, and dogs. Salt and perhaps the scent of pakalōlō hang in the air. Shack-style plate-lunch stops pepper the roadsides until you reach the colorful and funky little town of Hale'iwa, the "surfing capital of the world."

The North Shore Chamber of Commerce is happy to answer questions about North Shore businesses, although office hours are limited. Check out their Web site at GoNorthShore.org.

MEDICAL TREATMENT CENTERS Hale'iwa Family Health Center (637-5087), 66-125 Kamehameha Hwy., Hale'iwa. Tue. and Thu. 8–8; Mon., Wed., Fri., and Sat. 8–5.

✶ To See

ARCHAEOLOGICAL AND SACRED SITES ✪ Pu'u o Mahuka Heiau, off Pūpūkea Homestead Rd., Pūpūkea. We consider this hilltop heiau to be the most striking archaeological site on O'ahu, especially with its spectacular ocean-view setting. Measuring an enormous 575 feet by 170 feet, it's the largest on the island and a National Historic Landmark. History tells that several European sailors, probably from Captain Vancouver's ship, the *Daedalus*, were sacrificed here in 1794. The number of visitors to this site has increased greatly in recent years; please take extra care to help preserve its mystique. Touching or in any way altering remains at the site is against the law. Learn more about the heiau at HawaiiStateParks.org.

Take Pūpūkea Homestead Rd. (next to Foodland, near Waimea Bay) around the hairpin curve. Take the first cutoff right and continue to the end of the road.

Hale o Lono Heiau, Waimea Valley, 59-864 Kamehameha Hwy., across from Waimea Bay. Dating from AD 1470, Hale o Lono is the only fully restored Lono heiau in Hawai'i, although it's a very small one. It features a grass hale, tiki, an offering tower, and other elements that likely would have been part of the compound in its time. For more information, visit WaimeaValley.net. The heiau is at the back of the parking area. Do not disturb its features.

MUSEUMS & GALLERIES ✿ **North Shore Surf and Cultural Museum** (637-8888; northshoresurfmuseum.com), North Shore Marketplace, 66-250 Kamehameha Hwy., Hale'iwa. Open Tue.–Sun. noon–6. Free. Take a break from the beach at this funky little collectibles museum and get hip to the history of surfing and surf culture. Situated in the surfing capital of the world, this is the real deal. Glass Japanese fishing net floaters, old surfboards once belonging to the pros, and other curios convey the true North Shore lifestyle.

✳ To Do

BODYBOARDING, STAND-UP PADDLING, & SURFING Sunset Suzy (780-6963; sunsetsuzy.com). Learn to surf with North Shore lifeguard, *Blue Crush* surfer, and former *Baywatch* stunt person "Sunset Suzy." Private and group lessons are available for every experience level, as is a monthly surf camp for women and girls. Instruction takes place at the famed Sunset Beach.

A WILD BOAR AT PU'U O MAHUKA HEIAU

BICYCLE CRUISING Country Cycles (638-8866), 59-059 Pūpūkea Rd., Pūpūkea. Rent a beach cruiser bicycle and enjoy the long coastal bike path from Sunset Beach to Waimea Bay.

Turtle Bay Resort (293-8811; turtlebayresort.com), 57-091 Kamehameha Hwy., Hale'iwa. Mountain bikes and beach cruisers are available for rent by the hour or longer for use anywhere on the island.

✿ ✿ **CAMPING Camp Mokulēi'a** (637-6241; visitcampmokuleia.org), 68-729 Farrington Hwy., Mokulēi'a. Privately operated by the Episcopal Church, this beachfront campground is spectacular and very safe, and thus in high demand. In addition to tent camping, they have a lodge, cabins, a cottage, and a private beach house, plus a dining hall, which, considering you're far from Hale'iwa, is a definite plus. There's also a swimming pool, although the water fronting the camp is generally very swimmable. Reservations are required far in advance, and everyone's welcome.

DOLPHIN, SHARK, & WHALE WATCHING See our "Recreation" chapter for more information on these activities.

Deep Ecology (637-7946; 800-578-3992; deepecologyhawaii.com), 66-456 Kamehameha Hwy., Hale'iwa. Among other tours, this environmentally responsible company conducts whale-watching trips out of Hale'iwa Harbor. They often encounter dolphins along the way as a bonus. In addition to leading tours, they conduct marine animal rescues and are involved in community forums relating to both ecotourism and conservation issues.

Hawai'i Shark Encounters (351-9373; hawaiisharkencounters.com), Hale'iwa. The tour leaves Hale'iwa Boat Harbor and heads out about 3 miles offshore. You can remain on the boat and view sharks from above, or lower yourself into a submerged cage.

North Shore Catamaran Charters (351-9371; sailingcat.com), Hale'iwa. This small catamaran powers mostly via wind to make your whale-watching experience more peaceful. An underwater hydrophone enables riders to hear whale communications. The trip leaves from Hale'iwa Boat Harbor.

North Shore Shark Adventures (228-5900; sharktourshawaii.com). This is the first shark tour operator to have opened on O'ahu, founded by a Hale'iwa diveboat owner. Leave from Hale'iwa Boat Harbor for a short trip offshore, where you can either view sharks from the deck or enter a submerged cage.

FISHING Ku'uloa Kai Charters (637-5783; kuuloakai.com), 66-195 Ka'amo'oloa Rd., Waialua. Join real fishermen for a full big-game fishing experience in the deep waters of the North Shore. The boat can accommodate up to six passengers for full- or half-day charter trips.

GARDENS & PARKS ✿ **Waimea Valley** (638-9199; waimeavalley.net), 59-864 Kamehameha Hwy., Waimea. A cultural and botanical treasure with more than 700 years of habitation, Waimea Valley is that rare story of triumph over commercialization. Over the years, this once-sacred valley fell into the hands of various developers who erected a series of themed "adventure" parks; wealthy private homes and a tourist camp were next on the agenda. In 2002 the City and County of Honolulu acquired selected parcels through condemnation and leased them to the National Audubon Society. Backed by public demand, in 2006 the city, the military, and other organizations banded together to purchase the entire 1,875-acre valley from a New York developer for its preservation forever.

Visit the restored heiau temple at the entrance, walk its trails, and if the rain's been heavy enough around the streambed, swim in the valley's natural waterfall pool. Daily 9–5. $13 adults, $6 ages 4–12.

GOLF Kahuku Golf Course (293-5842; co.honolulu.hi.us/des/golf/kahuku .htm), 56-501 Kamehameha Hwy., Kahuku. Local favorite Kahuku Golf Course is a nine-hole, 35-par course and a great value for the money, despite its windiness. You'll get 2,699 yards of fun and easy walking, plus a view of the ocean. Green fees are only $11.50. At the time of writing, investors have purchased the land out from under this landmark golf course and may turn it and neighboring plantation countryside into a stretch of luxury development. Cross your fingers that doesn't happen.

Turtle Bay Golf (293-8574; turtlebayresort.com), 57-091 Kamehameha Hwy., Kahuku. With two championship 18-hole courses set against a beachfront, 880-acre landscape, Turtle Bay is an excellent place to play golf. The popular Palmer course offers a slope of 143 and par of 72. Green fees for the Arnold Palmer course are $140 for guests of the resort and $175 for visitors; for the George Fazio course, fees are $100 for guests and $125 for visitors. Carts are required and included in the above prices, which have dropped since our last edition. Combine your play with breakfast, lunch, or dinner at Lei Lei's, located right on the golf course.

HANG GLIDING, PARAGLIDING, GLIDERS, & ULTRALIGHTS See the "Recreation" chapter for more on these four activities, which let you get the wind in your hair without the distraction of roaring engines.

Original Glider Rides (677-3404; honolulusoaring.com). This 35-year-old operation can take you up in a glider, give you lessons, and rent you equipment if you are already licensed. Tours cruise the Wai'anae Range and North Shore and can be as mellow or as loopy and crazy as you like. Reservations recommended.

Paradise Air (497-6033; paradiseairhawaii.com). Denise and Tom Sanders have two awesome ultralight trikes that they run from Dillingham Airfield in Mokulē'ia. You'll learn how to operate them and go up tandem above the North Shore for as long as you and the weather conditions allow.

Soar Hawai'i Sailplanes (637-3147; soarhawaii.com). In business for 30 years, these folks own six gliders and can take you for a ride or even provide lessons. Sights include Waimea Bay and Mount Ka'ala, O'ahu's highest peak. Or perhaps you'd like an aerobatic experience; the pilot will tailor maneuvers to whatever you can handle. They also now offer Windward Coast motor-glider rides, which power up to reach altitude then cut the engine.

HIKING Ka'ena Point Trail, Ka'ena Point State Park, Mākua/Mokulē'ia. Hawaiians believed that Ka'ena Point was where souls jumped into the endless night after leaving their bodies; you'll feel the power of this remote, 800-acre nature preserve when you enter it.

The trail can be thought of as starting at two opposite points—on the northernmost tip of the Leeward Coast, and on the northernmost tip of the North Shore—and meeting in the middle at the otherwise inaccessible Ka'ena Point. You can also hike it from one end to the other. We recommend you hike halfway from either end, then turn back. Bus service stops long before either trailhead, so unless someone can pick you up, you'll be stuck on the other end.

Depending on which route you choose, you'll cover 3 to 5 miles of coastal landscape with rare native plants and birds, low sand dunes, tide pools, rugged coastline, large winter waves, and a lighthouse. In winter you might see whales; even the endangered Hawaiian monk seal visits the area occasionally. Swimming is not advised, as the water here can be dangerous. Any natural elements, including nests and flowers, should be left untouched.

The area can be really hot, windy, and dry, so bring lots of sunscreen and water. There are no bathrooms along the way or other services.

To get there: Approach on either side of Ka'ena Point. On the North Shore/Mokulē'ia side, follow Farrington Hwy. (930) to the end of the road. On the leeward side, you'll also follow Farrington Hwy. (93) to the end of the road. At either parking area, leave nothing in your car.

✔ **Turtle Bay Resort** (293-6000; turtlebayresort.com), 57-091 Kamehameha Hwy., Kahuku, has an underused trail system with about 12 miles of trails winding along coves and grassy beach dunes and through coastal groves. Do not disrupt the dunes, which have historical significance.

HORSEBACK RIDING It's against the law to ride horses on the beach in Hawai'i. However, the places that offer horseback riding on O'ahu walk you through picturesque settings, including alongside the ocean. All use western saddles for the safety of guest riders.

✔ **Happy Trails Hawai'i** (638-7433; happytrailshawaii.com), 59-231 Pūpūkea Rd., Pūpūkea. This friendly local company offers trail rides through rain forests

HORSEBACK RIDING AT TURTLE BAY

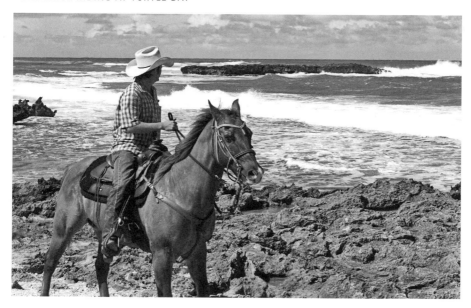

and orchards above the North Shore. They accept a maximum of 10 riders (6 years old and up) for 90-minute or two-hour trail trips.

Hawai'i Polo Oceanfront Trail Rides (220-5153; hawaiipolo.com/trailrides/asp), 65-411 Farrington Hwy., Mokulēi'a. Horse lovers looking for an exceptional experience will love riding a thoroughbred or quarter-horse polo pony belonging to the renowned Hawai'i Polo Club, as did President Obama on a recent trip home. Join an intimate riding group by day or at sunset, or book a moonlight ride for two. All take place on the club's 100-acre, oceanfront property, and beginning riders over age 8 are welcome. Polo lessons are also available.

🐴 **Turtle Bay Resort** (293-6000; turtlebayresort.com), 57-091 Kamehameha Hwy., Kahuku. This full-service resort offers several lovely riding opportunities, including shoreline and forest trail rides, private rides, and sunset and evening rides. Guides can take smaller children on pony walks.

SALONS & SPAS Spa Luana (447-6868; turtlebayresort.com), Turtle Bay Resort, 57-091 Kamehameha Hwy., Kahuku. Pregnancy massages, mud wraps, child manicures, makeup application, and waxing are just the beginning of the services offered here.

SCUBA DIVING & SNORKELING North Shore Catamaran Charters (351-9371; sailingcat.com). In the summer months, sail on a spacious catamaran along the beautiful North Shore to super snorkeling at Waimea Bay's marine preserve. Trips leave from from Hale'iwa Boat Harbor.

SKYDIVING For those of you who accept the risk associated with skydiving and want to take the plunge anyway, you'll be rewarded with stellar views and a memorable experience. Both outfits below can pick you up and return you to Waikīkī and photograph or videotape your descent, and both require tandem jumping unless you have a skydiving license. They can also teach you how to skydive.

Dillingham Airfield on the North Shore is the only authorized jumping site on the island.

Skydive Hawai'i (637-9700; hawaiiskydiving.com), 68-760 Farrington Hwy., Mokulēi'a. Hawai'i's oldest skydiving company features expert instructors licensed by the United States Parachute Association (USPA) and conducts jumps over the North Shore from its Cessna Caravan.

Pacific Skydiving Center (637-7472; pacific-skydiving.com), 68-760 Farrington Hwy., Mokulēi'a. This company runs the fastest-climbing plane of the two operators and also employs licensed, USPA expert instructors.

TENNIS Turtle Bay Resort (293-8811; turtlebayresort.com), 57-091 Kamehameha Hwy., Kahuku. This full facility offers 10 courts, equipment, and lessons. A fee is charged to play, and reservations are required.

Second in fame only to Waikīkī Beach, the beaches of the North Shore have become legendary, as have its most prominent surfers and lifeguards. On most winter days swimming is not advised, unless you enjoy bone-crushing waves some two stories high crashing down onto your head or being the center of search-and-rescue parties. In summer, even Waimea Bay can reduce to kitten-soft swells generally safe for decent swimmers.

When the waves are hot (and sometimes even when they're not), traffic can back up literally for miles along the coast's only thoroughfare, and beachside parking can be a nightmare. If you have a specific beach destination in mind and the news is reporting a really big surf day, consider taking TheBus instead of driving.

A note on turtle-watching, the North Shore's new "second industry." Laniākea, listed below, is the most popular place to do it these days, but the traffic's become so ridiculous that locals are no longer recommending it. For a less chaotic alternative that includes easy parking, head to Hale‘iwa Ali‘i Beach Park, just west of Hale‘iwa's landmark bridge. Turtles often visit the shoreline to the left of the lifeguard stand. These mellow creatures are federally protected; wherever you see them, please enjoy them from a distance.

Ali‘i Beach Park, 66-167 Hale‘iwa Rd., Hale‘iwa. Everyone goes to Laniākea to see turtles—but these creatures love to hang out on the left side of the lifeguard stand at Ali‘i Beach, too. And there's plenty of parking and fewer people. The beach hosts a segment of the Triple Crown of Surfing in winter, and waves and currents can be strong at that time of year.

❂ **‘Ehukai Beach**, 59-360 Kamehameha Hwy., Sunset Beach. Home of the legendary and hazardous "Banzai Pipeline" surf site. All roads seem to converge at ‘Ehukai's shoreline when the waves are prime. The Japanese word *banzai* means "10,000 years"—but its reputation as the World War II war cry "to the death," especially in suicide missions, is how the word is used around here. Needless to say, skip swimming and just savor the exciting experience of this renowned beach area.

Signs no longer mark the park. Look for a beachfront parking lot filled with cars several miles past Turtle Bay Resort if you're driving west, or several miles past Foodland if you're driving east. Sunset Beach Elementary School is across the street.

𝒶 **Kuilima Cove** (293-6000; turtlebayresort.com), Turtle Bay Resort, 57-091 Kamehameha Hwy., Kahuku. No matter what the waves are like on the rest of the North Shore, even in winter, Kuilima Cove is a generally safe swimming spot for your family. It's protected by a high reef shelf that has some good snorkeling but also a strong current suck. Stay closer in to the beach to be safe. We've seen turtles loll right on the shoreline, so you still might get to see cute critters in the shallow water. The beach is nice but crowded with hotel guests, and the delicious restaurant Ola is right there. For a quiet beach walk, head southwest around the corner, where crowds are virtually nonexistent because of dangerous swimming conditions.

Park in the resort lot, next to the hotel—just let them know at the tollbooth that you're going to the beach, which is public property.

Laniākea Beach Park, Kamehameha Hwy., Hale'iwa. Also called "Lani's" and "Turtle Beach." While not the best spot for swimming due to a rocky reef shelf, Laniākea has become a popular beach for turtle-watching. Find it about a mile before Hale'iwa heading west, along a sandy strip just before Pōhaku Loa Way and a horse pasture. You'll know you're there when you see millions of cars parked on both sides of the highway. Residents are at their wits' end over the traffic backup at this spot, so try to keep the flow.

✄ **Pūpūkea Beach Park**, 59-727 Kamehameha Hwy., Pūpūkea. The attraction here is Sharks Cove and Three Tables, full of tasty (and crowded) summer snorkeling and scuba nooks within a marine life conservation district. In winter its little pools can still be safe for swimming—but if waves are crashing on the rocks around you, stay out. The park sits across from Foodland, just east of Waimea Bay.

Mokulēi'a Beach Park, 68-901 Farrington Hwy., Mokulēi'a. Beyond the strip of the North Shore's star beaches and the town of Hale'iwa you'll find Mokulēi'a, an unpretentiously well-off country community with a polo field. The beach park area attracts illegal campers, homeless beachcombers, local families, and a few low-key visitors. The area can get some strong gusts and scary waves, but it's a relaxing getaway from the bustle. Not a great family beach due to remoteness. On Farrington Hwy. (930), pass Camp Mokulēi'a and look for the park entrance.

Sunset Beach Park, 59-104 Kamehameha Hwy., Sunset Beach. The majestic Sunset commands respect: It hosts a segment of the Triple Crown, surfing's crème de la crème mega-event, and because of gorgeous waves, it sees many a rescue. In any season it's the North Shore destination for admiring waves, watching the sunset, and deepening your tan. This is "hot stuff" country; although tour buses dump dozens of dazed visitors in sweater vests onto the sands every hour, most local folks are bronzed and in their best beach looks.

Sunset Beach isn't marked. Look an open stretch of beach, single row of cars, and white lifeguard tower about a mile east of Sunset Beach Elementary School.

TWENTY FEET AND UP AT WAIMEA BAY

✪ **Waimea Bay Beach Park**, 61-031 Kamehameha Hwy., Waimea. This is the granddaddy of the North Shore beaches in every way. The smooth, sweeping bay features lustrous golden sand, deep-aquamarine waters, and a gargantuan sea rock, all framed by a deep valley. The bay is part of a marine life conservation district, and the valley contains several significant archaeological remains.

In summer Waimea is a sleeping giant where families gather, tourists paddle about with snorkels, and the daring hike up the rock to jump into the groaning swells. But when the northern storms stir the ocean in the winter season, this world-class bay can occasionally turn into a yawning portal for mammoth waves up to 50 feet high.

Waimea is about 4 miles east of Hale'iwa, at a sharp inland curve in the highway. The park entrance is at the apex of the curve, so proceed slowly.

✳ Lodging

Ke Iki Beach Bungalows (638-8829; 866-638-8229; keikibeach.com), 59-579 Ke Iki Rd., Sunset Beach. Moderate. Ten one- and two-bedroom beachside bungalows and one studio bungalow await those who love the North Shore surf-house vibe. All have been recently renovated and are tropically tasteful, clean, and cozy—and in fact several are downright kickin' with dead-on ocean views. All have full kitchens and the essential beach scene elements such as barbecues, picnic tables, and hammocks. These little pads get good reviews from travelers. The owner can even coordinate on-site wedding ceremonies and receptions. Considering that you can fit up to five or six people in many of the units, the prices are great—split it with friends and enjoy a beach house for a few days.

🐚 **Turtle Bay Resort** (293-6000; 800-203-3650; turtlebayresort.com), 57-091 Kamehameha Hwy., Kahuku. Moderate–expensive. There is no full hotel or resort anywhere on Windward O'ahu or the North Shore except for the laid-back and gorgeously situated Turtle Bay. You'll think you've left O'ahu for a quieter neighbor island. As is typical of the windward side, which it straddles, it does get moody weather with many overcast or blustery days. Turtles and whales are frequently seen from the shorelines, however, and Kuilima Cove, abutting the property, is one of the North Shore's best swimming spots year-round.

The main hotel was built in the 1960s; it has undergone a dramatic upgrade in the last decade, and its generously sized, all-ocean-view rooms and lobby are truly lovely at last. The property spans 880 ocean-front acres of land and features hundreds of ocean-view hotel rooms, plus cottages, villas, a full spa, two world-class golf courses, tennis, horseback riding, and good restaurants.

The atmosphere here these days is touchy. Turtle Bay finally intends to make good on their 25-year-old, very controversial plan to build thousands of new time shares and other luxury hotels along the pristine coastline. The rural and economically depressed nearby community of Kahuku, as well as longtime North Shore residents, are struggling to decide whether they need low-paying service jobs more than their treasured country lifestyle, and some folks are fighting back.

Turtle Bay Condos (293-2800; 888-266-3690; turtlebaycondos.com), 57-091 Kamehameha Hwy., Kahuku. Moderate. On the expansive property of Turtle Bay Resort you'll find a series of two-story studio, one-, two-, and three-bedroom golf-course condos that you can rent for a minimum of two nights. Although sharing land space with the resort, they are rented separately. Each unit offers a fully equipped kitchen and a washer and dryer. A one-bedroom unit typically features a king or queen bed plus sleeper sofa, and prices are very reasonable for the large amount of living space. None has ocean views and each is privately owned, meaning that decor can vary widely. The condo development maintains its own pool and tennis courts. You'll need to arrange to pick up the unit key yourself from an office in the community of Kahuku, down the road.

✹ Where to Eat

DINING OUT 21 Degrees North (293-6000; turtlebayresort.com), Turtle Bay Resort, 57-091 Kamehameha Hwy., Kahuku. Open for dinner Tue.–Sat. Reservations recommended. This is the North Shore's most elegant restaurant, located at the oceanfront Turtle Bay Resort. The hotel-atmosphere hexagonal dining room is simple, with framed, full-glass window views onto both the resort's pool deck and ocean—so arrive before sunset if you can. The menu is formal and elegant, with dishes such as oysters, blackened 'ahi, organic greens with macadamia nut crusted goat cheese, filet mignon, Muscovy duck

breast, braised Kona lobster, and crab-crusted Hawaiian sea bass. Home-made ice creams are not to be missed. Five-course menus are available, and the entrée menu offers suggested wine pairings.

✐ **Haleʻiwa Joe's** (637-8005; haleiwajoes.com), 66-011 Kamehameha Hwy., Haleʻiwa. Open daily for lunch and dinner. Moderate. No reservations. Mellow tourist eatery by day, popular local restaurant by night, Haleʻiwa Joe's seems to appeal to almost everyone, although we find the food only fairly good. The decor is somewhat generic, but views are tasty—request seating on the open-air patio to gaze onto nearby Haleʻiwa Harbor.

Most folks find that Joe's is one of the best area picks for sit-down dining, and without much else to do at night on the North Shore, making an evening out of your meal is a good idea. Dishes include Sumatran beef salad, crunchy coconut shrimp, grilled salmon, signature whole moi, fire shrimp, tempura crab roll, and seared 'ahi. For dessert, try the "love" cake, filled with hot cream cheese and chocolate and smothered in raspberry sauce. Joe's also has a bar off to the side.

Jameson's by the Sea (637-6272; jamesonshawaii.com), 62-540 Kamehameha Hwy., Haleʻiwa. Open daily for lunch and dinner; Sun. brunch. Moderate–expensive. Reservations recommended. Jameson's has been around forever, and it used to be such a quality restaurant that this author's parents would drive all the way from town to eat there. It's still not bad, although it feels touristy these days. Known for its fresh fish dishes and ocean views (from across the road), at cocktail hour the patio is lined with visitors timing the last drop of liquor with the sunset, which paints the sky brilliantly over the ocean vista. Some of its best menu items are the 'ōpaka-paka poached in white wine and mahimahi. All dining takes place on the streetfront patio and first floor interior these days.

Lei Lei's (293-2662; turtlebayresort .com), Turtle Bay Resort, 57-049 Kuilima Dr., Kahuku. Open daily for all three meals. Moderate–expensive. Reservations are recommended for dinner. Lei Lei's is a casual golf-course restaurant and one of the best places to eat on the entire North Shore, with a surprisingly top-rack selection of savory dishes. Although located on Turtle Bay Resort property, it's independently and locally owned and exhibits true aloha for customers as well as for its loyal staff and the community.

For breakfast, try the Hawaiian sweet bread French toast and plantation iced tea; lunch offers a step up in selection and price, with fresh grilled Hawaiian fish plate, seared 'ahi sashimi Caesar salad, and shrimp cocktail; dinner ramps it up further with dishes like escargots, oyster shots, crab-stuffed salmon, prime rib, and double-cut pork loin chop. During the day and twilight hours the view onto the golf course is very pleasant.

 Ola (293-0801; olaislife.com), Turtle Bay Resort, 57-091 Kamehameha Hwy., Kahuku. Open daily for lunch and dinner. Moderate–expensive. Reservations recommended. Well-known island chef Fred DeAngelo opened Ola in 2005 and presides over its excellent and award-winning kitchen. Although located at Turtle Bay Resort, the restaurant is independent and the menu more playful, trendy, and regional than the resort's lauded restaurant, 21 Degrees North (described above). Ola sits right on the sandy beach fronting the resort. Both the dining and lounge patio are completely open air with views directly onto the ocean.

OLA

Courtesy Debbie Friedrich Photography

Lunch prices are moderate, with delectable items like traditional 'ahi poke, bruschetta salad, and fresh Island fish sandwich. Be sure to order Kahuku corn whenever it's listed—it's grown right in the area and is sweet and very good. At dinnertime you'll find high-end dishes such as roasted garlic edamame, lomi salmon salad, misoyaki butterfish, grilled lobster tail, and seared scallops. Fresh local ingredients, characteristic of the cuisine, are paramount in Ola's preparations. Service can be a little lax.

EATING OUT Café Hale'iwa (637-5516), 66-460 Kamehameha Hwy., Hale'iwa. A Hale'iwa landmark eatery, casual and surf-fiesta in decor and flavor. Breakfasts are hearty American, and lunches are local plate-lunch-style.

✔ **Cholo's Homestyle Mexican** (637-3059; cholosmexican.com), 66-250 Kamehameha Hwy., Hale'iwa. Perhaps the most festive dining spot on the North Shore, Cholo's draws both residents and visitors. The food's pretty good, although not entirely authentic, but outdoor seating makes it fun.

🦐 **Grass Skirt Grill** (637-4852; grass skirtgrill.com), 66-214 Kamehameha Hwy., Hale'iwa. One of the best choices for fresh shrimp, salads, fish plates, and more, with local flair. A clean and cute interior for dining is a bonus.

✔ **Kua 'Āina** (637-6067), 66-160 Kamehameha Hwy., Hale'iwa. A local favorite for well-made burgers and earthier sandwich selections. Great fries.

Paradise Found Café (637-4540), 66-483 Kamehameha Hwy., Hale'iwa. An awesome find in the back of Celestial Natural Foods, a health food store. This hippie-surf café conveys the true free spirit and warmth of the North Shore and makes some of the most delicious and healthiest vegetarian food around, using ingredients from local organic farmers.

✪ 🦐 **Sharks Cove Grill** (638-8300; sharkscovegrill.com), 59-712 Kamehameha Hwy., Hale'iwa. A simple roadside truck serving breakfast, lunch, and dinner on picnic benches under a tarp, and it's just across from, you guessed it, Sharks Cove. It's one of our favorite stops on the North Shore, with fresh 'ahi, grilled skewers, smoothies, and great salads. Co-diners might include clucking chickens, a few cats, and plenty of shirtless surfers.

SWEETS & TREATS ✔ **Aoki's Shave Ice** (637-7017; aokisshaveice .com), 66-117 Kamehameha Hwy., Hale'iwa. The Aoki family has been selling shave ice since the 1930s. Try Hawai'i-style flavors like lychee and li hing mui, with or without ice cream and azuki beans.

✔ **Matsumoto Shave Ice** (637-4827; matsumotoshaveice.com), 66-087 Kamehameha Hwy., Hale'iwa. Like Aoki's, Matsumoto's is a landmark, serving an average of 1,200 shave ices each day.

✔ **Ted's Bakery** (638-5974; teds bakery.com), 59-024 Kamehameha Hwy., Sunset Beach. Enter and speak the magic words: *chocolate-haupia cream pie.*

TEA & COFFEE Coffee Gallery (637-5355; roastmaster.com), North Shore Marketplace, 66-250 Kamehameha Hwy., Hale'iwa. A North

SHAVE ICE IS COOL ON A HOT HAWAIIAN DAY.

two-lane highway in front of you, the ocean view would be really good.

Ola (293-0801; olaislife.com), Turtle Bay Resort, 57-091 Kamehameha Hwy., Kahuku. By day, Ola serves high-quality pupu, full dishes, and excellent drinks. It's our best and most classic pick for the North Shore, although far from Hale'iwa. Your table might literally be on the sand, surrounded by tiki torches and fronting a swimmable beach. The restaurant serves award-winning "contemporary Hawaiian" cuisine for lunch and dinner (see *Dining Out*).

✳ Selective Shopping

ALOHAWEAR Kohala Bay Collections (293-2728), Turtle Bay Resort, 57-091 Kamehameha Hwy., Kahuku. This shop is located in the hotel lobby and has a selection of Tori Richard aloha shirts, as well as other resort wear items.

FARMERS' MARKETS Hale'iwa Farmers' Market (388-9696; haleiwa farmersmarket.com). One of three North Shore farmers' markets, this one's the biggest, at Kamehameha Hwy. and Cane Haul Rd. in Hale'iwa Town every Sun. 9–1.

HOME DECOR Bali Moon Hawai'i (637-6666; balimoonhawaii.com), Hale'iwa Shopping Center, 66-145 Kamehameha Hwy., Hale'iwa. Brazilian owned Bali Moon features unique lamps, kiln-dried teak furnishings, and even recycled teak pieces, most in unusual designs and dimensions.

KID STUFF ✐ **The Growing Keiki** (637-4544; thegrowingkeiki.com), 66-051 Kamehameha Hwy., Hale'iwa.

Shore institution that roasts its coffees on site.

✳ Entertainment

SUNSET PATIOS Hale'iwa Joe's Seafood Grill (637-8005; haleiwajoes .com), 66-011 Kamehameha Hwy., Hale'iwa. Not a lot of atmosphere here, but the ocean-view terrace is a nice place to wind down the day. Brightly colored drinks abound, especially 4:30–6:30 PM.

Jameson's by the Sea (637-6272; jamesonshawaii.com), 62-540 Kamehameha Hwy., Hale'iwa. A North Shore landmark restaurant that in our opinion has passed its prime, it's still one of your better bets for a sunset drink. Everyone sits on the outdoor lānai these days, and by everyone, we mean tourists. If it weren't for that

THE FINANCIAL DISTRICT DRESS CODE: ALOHAWEAR

AN ALOHAWEAR PRIMER

If you're not from Hawai'i, all aloha shirts and mu'umu'u probably look alike. If you're from Hawai'i, you know that "real" alohawear is serious business, beginning with superior fabrics and ending with specific patterns and colors. We warn you that most alohawear sold in Waikīkī, especially in its many cheap-looking trinket shops, is Tourist Garb. Unless you'd like to make a funky fashion statement, avoid polyester, screaming colors, parrot patterns, and any-

SURF N SEA

This little boutique for the tiny carries hip clothing like Paul Frank PJs, full-body rash guards, and well-made aloha shirts, along with fun little gifts.

SURF & OTHER SPORTING GEAR

North Shore Boardriders Club (637-5026; northshoreboardridersshop .com), North Shore Marketplace, 66-250 Kamehameha Hwy., Hale'iwa. Owned by legendary big-wave surfer Barry Kanaiaupuni. You'll find Quiksilver, Roxy, and other cool surf clothing plus racks of surfboards.

Surf N Sea (637-7873; surfnsea.com), 62-595 Kamehameha Hwy., Hale'iwa.

thing that reminds you of Jimmy Buffett, Magnum PI, or Florida.

Classic aloha shirts are made of sturdy, good-quality cotton (and occasionally linen or silk), often with large or small muted organic patterns that blur at a distance. Some newer looks draw from the 1960s, when big, bold, and simple colors and patterns were popular. We would consider these "vintage inspired."

The straight-bottom shirt can be worn untucked with shorts or pants, if the length's right, or tucked in and worn with a belt for a more formal look. Most men in Honolulu wear aloha shirts to work on a daily basis—even those who moved here recently from the Mainland. A good shirt will set you back between $45 and $90. Some of the best are Kāhala, Ono, Tori Richard, Diamond Head, Cooke Street, and Reyn's.

Mu'umu'u are on the way out as daily wear. Still, elegant cotton or rayon mu'umu'u remain very appropriate at traditional family celebrations, Christmas dinners at the country club, and Hawaiiana events. Worn by older Hawaiian women, especially paired with Island treasures like Ni'ihau-shell necklaces or woven hats with haku lei bands, mu'umu'u look absolutely venerable and timeless to us. Like the best aloha shirts, classic patterns and colors are muted, although newer models sometimes go bright, bold, and simple. Look for designs by Mamo Howell, Manuheali'i, and Princess Ka'iulani. Quality full-length mu'umu'u usually cost well over $150.

One last nugget of alohawear information: Unless you plan to perform in a Hawaiian music trio or Japanese punk-rock band, avoid buying matching sets.

A North Shore surf shop deluxe with more than 40 years behind it. Browse through stacks of surfboards and racks of surf clothing; rent a longboard, kayak, snorkel, or scuba tank; or join in one of their many sporting and adventure tours.

Tropical Rush (637-8886; tropical rush.com), 62-620 Kamehameha Hwy., Hale'iwa. A mini compound of shacks—one filled with skateboards, another with surfboards, and another with this-and-that. You can get a new or used board by some of today's hottest makers, plus surf clothing.

SWIMWEAR North Shore Swimwear (637-7000; northshore swimwear.com), North Shore Marketplace, 66-250 Kamehameha Hwy., Hale'iwa. Tons of styles, tons of fabrics, tons of patterns—take one to go or design your own for a custom-built bikini or one-piece at a price you can afford.

Central O'ahu 5

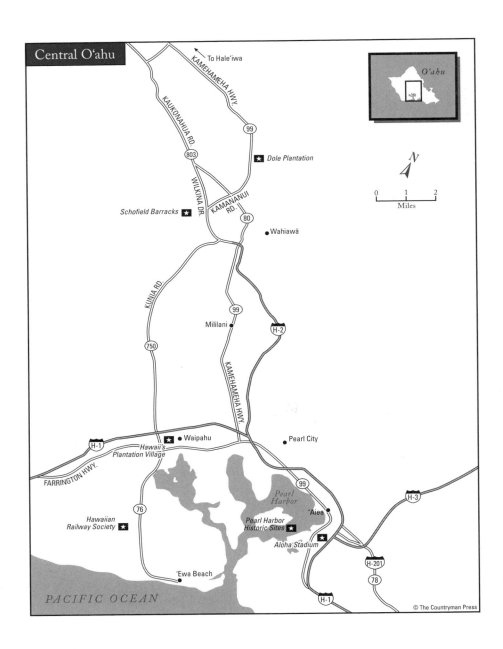

Central O'ahu

To Hale'iwa

KAMEHAMEHA HWY.

KAUKONAHUA RD.

99

803

WILKINA DR.

KAMANANUI RD.

★ Dole Plantation

Schofield Barracks ★

80

• Wahiawā

KUNIA RD.

99

H-2

Mililani •

750

KAMEHAMEHA HWY.

H-1

★ • Waipahu

Hawaii's
Plantation Village

• Pearl City

99

FARRINGTON HWY.

76

Pearl
Harbor

H-3

Hawaiian
Railway Society ★

Pearl Harbor
Historic Sites ★

'Aiea •

★

Aloha Stadium

H-201

78

'Ewa Beach

H-1

PACIFIC OCEAN

© The Countryman Press

O'ahu

N

0   1   2
Miles

CENTRAL OʻAHU

Central Oʻahu stretches between the wide plains of the Waiʻanae and Koʻolau Ranges and southward to Pearl Harbor. Dotted with unpretentious suburban communities like Wahiawā, Mililani, Pearl City, ʻAiea, and Waipahu, this is our equivalent of "the heartland."

And indeed this has long been Oʻahu's agricultural zone, swathed mainly in pineapple until they could grow them cheaper elsewhere. Many older residents were once themselves plantation hands. Hawaiʻi Plantation Village in Waipahu shares their story, one which hundreds of thousands of Hawaiʻi residents can call part of their family history.

Also here is Pearl Harbor, bombed nearly to bits by Japan in World War II. You can still see bullet holes in the windows of Ford Island airplane hangars. Spend the day experiencing the USS *Arizona* Memorial, the submarine USS *Bowfin*, the battleship USS *Missouri*, and the Pacific Aviation Museum and learn up close and personal about that poignant historic event.

HOSPITALS Wahiawā General Hospital (621-8411), 128 Lehua St., Wahiawā.

MEDICAL TREATMENT CENTERS Haleʻiwa Family Health Center (623-2435), Mililani Towne Center, 95-1249 Meheula Parkway, Suite B10, Mililani. Mon. noon–8; Tue. 8–noon; Wed.–Thu. 8–3; Fri. 8–noon; Sat. 8–11.

✳ To See

ARCHAEOLOGICAL & SACRED SITES Keaīwa Heiau, Keaīwa Heiau State Recreation Area, ʻAiea Heights Dr., ʻAiea. Keaīwa is believed to have been a heiau hoʻola, or ancient healing temple, built at least 400 years ago. It would have also served as a facility for apprentices, who might have trained for 15 years or more to learn the healing arts. The main foundation wall measures 100 by 160 feet. Badly damaged by the military during World War II, the heiau has since been restored and now features an exhibition garden of medicinal plants and other replicas of structures that would have stood here in its day. Do not touch or otherwise disturb the area.

From Waikīkī, take the H-1 Freeway to exit 19B, which puts you on the Moanalua Freeway (201/78). Take the Stadium/ʻAiea exit to Moanalua Rd. From there, turn right onto ʻAiea Heights Dr. and follow it upward to the end.

✒ ✪ **HISTORIC SITES Pearl Harbor.** Hawaiians called Pearl Harbor Wai Momi, or "Water of the Pearl." The United States began secretly scouting the site in the mid-1800s after reports indicated it could serve as an excellent harbor and defense area, and in 1887 the Hawaiian kingdom granted the lagoon to the United States through a controversial reciprocal arrangement. Over the years it has served as a naval fleet support system for sheltering, repairing, and arming submarines and aircraft. Pearl Harbor is a National Historic Landmark.

Whether or not you're interested in Hawaiʻi's past, the military, or even world history, visiting the sites at Pearl Harbor is still a one-of-a-kind experience. Budget a full day to explore the **USS *Arizona* Memorial**, battleship **USS *Missouri***, submarine **USS *Bowfin***, and new **Pacific Aviation Museum**. Note that both the battleship and submarine will present physical challenges, such as small port doorways and harrowingly steep stairways, which may not be appropriate for some visitors. At the *Arizona*, children will be expected to move about quietly.

We recommend you arrive fairly early, via car or city bus. Wear tennis shoes or closed sandals. Leave belongings at your hotel; increased security permits no purses, backpacks, or other large equipment. Small cameras and wallets are fine. Lockers are available if necessary.

Head to the main ticket booth, next to the USS *Bowfin*, for one-stop ticket purchases. The USS *Arizona* Memorial is free, but you'll be given a ticket good for a certain time of day—use the time in between to visit the submarine and take the audio tour of the *Arizona*'s visitors center and surroundings or, if you have at least a four-hour wait, take the shuttle to the *Missouri* and Pacific Aviation Museum first. The latter has the best lunch café.

For more information about each site, please read below. The Pacific Aviation Museum is covered in this chapter under *Museums & Galleries*.

Battleship *Missouri* Memorial (455-1600; 877-644-4896; ussmissouri.com), 63 Cowpens St., Ford Island, Pearl Harbor. Open daily 9–5. $20 adults, $10 ages 4–12. On the National Register of Historic Places. Café and gift shop. The 887-foot-long "Mighty Mo" is a battleship that served both in World War II and the Persian Gulf War, housing as many as 2,400 men at one time. While the ship was anchored in Tokyo Bay in 1945, Japanese officials boarded and formally surrendered to the Allies.

Exploring the *Missouri* is exciting. It's full of nooks and crannies, steep stairways (not for the slippery-footed), solid-steel doors, and cultural artifacts—in fact, you can easily get lost, like we did. That made it even more fun. Basic admission includes access to one of several tours, and we recommend you take advantage of their offer. Learning the history of the ship and the times in which it served will greatly enrich the experience. Or pay a little extra upfront and get a deluxe tour, including access to areas otherwise off-limits. A lift can bring mobility-impaired individuals up to the main and upper decks.

An $18 million renovation of the ship took place in 2009, so everything's ship-shape.

USS *Arizona* Memorial (422-0561; nps.gov/usar), 1 Arizona Memorial Pl., Pearl Harbor. Visitors center open 7–5 daily; tours 8–3. Free; tickets are offered on first-come, first-served basis. National Historic Landmark. Museum and gift shop. Pick up your free ticket at the main booth near the USS *Bowfin*. It will be good only for the date and time designated. At the USS *Arizona* Memorial, a few minutes' walk from the *Bowfin*, explore the newly renovated visitors center, which features a small museum, bookstore, and optional audio tour of war arti-facts around the property. The museum tells the story of World War II and Pearl Harbor through personal accounts and relics, bringing you closer to the attack on Hawai'i.

The tour itself begins with a brief and powerful documentary on Pearl Harbor's attack and culminates at a memorial platform built above the sunken remnants of the USS *Arizona*, accessible only by boat. The *Arizona* was one of many bat-tleships bombed in Pearl Harbor by Japanese fighters during World War II, and it sank in several minutes with more than 1,100 men trapped inside. Their names are listed at the site itself, and you'll see the dark hulk of the ship beneath you. The memorial is actually a national park, operating under the National Park Service.

On most days, one or more survivors of the attack—civilians who lived here dur-ing the war as well as veterans—are at the visitors center sharing stories about their experiences.

USS *Bowfin* Submarine Museum & Park (423-1341; bowfin.org), 11 Arizona Memorial Dr., Pearl Harbor. Open daily 8–5; last tour is at 4:30. $10 adults, $4 ages 4–12 (children under 4 not permitted on board). National Historic Land-mark. Museum and gift shop. The 312-foot USS *Bowfin* is a real-life World War II submarine and one of only about 15 still in existence. It once housed nearly 100 volunteer men within its confines and it sank 44 enemy ships during the war. Entry fee to the submarine also includes a digital audio player, which guides you from room to room through the length of the sub. Be prepared for ducking, climbing, and cramped spaces, but it's totally worth it.

Preface or complete the experience with a visit to the adjacent 10,000-square-foot museum, which exhibits submarine-related artifacts such as a Poseidon C-3 missile (the only one on display anywhere). Tickets to the submarine also include entry to the museum, but you can also purchase less expensive tickets if you want to only visit the museum.

MUSEUMS & GALLERIES Hawai'i's Plantation Village (677-0110; hawaii plantationvillage.org), 94-695 Waipahu St., Waipahu. Open Mon.–Sat. for guid-ed tours on the hour, 10–2. $13 adults, $10 seniors, $5 ages 4–11. Selected build-ings are on the National Register of Historic Places. Gift shop. Several hundred thousand people from China, Japan, Portugal, Puerto Rico, Okinawa, Korea, the Philippines, and other nations arrived in Hawai'i between about 1850 and 1940 to work on its sugar plantations. They lived in "camps" near the fields and performed backbreaking work for low pay. Many people living in Hawai'i today descend from these immigrant laborers or were plantation laborers themselves.

This unusual outdoor museum tells their story. Both original and precisely re-created plantation camp buildings, such as the community bath, plantation store, and houses, as well as numerous artifacts, a film, and other memorabilia, unfold the workers' lives in detail.

Also moving are the stories of picture brides from Japan, Okinawa, and Korea, who arrived at the Honolulu docks to be married to laboring men they'd never met. If you've never seen the 1994 film *Picture Bride* by Hawai'i-born director Kayo Hatta, rent it before your visit for a good introduction to sugar plantation life.

The museum is located in the old sugar mill town of Waipahu, further authenticating your experience.

Pacific Aviation Museum (441-1000; pacificaviationmuseum.org), Hangar 37, Ford Island, 319 Lexington Blvd., Pearl Harbor. Open daily 9–5. $15 adults, $8 ages 4–12. Guided tours cost extra. Café and gift shop. The $90 million Pacific Aviation Museum is the nation's first aviation battlefield museum. The museum is situated in the middle of Pearl Harbor on the 433-acre Ford Island, a National Historic Landmark that still looks much like it did in World War II. The first phase opened in 2006, on the 65th anniversary of the Japanese attack on Pearl Harbor. The museum is a significant and complementary addition to the trilogy of fascinating sites already at Pearl Harbor and is earning accolades for its historical accuracy and striking presentations, such as aircraft backdrops painted by Hawai'i's opera technical director.

Three hangars will comprise the museum upon its final phases of completion. At the time of writing, only Hangar 37 was fully open. It features a film on the war, seven World War II aircraft, and other artifacts, plus flight simulators fun for kids. Hangars 79 and 54 will follow when funding can cover the enormous costs. They also plan to renovate a historic military diving tower near the entrance.

Pay a little extra to get a docent tour, which includes "secret" access into Hangar 54. It feels like slipping backstage at a theater performance. You'll see real bullet holes in the glass left over from the attack, and a series of jets and helicopters in the process of being restored for display. The docents themselves are often former veterans and pilots, making stories educational and real.

Tropic Lightning Museum (655-0438; 25idl.army.mil/tropic lightning museum/museum.htm), Schofield Barracks, Building 361, Wai'anae Ave., Wahiawā. Open Tue.–Sat. 10–4. Free. Learn more about the US Army's famed 25th Infantry Division, the first infantry activated upon the bombing of Honolulu. It sits on historic Schofield Barracks, featured in films such as *Pearl Harbor* and *From Here to Eternity*. This interesting little museum houses displays of uniforms, artillery guns, equipment, and military vehicles. They also can send you on a self-guided walking tour of the barracks, a great opportunity to see life behind the scenes as well as historical sites.

USS *Bowfin* **Submarine Museum & Park** (423-1341; bowfin.org), 11 Arizona Memorial Dr., Pearl Harbor. Open daily 7–5. $5 adults, $3 children (museum only). National Historic Landmark. Gift shop. The museum is really designed to go hand-in-hand with a visit to the adjacent 312-foot USS *Bowfin*, a real-life World War II submarine docked outside, but it stands well on its own, too. It offers 10,000 square feet of submarine-related artifacts, such as a Poseidon C-3 missile (the only one on display anywhere). If you're up for climbing through portals and down steep stairs, purchase a ticket to the *Bowfin* instead, which gives you access to both the sub and the museum.

✸ To Do

FOR FAMILIES ♫ **Dole Plantation** (621-8408; doleplantation.com), 64-1550 Kamehameha Hwy., Wahiawā. Even though the pineapple is neither a Hawai'i native nor extensively cultivated here anymore, our plantation history has made it a lasting icon of the Islands. Dole Plantation pays homage to its spiny friend through this tourist-filled commercial activity center, once just a humble fruit stand. Activities include a narrated train tour through fields of pineapple, one of the world's largest mazes, and a plantation garden. Open daily 9–5:30. Attraction prices vary and are nominal.

HIKING **'Aiea Loop Trail**, Keaīwa Heiau State Recreation Area, 'Aiea Heights Dr., 'Aiea Heights. A fairly easy uphill route that includes views, native trees, an old Hawaiian temple remain—definitely the highlight of the walk—and plane wreckage dating from 1943. The well-marked 4.5-mile loop path is mostly forested, shady, and level, although it can be windy and muddy at times. For the easiest trek, enter through the upper trailhead and exit through the lower, by the campground. Keaīwa Heiau is believed to have been a medicinal, or healing, temple site dating from perhaps 400 years ago. Do not disturb anything at the site.

To get there: From Waikīkī, take the H-1 Freeway to exit 19B, which puts you on the Moanalua Freeway (201/78). Take the Stadium/'Aiea exit to Moanalua Rd. From there, turn right onto 'Aiea Heights Dr. and follow it upward to the end.

TENNIS Real tennis heads will want to play at the **Central O'ahu Regional Park Tennis Complex & Archery Range** (677-8849), 94-801 Kamehameha Hwy., Waipahu. This amazing and relatively new complex features 18 field courts, a lit clubhouse court, and a lit show court. Bring your own equipment—courts are available on a first-come, first-served basis.

✸ Where to Eat

DINING OUT **Phuket Thai** (623-6228; phuketthaihawaii.com), Mililani Town Center, 95-1249 Meheula Prkwy., Mililani. Open daily for lunch and dinner. Inexpensive–moderate. Reservations recommended for dinner. If you've never been to Thailand, you might not know that this regional name is pronounced approximately *poo-KET*. That issue aside, this is a delicious, tasteful, contemporary choice in Central O'ahu, and a sister location of Phuket Thai near Waikīkī. It serves standard family-sized dishes of mee krob, crab legs, sweet-and-sour fish, shrimp rolls, tom yum gai, rice noodles, and paht Thai. Curries can be ordered mild on up. They also serve nice little desserts, such as Thai sticky rice with coconut milk and ice cream.

EATING OUT Molly's Smokehouse (621-4858), 23 S. Kamehameha Hwy., Wahiawā. We're hearing mixed reviews of Molly's these days, but give it a try if you're in the area.

🍴 **Poke Stop** (676-8100; elmerguzman.com), 94-050 Farrington Hwy., Waipahu. Famous for its local-style poke (POH-keh) dishes prepared by a well-known Island chef. They also serve delicious gourmet sandwiches and plate lunches. Also in Mililani (626-3400), 95-1840 Meheula Pkwy.

✳ **Entertainment**

MOVIE HOUSES Consolidated Theatres Mililani Stadium (627-0200), Town Center of Mililani, 95-1249 Meheʻula Pkwy., Mililani. Big releases.

✱ **Selective Shopping**

SHOPPING CENTERS Waikele Premium Outlets (676-5656; premiumoutlets.com), 94-790 Lumiaina St., Waikele. Way off the beaten path is a compound loaded with deep industry discounts. Shop more than 50 stores, include BCBG Max Azria, Saks Fifth Avenue Off 5th, Barneys New York, Adidas, Puma, Izod, and Coach. Parking is free.

Leeward Oʻahu 6

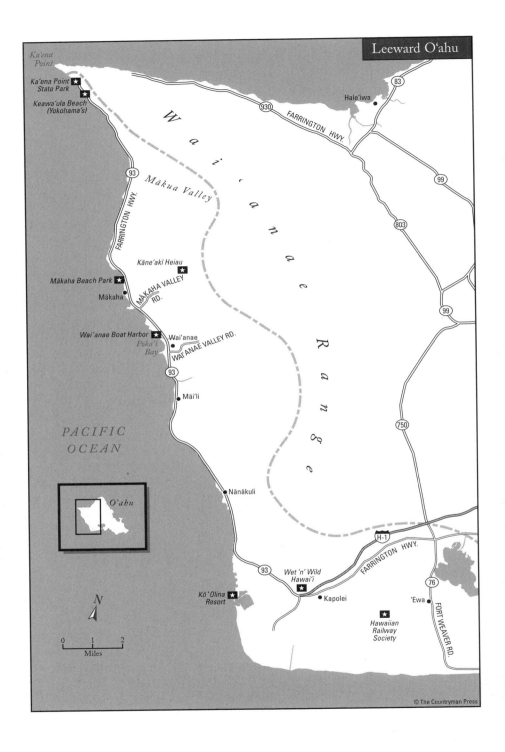

LEEWARD OʻAHU

Leeward Oʻahu—which runs down the southern and western flank of the Waiʻanae Range—is slowly gaining notice as one of the island's last havens from commercialism and crowds. We're including in our coverage of this region the neighborhoods of ʻEwa Beach and commuter Kapolei as well as the Leeward Coast (also called the Waiʻanae Coast), where you'll find the Native Hawaiian homesteading communities of Nānākuli and Waiʻanae. The region also includes Mākaha, popular with big-wave surfers and Mainland retirees in addition to local families, and the ever-expanding and high-commercial Kō ʻOlina Resort, a jewel of the coastline.

The Leeward Coast is generally hot and dry, with miles of pristine, virtually empty beaches and deep-blue water populated by spinner dolphins. It also has particularly high unemployment and poverty rates, as well as a reputation for some roughness. You'll find plenty of friendly folks "talking story" at the supermarket, hopping the bus to go work, hanging out at the beach with their families and friends, and generally enjoying life, but you may also see extensive homeless encampments along the beach parks. Needless to say, merrymaking Mainlanders tooling through in red convertibles are not always a welcome sight. Respect and discretion are valued in every community, but here they are not only polite, but also wise.

MEDICAL TREATMENT CENTERS Kapolei Health Care Center (697-3800), 91-525 Farrington Hwy., Suite 102, Kapolei. Mon. 7:30–8, Tue. and Thu. 7:30–5:30, Wed. and Fri. 7:30–6, Sat. 7:30–4.

Waiʻanae Coast Health Center (696-7081), 86-260 Farrington Hwy., Waiʻanae. Emergency room open 24/7. Clinic and walk-ins 8–8. Also offers traditional Hawaiian healing services.

✳ To See

ARCHAEOLOGICAL AND SACRED SITES Kāneʻākī Heiau (695-8174), Mauna Olu Estates Ala Hele St., Mākaha. The most visited archaeological site on the Leeward Coast, this heiau has been restored to closely resemble its original layout, including a drum house, house of spiritual power, an offering stand, an oracle tower, and an image of the god Kū. It's estimated to be at least 500 years old and was used for both agricultural and sacrificial purposes. Please take care not to disturb the site.

Kāneʻaki is on private land and open to the public on selected days and hours only. Call the above number before you make the trek. From Farrington Hwy. (93) in Mākaha, take Mākaha Valley Rd. Follow it until you see a right turn for the estates and heiau.

MUSEUMS & GALLERIES *&* **Hawaiian Railway Society** (681-5461; hawaiian railway.com), 91-1001 Renton Rd., ʻEwa Beach. Open Sun. Train departs at 1 and 3. $10 adults, $7 seniors and children 3 and older. $20 for parlor car. On the National Register of Historic Places. That's right, there used to be a railroad on Oʻahu—in fact, the railroad was key in the development of the sugar industry across the state. In addition to public carrier lines and military routes, 47 plantations had their own systems. Nearly 7 miles of Oʻahu tracks from ʻEwa to Nānākuli have been restored. The 90-minute trip is fully narrated and a nice complement to Hawaiʻi's Plantation Village, located in nearby Waipahu (see Central Oʻahu). Views from the trains are less interesting than the trains themselves.

As you approach the museum down Renton Road, you'll pass through a historic plantation village from the old sugar days.

✳ To Do

BICYCLE CRUISING Hale Nalu Surf & Bike (696-5897; halenalu.com), 85-876 Farrington Hwy., Waiʻanae. Rent a bike short term, or even pick up a used or new bike for sale.

BODYBOARDING, STAND-UP PADDLING, & SURFING Hale Nalu (696-5897; halenalu.com), 85-876 Farrington Hwy., Waiʻanae. *The* place on the Waiʻanae Coast for surfboards, bodyboards and more.

DOLPHIN-, SHARK-, & WHALE-WATCHING ✪ **Wild Side Specialty Tours** (306-7273; sailhawaii.com), Waiʻanae. If you want to get close to wild dolphins in the most sensitive, nontouristy, and educated manner possible, this is the right outfit. Conducted by a marine biologist, Wild Side takes a handful of people aboard their spacious, 42-foot catamaran for a four-hour sail along the coast; conditions and dolphin curiosity permitting, you might even swim in the vicinity of these beautiful mammals. They also offer snorkeling, stargazing journeys, and seasonal whale-watching. Trips leave from Waiʻanae Boat Harbor.

GOLF Hawaiʻi Prince Golf Club (956-1111; princeresortshawaii.com), 91-1200 Fort Weaver Rd., ʻEwa Beach. Designed by Arnold Palmer and Ed Seay and built in 1992, this 27-hole course occupies 270 acres, much of which is studded by lakes. The three nines offer a variety of other exciting challenges as well. Green fees start at $80 for guests of the Hawaiʻi Prince Hotel in Waikīkī and $160 for all other visitors, including cart fees.

Kō ʻOlina Golf Club (676-5300; koolinagolf.com), 92-1220 Aliʻinui Dr., Kapolei. This challenging, 18-hole championship course has hosted the Senior PGA and was cited by *Golf Digest* as one of the United States' "top 75 resort courses." It also features an excellent golf shop. Designed by Ted Robinson, the course measures 6,867 yards with a slope of 135 and par of 72. Food and beverages can be ordered from the 9th and 18th holes. Green fees are $145 for guests, $170 for visitors.

Mākaha Resort & Golf Club (695-9544; makaharesort.net), 84-626 Mākaha Valley Rd., Waiʻanae. A William Bell–designed facility that suits its beautiful valley setting, this 18-hole, par-72, 122-slope championship course offers 7,077 yards of play. It's been nationally rated as one of Hawaiʻi's top 10 courses, and by *Honolulu Magazine* readers as Oʻahu's best course. Green fees are $95, including cart.

Māhaka Valley Country Club (695-7111; makahavalleycc.com; 84-627 Mākaha Valley Rd., Waiʻanae. Also a William Bell–designed course and just next door to the above resort links, this is 18 holes of peaceful country bliss. Look out for the occasional peacock on the fairways. Green fees start at $65, including cart.

FOR FAMILIES ✒ **Wet ʼnʼ Wild Hawaiʻi** (945-3928; wetnwildhawaii.com), 400 Farrington Hwy., Kapolei. Now under Australian ownership, this high-octane, kid-friendly water park offers 29 acres and more than 25 slides and rides. The most notable include the Tornado, which catapults riders through a 130-foot tunnel; Da Flowrider, where you can simulate riding an enormous wave; and Hawaiian Waters, a 400,000-gallon wave pool. Closed Tue.–Wed. Open hours 10:30–3:30. Basic admission is $41.99 adults, $31.99 ages 3–11.

SALONS & SPAS **ʻIhilani Spa** (626-4446; ihilani.com), JW Marriott ʻIhilani Resort & Spa, 92-1001 ʻŌlani St., Kapolei. A multi-award-winning, 35,000-square-foot facility with men's and women's Roman-style pools, anti-stress facials, Hawaiian tī-leaf wraps, medicinal massages, thalasso baths, and more.

SCUBA DIVING & SNORKELING **Wild Side Specialty Tours** (306-7273; sailhawaii.com), 87-1286 Farrington Hwy., Waiʻanae. Head out with marine-trained specialists on an intimate excursion to observe dolphins in the deep trenches of Mākaha and snorkel offshore at Electric Beach.

TENNIS Play at the **JW Marriott ʻIhilani Resort and Spa** (679-3197; ihilani tennis.com), 92-1001 ʻŌlani St., Kapolei. Rent a racket from the resort and book time on one of their six quality courts. A court fee is charged, and reservations are required.

✳ Beaches

The Waiʻanae Coast is lined with wide, white sand beaches that look surprisingly Californian. Virtually empty of people and shrouded by scrub brush, they exude allure and mystery. Even if you're driving an old Toyota with local plates and a KAU INOA bumper sticker, however, admire these stretches of buff and blue from the road and pullouts only. Do drive to the end of Farrington Hwy. to admire the entire coastline (keeping an eye out for dolphin pods the farther along you go), then turn back and settle into one of the safe-swimming, well-populated beach spots we recommend.

 **Kō ʻOlina Lagoons** (679-0079), Aliʻinui St., Kapolei. These four perfect beach coves turn off the chaos of the world. Set against the mega-resort property of Kō ʻOlina Resort & Marina, the lagoons are probably the most visitor- and family-friendly beach zones on the entire island. Unfortunately, they're man-made; Kō ʻOlina blasted them out of the prehistoric-reef shoreline and layered them with tons of powdery, white sand. We'll put the environmental issues of that effort aside and comment that they are indeed gorgeous, pond-like, perfect for kids of all ages and swim abilities, and even have great snorkeling by the rock piles. Plus, you'll have easy access to restrooms and resort cafés. Try the first or second cove, near the Marriott ʻIhilani.

The downside? If you're not staying at Kō ʻOlina, scoring parking can be difficult. Each cove has a small, free lot that fills quickly. If you don't mind paying hotel prices for parking, visit the first lagoon and use the ʻIhilani's lot. When the adjacent Disney resort is complete, there may more public beach access along its shorefront.

Take the H-1 Freeway west toward Waiʻanae, exiting at Kō ʻOlina. At the security gate let them know you're headed to the lagoons, then follow the signage to the lagoon of your choice.

Mākaha Beach Park, 84-369 Farrington Hwy., Mākaha. Mākaha Beach is famous in the international surfing community as the site of several major com-

THE LEEWARD COAST

petitions. In winter riptides and powerful waves can make swimming hazardous, but in summer it's generally safe. On weekends, the beach attracts local residents and a smattering of visitors. The sand's bright white, the water's deep blue, and the atmosphere is relaxed and friendly. You might even see a dolphin pod far offshore here if you're lucky.

Take the H-1 Freeway west toward Wai'anae, following Farrington Hwy. (93) up the coast. Shortly after Mākaha Valley Rd., look for cars lining a sand beach just before a low-rise hotel.

Pōka'i Bay Beach Park, 85-037 Wai'anae Valley Rd., Wai'anae. Got young keiki? On the Leeward side, one of the best swimming spots for kids is at sheltered and shallow Pōka'ī Bay, a sandy beach cove with a beautiful mountain vista. The beach is popular with local families and exudes a great deal of rural community charm.

Take the H-1 Freeway west toward Wai'anae, following Farrington Hwy. (93) up the coast. Turn left on Wai'anae Valley Rd. to reach the parking area.

✳ Lodging

Aulani, a Disney Resort & Spa (714-520-7001; resorts.disney/go .com). The first phase of this new Kō 'Olina resort is set to open in late 2011. At the time of writing, all we can say is that it's absolutely enormous and already taking reservations as of late 2010. The contact information above may change once it's in full operation.

Hawaiian Princess at Mākaha (696-1234; 800-365-9190; hawaiian princessmakaha.com), 84-1021 Lahilahi St., Mākaha. Moderate. The Hawaiian Princess is by no means a resort—or even much of a hotel, for that matter. Think older medium-rise. Choose from a variety of privately owned and decorated condos that are rented for a minimum of four nights. The modest one- and two-bedroom units do have awesome views of a sandy beach and the deep-blue ocean, plus convenient appliances. You might even see dolphin pods offshore if you keep an eye out. The property also offers tennis courts, a pool, and a hot tub.

JW Marriott 'Ihilani Resort & Spa at Kō 'Olina (679-0079; 800-626-4446; ihilani.com), 92-1001 'Ōlani St., Kapolei. Expensive. Part of the 640-acre Kō 'Olina "empire," the

JW MARRIOTT 'IHILANI RESORT & SPA
Courtesy John DeMello

'Ihilani is a 17-story, 387-room hotel on the ocean and is surrounded by an excellent golf course, villas, and other high- and low-rise accommodations. Built out of coastal scrubland, it's the only luxurious place to stay on the entire southwestern or western half of the island (the Disney resort may change that) and offers pretty much everything you'd need for a restful vacation. Standard rooms average a whopping 640 square feet and have either mountain or ocean views, although most have at least some view of the water. The hotel also features a renowned 35,000-square-foot spa and activities such as catamaran cruising.

The hotel is grand, the lagoons are picture perfect, and the 35,000-square-foot spa offers rest deluxe. It's all pretty far from town and the North Shore, however, so make sure you're okay with either isolation or lots of freeway driving during your stay.

✴ Where to Eat

DINING OUT Azul (679-3166; ihilani.com), Kō 'Olina Resort & Marina, JW Marriott 'Ihilani Resort & Spa, 92-1001 Ali'inui Dr., Kapolei. Open for dinner Wed.–Sat. Expensive. Reservations recommended. Azul is a surprisingly excellent choice for dining, considering the lack of competition in the area and the fact that it's a hotel restaurant. The restaurant ambience is soothing and classic, with a touch of sophistication. The food goes one up from expectations upon entering.

Chef Blaine Wilkinson insists on the freshest and highest quality of ingredients and meats, all purchased from top local farms whenever possible. For example, the beef they serve is entirely organic and hormone-free; the fish only comes from day boats and short-trip longline boats. Recent dishes have included lobster avocado, braised wagyu short ribs, beef tenderloin, shrimp scampi, Pacific lobster tail, veal saltimbocca, and Maui gold pineapple tarte tartin.

🌸 ✎ **Hapa Grill** (674-8400; hapa grill.net), The Marketplace at Kapolei, 590 Farrington Hwy., Kapolei. Open daily for all three meals. Inexpensive–moderate. Reservations are accepted. A local favorite and deservedly so, Hapa Grill is Hawai'i in spirit and eats. It's located at an off-the-tourist-path strip mall and the interior's pretty much unpretentious coffee shop decor, so expect casual tone and Island families. The menu features popular dishes that owner Shannon's parents used to serve from their Sassy Kassy lunch wagon, which was parked in the area for decades. The Tangonans themselves can often be found in the kitchen whipping up favorites like teriyaki beef and mochiko chicken. Other well-made classic Hawai'i dishes include Portuguese bean soup, 'ahi tower, lumpia, and grilled mahimahi, plus a host of standard American fare.

❂ **Roy's Restaurant** (676-7697; roys restaurant.com), Kō 'Olina Resort & Marina, 92-1220 Ali'inui Dr., Kapolei. Open daily for lunch and dinner. Expensive. Reservations recommended. Roy's is hands-down one of Hawai'i's top restaurants, and hip founder Roy Yamaguchi is known internationally as a culinary pioneer.

Even if the Leeward Coast weren't lacking great restaurants, Roy's would still be an obvious choice for fine dining, especially for dinner. Off the beach, the restaurant offers a mellow golf-course view. Signature dishes include crisped seafood potstickers, yellowfin ʻahi poketini, roasted macadamia nut mahimahi, and hibachi-style grilled salmon. Roy's also features an outstanding wine list, so prepare your palate. The lower restaurant level is handicapped accessible.

EATING OUT Tacos & More (697-8800), 85-993 Farrington Hwy., Waiʻanae. Mexican food by Mexicans on the dry side of the island. A cantina-fiesta environment, friendly and tasty, with all the dishes you're used to, plus margaritas served with the local-style li hing touch.

✳ Entertainment

MOVIE HOUSES Consolidated Theatres Kapolei (674-8031; 890 Kamōkila Blvd., Kapolei). First-run movies.

INFORMATION

Sometimes we just need a few facts at our fingertips—even on vacation. Below you'll find information to keep you clued in and ready for just about anything.

BANKS If you have a bank debit card, you'll find hundreds of bank machines you can use throughout the state; most businesses will honor your debit card as well. Below we list the systems their bank machines accept. If you need to enter a bank, main branch information for each is listed below. All are located downtown. Call for regional branch locations.

American Savings Bank (523-6844; 800-272-2566; asbhawaii.com), 1001 Bishop St., downtown. Linked to Cirrus, Plus, and Star systems; selected machines may accept additional systems.

Bank of Hawai'i (538-4171; 888-643-3888; boh.com), 111 S. King St., downtown. Linked to American Express, Armed Forces Financial Network, Cirrus, Discover, Maestro, MasterCard, Novus, Plus, Quest, Star, and Visa.

Central Pacific Bank (544-0510; 800-342-8422; centralpacificbank.com), 220 S. King St., downtown. Linked to American Express, Cirrus, Discover, Maestro, MasterCard, Plus, Quest, Star, and Visa.

First Hawaiian Bank (525-6340; 888-844-4444; fhb.com), 999 Bishop St., downtown. Linked to American Express, Cirrus, Discover, MasterCard, Plus, Quest, Star, and Visa.

HAWAIIAN GINGER

BOOKS ABOUT HAWAI'I There are thousands of books published on topics relating to Hawai'i, from nostalgic neighborhood remembrances to Native Hawaiian sovereignty, indigenous flora, and legends. Another new book hits the market practically every day. Below we offer a variety of recommendations to get you started.

Archaeology

James, Van. *Ancient Sites of O'ahu*. Bishop Museum Press, 1992.

Kirch, Patrick Vinton. *Feathered Gods and Fishhooks: An Introduction to Hawaiian Archaeology and Prehistory*. University of Hawai'i Press, 1985.

Sterling, Elspeth P., and Catherine C. Summer. *Sites of O'ahu*. Bishop Museum Press, 1993.

Autobiographies, Biographies, & Personal Accounts

Allen, Helena G. *The Betrayal of Lili'uokalani: Last Queen of Hawai'i 1838–1917*. Mutual Publishing, 1982.

Bird, Isabella Lucy. *Six Months in Hawai'i*. Mutual Publishing, 1998.

Ellis, William. *Journal of William Ellis: A Narrative of an 1823 Tour Through Hawai'i or Owhyhee*. Mutual Publishing, 2004.

Lili'uokalani. *Hawai'i's Story by Hawai'i's Queen*. Mutual Publishing, 1991.

London, Jack. *Stories of Hawai'i*. Mutual Publishing, 1984.

Stevenson, Robert Louis. Edited by A. Grove Day. *Travels in Hawai'i*. University of Hawai'i Press, 1973.

Twain, Mark. Edited by A. Grove Day. *Mark Twain in Hawai'i: Roughing It in the Sandwich Islands*. Mutual Publishing, 1995.

Children's Books

Coste, Marion. *Kōlea: The Story of the Pacific Golden Plover*. University of Hawai'i Press, 1998.

Crowe, Ellie, and Don Robinson. *Kamehameha, the Boy Who Became a Warrior King*. Island Heritage Publishing, 2003.

Hayashi, Leslie Ann. *Fables from the Deep*. Mutual Publishing, 2002.

Knudsen, Eric, and Guy Buffet. *Spooky Stuffs*. Island Heritage Publishing, 2003.

Stender, Joshua Kaiponohea. *Nā Makana a Nā I'a/The Fish and Their Gifts*. Kamehameha Schools Press, 2004.

Tabrah, Ruth. Edited by Kirsten Whatley. *Momotaro: Peach Boy*. Island Heritage Publishing, 1995.

Cultural Identity

Dudley, Michael K., and Keoni K. Agard. *A Hawaiian Nation: Man, Gods, and Nature*. Nā Kāne o Ka Malo Press, 1993.

Halualani, Rona Tamiko. *In the Name of Hawaiians: Native Identities & Cultural Politics*. University of Minnesota Press, 2002.

Hartwell, Jay C. *Nā Mamo: Hawaiian People Today*. 'Ai Pōhaku Press, 1996.

Kanahele, George H. S. *Kū Kanaka, Stand Tall: A Search for Hawaiian Values.* University of Hawai'i Press, 1993.

McGregor, Davianna Pomaika'i. *Nā Kua'āina: Living Hawaiian Culture.* University of Hawai'i Press, 2007.

Historical/Cultural Explorations

Chambers, John H. *Hawai'i, On-the-Road Histories Series.* Interlink Publishing Group, 2006.

Ching, Carrie. *Things Hawai'i: A Celebration of the History, Landmarks, Flavors, Trends, and Traditions That Make Hawai'i Special.* Mutual Publishing, 2004.

Daws, Gavan. *Honolulu: The First Century.* Mutual Publishing, 2006.

————. *Shoal of Time: A History of the Hawaiian Islands.* University of Hawai'i Press, 1974.

Day, A. Grove. *Hawai'i and Its People.* Mutual Publishing, 2005.

Dorrance, William H. *O'ahu's Hidden History.* Mutual Publishing, 1999.

Kanahele, George H. S. *Waikīkī 100 BC to 1900 AD: An Untold Story.* University of Hawai'i Press, 1996.

Loomis, Albertine. *Grapes of Canaan.* Dodd, Mead, 1951.

Malo, David. *Hawaiian Antiquities: Mo'olelo Hawai'i.* Bishop Museum Press, 1997.

Nordyke, Eleanor C. *The Peopling of Hawai'i.* University of Hawai'i Press, 1989.

Prange, Gordon W. *At Dawn We Slept: The Untold Story of Pearl Harbor.* Penguin, 2001.

Folklore

Beckwith, Martha Warren. *Hawaiian Mythology.* University of Hawai'i Press, 1970.

Kalākaua, David. Edited by Glen Grant. *The Legends and Myths of Hawai'i.* Mutual Publishing, 1990.

Kawaharada, Dennis, ed. *Ancient O'ahu: Stories from Fornander and Thrum.* Kalamaku Press, 2001.

Westervelt, William D. *Legends of Old Honolulu.* Mutual Publishing, 2003.

Food & Cooking

Hee, Jean Watanabe. *Hawai'i's Best Local Dishes.* Mutual Publishing, 2002.

Laudan, Rachel. *The Food of Paradise: Exploring Hawai'i's Culinary Heritage.* University of Hawai'i Press, 1996.

Wong, Alan, and John Harrisson. *Alan Wong's New Wave Luau.* Ten Speed Press, 2003.

Hawaiian & "Pidgin" Language

Pukui, Mary Kawena. *'Ōlelo No'eau: Hawaiian Proverbs and Poetical Sayings.* Bishop Museum Press, 1997.

Pukui, Mary Kawena, and Samuel H. Elbert. *Hawaiian Dictionary.* University of Hawai'i Press, 1986.

————. *Hawaiian Grammar*. University of Hawai'i Press, 1979.

Pukui, Mary Kawena, Samuel H. Elbert, and Esther T. Mo'okini. *Place Names of Hawai'i*. University of Hawai'i Press, 1974.

Sakoda, Kent, and Jeff Siegel. *Pidgin Grammar: An Introduction to the Creole Language of Hawai'i*. Bess Press, 2003.

Simonson, Douglas, Pat Sasaki, and Ken Sakata. *Pidgin to da Max, 25th Anniversary Edition*. Bess Press, 2005.

Tonouchi, Lee A. *Da Kine Dictionary*. Bess Press, 2005.

Wight, Kahikahealani. *Learn Hawaiian at Home*. Bess Press, 2005. Includes CD.

Hawai'i Architecture, Design, & Fashion
Brown, DeSoto, and Linda Arthur. *The Art of the Aloha Shirt*. Island Heritage Publishing, 2003.

McGrath, Mary, Kaui Philpotts, and David Duncan Livingston. *Hawai'i, a Sense of Place*. Mutual Publishing, 2005.

Sandler, Robert. Edited by Frank Haines. *Architecture in Hawai'i*. Mutual Publishing, 2008.

Literature
Cataluna, Lee. *Folks You Meet in Longs and Other Stories*. Bamboo Ridge Press, 2005.

Chock, Eric, et al. *Growing up Local: Anthology of Poetry & Prose from Hawai'i*. University of Hawai'i Press, 1998.

Daws, Gavin, and Bennet Hymer, eds. *Honolulu Stories: Voices of the Town Through the Years: Two Centuries of Writing*. Mutual Publishing, 2008.

Harstad, James R., and Cheryl A. Harstad. *Island Fire: An Anthology of Literature from Hawai'i*. University of Hawai'i Press, 2002.

Yamanaka, Lois-Ann. *Saturday Night at the Pāhala Theatre*. Bamboo Ridge Press, 1993.

Nature & Natural History
Culliney, John L. *Islands in a Far Sea: The Fate of Nature in Hawai'i*. University of Hawai'i Press, 2005.

Hoover, John P. *Hawai'i's Fishes: A Guide for Snorkelers, Divers, and Aquarists*. Mutual Publishing, 2005.

Howarth, Francis G. *Hawaiian Insects and Their Kin*. University of Hawai'i Press, 1992.

Liittschwager, David, and Susan Middleton. *Archipelago: Portraits of Life in the World's Most Remote Island Sanctuary*. National Geographic, 2005.

Pratt, Douglas H. *Enjoying Birds and Other Wildlife in Hawai'i*. Mutual Publishing, 2002.

Wood, Paul. *Flowers and Plants of Hawai'i*. Island Heritage Publishing, 2006.

Recreation
Ambrose, Greg. *Surfer's Guide to Hawai'i*. Bess Press, 2006.

Ball, Stuart M. Jr. *The Hikers Guide to O'ahu*. University of Hawai'i Press, 2000.

Allen, Tricia. *Tattoo Traditions of Hawai'i*. Mutual Publishing, 2006.

Buck, Sir Peter. *Arts and Crafts of Hawai'i (The Complete Collection)*. Bishop Museum Press, 2003.

Elbert, Samuel H. *Na Mele o Hawai'i Nei*. University of Hawai'i Press, 1970.

Finney, Ben. *Sailing in the Wake of the Ancestors: Reviving Polynesian Voyaging*. Bishop Museum Press, 2003.

Hula: Hawaiian Proverbs and Inspirational Quotes Celebrating the Hula in Hawai'i. Mutual Publishing, 2003.

Ide, Laurie Shimizu. *Hawaiian Lei Making Step-by-Step Guide*. Mutual Publishing, 2006.

CHILD CARE There are several options for parents who need child care during a visit to O'ahu. If you're staying in a higher-end hotel, begin by inquiring whether they have babysitter options in-house—some do. Or contact the reputable agencies below for child care anywhere on the island.

Keiki Sitters (861-7294; keikisitters.com). In business since 2007, Keiki Sitters care for newborns up to age 14, have no minimum time requirement, and are open 24/7. Their sitters have clean background checks, are CPR/first-aid certified, and have a minimum of five years experience in child care. Most are students, recruited from local colleges. An initial membership fee is required.

Sitters Unlimited of Hawai'i (674-8440; sittershawaii.com). This organization has served O'ahu for more than 20 years and offers clients carefully chosen sitters with CPR/first-aid certification, experience, references, TB clearance, and criminal/child abuse background clearance. They can provide day, evening, or even overnight care. There is a four-hour minimum.

CLIMATE OVERVIEW & WEATHER REPORTS The main Hawaiian Islands sit across the Tropic of Cancer and are officially in the northern tropics. Clouds are a way of life here, and they usually come and go all day long. If the sky looks bad when you peek out the window, wait an hour and see if it doesn't change entirely—often it will.

The overall average day's weather on O'ahu at any time of year could be described as warm to hot, with day temperatures averaging between 74 and 88 degrees Fahrenheit. We have generally moderate humidity, partly sunny skies, mountain-area rain showers (with single or even double rainbows), and gentle to somewhat strong northeasterly trade winds. Not too shabby!

Summer temperatures islandwide usually hover in the mid- to high-80s during the day and dip into the high 70s at night; strong rain is infrequent and breezes increase, cooling the heat. During winter, day temperatures fluctuate between the 70s and low 80s, and at night it can drop into the mid- to low-60s range. Although brief rain showers are common across the island year-round, extremely heavy rains and thunderstorms do occasionally occur, especially in winter months. Hurricanes are rare. Once in a while "kona winds" blow from the south, bringing excessive mugginess often followed by a cleansing rain. These winds can also drag with them heavy "vog"—volcanic haze—from the Big Island's volcanoes. If the sky's a hazy orange during your visit, instead of the bright and clear air-quality days we normally have, you can thank Mother Nature for blowing her top.

O'ahu is made up of many microclimates that are most easily characterized by region. The Honolulu area typically has sunny skies, cooling trade winds, and modest rainfalls, while Windward O'ahu is known for blustery, overcast weather many days of the year and excessive rain. The North Shore is relatively dry, with a high percentage of sunny days, and Leeward O'ahu hits some of the island's hottest temperatures and often lacks the cooling trade winds.

Ocean temperatures along the coasts are consistently in the mid- to high 70s year round. Currents around the island are very complex, and the tide reaches two highs and two lows of different heights each day. Weather reports usually announce only the highest and lowest points and when to expect them; this information can help you decide when to go tide pooling, beachcombing, and so forth.

Significant tsunamis rarely occur in Hawai'i, but sirens are positioned across the state for emergency notification.

National Weather Service Forecast for Hawai'i (973-4380; prh.noaa.gov/hnl). The phone recording and Web site each provide a range of information on watches, advisories, warnings, O'ahu weather forecasts, O'ahu surf forecasts, O'ahu coastal wind observations, buoy reports, current weather conditions in selected locations, tides, sunrise, sunset, coastal water forecast, a general overview of Hawai'i weather, and more.

Surf News Network (596-7873; surfnewsnetwork.com). Check out surf conditions at specific spots, like Chun's Reef, via Web cam. Also get access to information on upcoming weather, swells, tides, and buoys.

EMERGENCY SERVICES As on the Mainland, dialing 911 will mobilize any emergency assistance unit, including the police, fire department, or ambulance. It also serves as a non-emergency dispatch.

For more complicated situations ranging from criminal victimization to a death in the family, contact the **Visitor Aloha Society of Hawai'i** (926-8274; visitoralohasocietyofhawaii.org), Waikīkī Shopping Plaza, 2250 Kalākaua Ave., Suite 403-3. They can help you figure out where to turn (after emergency care has been rendered) and help you through the process.

GROCERIES, SUNDRIES, & PRESCRIPTIONS When you need fixin's to cook dinner at your vacation rental or that box of midnight cookies, where do you turn? See below for area supermarkets, as well as sundry stores with pharmacies. Most open between 6 and 8 AM, but several operate 24 hours a day.

In addition to these listings, Waikīkī has several 24-hour 7-Eleven stores and about a trillion late-night ABC Stores, both of which offer snacks, aspirin, trinkets, and so forth.

Waikīkī

Food Pantry (923-9831), 2370 Kūhiō Ave. Daily 6 AM–1 AM.

Food Pantry (947-3763), 438 Hobron Ln. Daily 6 AM–11:30 PM.

Kūhiō Pharmacy (923-4466), 23300 Kūhiō Ave. Prescriptions Mon.–Sat. 9 AM–5 PM.

Greater Honolulu

Foodland (949-5044), Ala Moana Center, 1450 Ala Moana Blvd., Ala Moana. Mon.–Sat. 5 AM–10 PM, Sun. 6–8.

Longs Drugs (941-4433), Ala Moana Center, 1450 Ala Moana Blvd., Ala Moana. Mon.–Fri. 8 AM–10 PM, Sat. 8–9, Sun. 8–8.

Longs Drugs (536-7302), 1330 Pali Hwy., downtown. Open 24/7.

Safeway (733-2600), 870 Kapahulu Ave. Open 24/7.

Whole Foods (738-0820), Kāhala Mall, 4211 Wai'alae Ave., Kāhala. Daily 7 AM–10 PM.

Windward O'ahu

Down to Earth (262-3838), 201 Hamakua Dr., Kailua. Daily 8–7.

Foodland (261-3211), 108 Hekili Street, Kailua. Open 24/7.

Longs Drugs (261-8537), 609 Kailua Rd., Kailua. Daily 7 AM–10 PM.

Tamura's (232-2332), 54-316 Hau'ula Kai Shopping Center, Kamehameha Hwy., Hau'ula. Daily 8–9.

Whole Foods is scheduled to open in Kailua by late 2011 or early 2012 on Kailua Rd.

The North Shore

Foodland (638-8081), 59-720 Kamehameha Hwy., Pūpūkea. Daily 6 AM–11 PM.

Mālama Market (637-4520), 66-190 Kamehameha Hwy., Hale'iwa. Daily 7 AM–9 PM.

Central O'ahu

Longs Drugs (623-6466), Mililani Marketplace, 94-780A Mehe'ula Pkwy., Mililani. Mon.–Fri. 8 AM–9 PM, Sat.–Sun. 8–7.

Times Supermarket (564-7166), Mililani Marketplace, 95-1249 Mehe'ula Pkwy., Mililani. Daily 5 AM–midnight.

Leeward O'ahu

Longs Drugs (674-0069), Kapolei Shopping Center, 91-590 Farrington Hwy., Kapolei. Daily 7 AM–midnight.

Safeway (674-0070), Kapolei Shopping Center, 91-590 Farrington Hwy., Kapolei. Open 24/7.

Tamura Superette (696-3321), 86-032 Farrington Hwy., Wai'anae. Daily 7 AM–8 PM.

HANDICAPPED SERVICES A great resource for disabled services information is the Hawai'i State Department of Health's **Disability and Communication Access Board** (586-8121; hawaii.gov/health/dcab/travel), 919 Ala Moana Blvd., Room 101, Kaka'ako. Be sure to check it out in advance for a comprehensive PDF file you can print out, or at least give them a call when you arrive.

All major car rental companies these days can provide vehicles equipped for disabled drivers if you request one in advance. Remember to bring your parking placard with you and identification to prove it's yours. For more information on getting around town, please see the "Transportation" chapter.

HOLIDAYS Hawai'i observes American national holidays, as well as several unique Hawai'i holidays. While most banks remain open on state holidays, expect to find selected businesses, government agencies, and schools closed on either the holiday itself or the closest working day to it.

January 1	New Year's Day
Third Monday in January	Martin Luther King Jr. Day
Third Monday in February	Presidents' Day
March 26	Prince Kūhiō Day
Late March/April	Good Friday–Easter
Last Monday in May	Memorial Day
June 11	Kamehameha Day
July 4	Independence Day
Third Friday in August	Statehood Day (Admissions Day)
First Monday in September	Labor Day
Second Monday in October	Discoverers' Day
November 11	Veterans' Day
Fourth Thursday in November	Thanksgiving Day
December 25	Christmas Day

HOSPITALS & OTHER MEDICAL TREATMENT O'ahu has numerous 24-hour hospitals and limited-hours medical care centers. For emergencies, head for the nearest hospital or call 911 for an ambulance.

Kaiser Permanente (432-0000) operates several Kaiser-member-only, non-urgent day clinics on O'ahu. Call the 24-hour switchboard and let them know what area you're staying in so they can direct you to the nearest clinic. You can also call the **Kaiser 24-Hour Advice Nurse** (432-7700).

LANGUAGE GLOSSARY What, no can understand when Hawai'i folks talk story? No worry, brah. The list below is a mix of commonly used Hawaiian words and some popular pidgin words. What we call "pidgin" in Hawai'i is in fact a creole dialect with old origins in trading and plantation life. Some people speak it heavily, some speak it lightly, and some don't speak it at all. Most long-timers in Hawai'i do have a regional inflection and pepper their speech with regional vocabulary, even if they don't actually speak pidgin. Your best bet is to listen and enjoy, not try.

This basic pronunciation guide approximates the way words are most frequently pronounced by residents and their general meanings in everyday conversation.

ʻāina (EYE-nah)	land
aliʻi (ah-LEE-ee)	traditional ruling class, or "important person"
aloha (ah-LOH-hah)	hello, good-bye, love, fondness
da kine (dah-KYNE)	used in context typically to refer to a person or thing
grind/grinds	"to chow down"/"chow"
hālau (hah-LAOO)	hula school/troupe, long house for canoes
hale (HAH-leh)	house
hana hou (HAH-nah-HOH)	do it again
hānai (hah-NYE)	adopted
haole (HOW-leh)	Causasian
hapa (HAH-pah)	half or part, as in *hapa-haole*, or "part Caucasian"
hāpai (hah-PYE)	pregnant
howzit (HOW-zit)	how's it going (casual)
hui (HOO-ee)	club, association, group
kamaʻāina (kah-mah-EYE-nah)	official state resident or longtimer
kāne (KAH-neh)	man
kapu (KAH-poo)	taboo or off-limits
keiki (KAY-kee)	child or children
kōkua (koh-KOO-ah)	help
kumu (KOO-moo)	teacher, especially of Hawaiian cultural or spiritual aspects
kupuna (koo-POO-nah)	elder or elders
lānai (lah-NYE)	porch or veranda
lei (LAY)	flower garland
mahalo (mah-HAH-loh)	thank you
makai (mah-KYE)	toward the sea or on the sea side of
malihini (mah-lee-HEE-nee)	"newcomer," usually from the Mainland
mauka (MAOO-kah)	toward the mountains or on the mountain side of
muʻumuʻu (moo-oo-MOO-oo)	a loose gown, traditionally floor length
ʻohana (oh-HAH-nah)	family
pau (PAOO)	finished
pidgin (PIH-jin)	common term for Hawaiʻi's vernacular language/dialect
pono (POH-noh)	justness, righteousness, making things "right"
shaka (SHAH-kah)	hand gesture for "things are great," "thanks," or "hey there"
slippers	flip-flops or go-aheads
talk story	"shooting the breeze," or casual sharing of personal stories
tūtū (TOO-too)	grandmother
wahine (wah-HEE-neh)	woman (sometimes pronounced va-HEE-neh)

LIBRARIES Whether you need obscure reference materials on Hawaiian nose-flute designs or a reading break from sun and surf, you'll find several excellent libraries around Honolulu.

Greater Honolulu

Hawai'i State Library (586-3500; librarieshawaii.org), 553 S. King St., downtown. Built in 1913 from funds provided by Carnegie, the Hawai'i State Library is the main branch of the only statewide library system in the United States. Visitors may purchase temporary library cards, borrow Hawaiian music CDs, browse hundreds of volumes on Hawai'i and other Pacific islands, or surf the Internet from one of its public computers (reserve in advance). The library is on the National Register of Historic Places.

Bishop Museum Library and Archives (848-4148; bishopmuseum.org), Bishop Museum, 1525 Bernice St., Kalihi. An excellent research resource, with vast amounts of books, periodicals, newspapers, music, art, and more relating to Hawai'i and the Pacific. Limited hours.

Hawaiian Historical Society (537-6271; hawaiianhistory.org), 560 Kawaiaha'o St., downtown. The organization holds a large historical collection of materials on the grounds of the Mission Houses Museum. Get access to 25,000 books, newspapers, photos and other items, with an especially strong collection of material on early voyages and travels. Both English- and Hawaiian-language resources are available.

Hawaiian Mission Children's Society Library (531-0481; missionhouses.org), Mission Houses Museum, 553 S. King St., downtown. This is a collection belonging to the Mission Houses Museum, a treasure trove of more than 12,000 books and other materials relating to Hawaiian and mission history.

Hawai'i State Archives (586-0329; hawaii.gov/dag/archives), 'Iolani Palace Grounds, Kekauluohi Bldg., 364 S. King St., downtown. A massive collection of state government historic records, genealogical indexes, photographs, and other fascinating volumes all available for reference viewing.

Robert Allerton Art Research Library (532-8754; honoluluacademy.org), Honolulu Academy of Arts, 900 S. Beretania St., Makiki. The academy houses a noncirculating collection of art-related materials that you can browse. Hours are limited.

University of Hawai'i Hamilton Library (956-7204; uhm.hawaii.edu), University of Hawai'i at Mānoa, 2550 McCarthy Mall, Mānoa. This is the largest collection of reading materials in the state, with approximately 3.5 million volumes, periodicals, and documents on every subject.

MAGAZINES, NEWSPAPERS, RADIO, TELEVISION, & WEB Below are the names and contact information for major local magazines and newspapers to pick up during your visit and perhaps subscribe to when you're back home. Most of the newspapers are available at newsstands; the magazines are on shelves at local bookstores and selected sundry shops, or order direct. Also, we've included a list of radio stations and television channels so you're hooked into the action while in town.

MAGAZINES *Hana Hou!* (733-3333; hanahou.com). This is Hawaiian Airlines' glossy inflight magazine, and it's filled with well-written articles on life in Hawai'i and other information.

Hawai'i Magazine (537-9500; hawaiimagazine.com). A quality, locally produced magazine geared toward visitors, and full of Hawai'i news, insider travel scoops, and other stories.

Hawai'i Business (534-7520; hawaiiabusiness.com). Honolulu's a small city—reading *Hawai'i Business* is a great way to learn who's who and how things work.

Honolulu Magazine (534-7520; honolulumagazine.com). The definitive "sophisticated" Hawai'i-living magazine, featuring articles on everything from legendary island musicians to urban development issues.

NEWSPAPERS *Pacific Business News* (955-8100; bizjournals.com/pacific). This little weekly paper is in every executive office waiting room and keeps readers up to date on local business activity.

Honolulu Star-Advertiser (529-4747; staradvertiser.com). Now Hawai'i's only daily, delivered hot off the presses every morning.

Honolulu Weekly (528-1475; honoluluweekly.com). Our locally written and owned, heavily read, free alternative weekly pumps out relevant, liberal, and timely pieces on everything from fashion to politics.

MidWeek (235-5881; midweek.com). Widely read, this free paper includes everything but the kitchen sink. Its syndicated and locally written articles range from moderately liberal to conservative.

RADIO STATIONS Selected popular or unique radio stations, both FM and AM.

KHPR 88.1 FM	Hawai'i Public Radio's classical music and NPR news, no commercials.
KIPO 89.3 FM	Hawai'i Public Radio's world music, jazz, NPR, BBC, no commercials.
KTUH 90.3 FM	University of Hawai'i's Hawaiian, jazz, and alternative programming.
KSSK 92.3 FM	Adult contemporary-music mix and local talk.
KCCN 100.3 FM	Island music and reggae.
KINE 105.1 FM	Classic and contemporary Hawaiian music.
KPOI 105.9 FM	Classic rock.
KKOL 107.9 FM	Oldies.
KKNE 940 AM	Classic Hawaiian music and commentary, few commercials.
KNDI 1270 AM	Samoan, Tongan, Laotian, and other multi-ethnic programming.
KKEA 1420 AM	Local and national sports and talk radio.

TELEVISION In addition to nationally broadcast stations from ABC to TCM to MTV, O'ahu has several interesting local-programming stations, listed below. Channel numbers can differ according to subscriber service.

KBFD	**4**	Independent Korean-language programming.
KIKU	**9**	Japanese-language and other culturally diverse programming.
KHET	**10**	Hawai'i public television.
OC16	**16**	Youth-oriented, local-style programming focusing on Hawai'i topics.
FOCUS	**49**	Hawai'i community programming and coverage of state legislature.
OAHU	**52**	Hawai'i cultural topics from the arts to local sports.
NATV	**53**	Pacific-culture programming, plus Deutsche Welle.
VIEWS	**54**	Local issues, city council board meetings.
TEC	**55**	Educational programming, including local university courses.
TEACH	**56**	Department of Education classes and other educational programs.

WEB Most of the above media are also online. Below are our top-pick Web-only sites that offer helpful resources for visitors and special coverage of Hawai'i for residents and visitors both.

GoHawaii.com. Produced by the Hawai'i Visitors and Convention Bureau, the site has a good collection of calendar items as well as other visitor-oriented Hawai'i information.

PacificNetwork.tv. Founded by well-known local filmmaker Edgy Lee, Pacific Network is an ongoing series of reports and broadcasts billed as "the Native Hawaiian portal to the world." It's high quality and educational.

MARRIAGE IN HAWAI'I More than 750,000 people come to Hawai'i each year to wed or honeymoon—so trust us that elements are in place to facilitate yours. You would be wise to hire a local wedding consultant, who can guide you through the entire process and set everything up. Many of Hawai'i's hotels are fully capable of planning and executing your wedding as well. And yes, they can coordinate a beach ceremony.

Assuming you're planning the event far in advance, you might enjoy the book *Hawai'i Weddings Made Simple* by Keri Shepard (Mutual Publishing, 2003), which covers all the basics and includes local contacts for every area of need. The magazine *Hawai'i Bride & Groom* (428-1596; hawaiibride.com) comes out twice each year and is filled with local wedding planning facts.

Check out the **O'ahu Wedding Association** (oahuweddingassociation.com), an association of numerous Hawai'i wedding industry businesses with a beautiful Web site full of information and discriminating contacts. In Honolulu visit the **The Wedding Café** (591-1005), Ward Warehouse, 1050 Ala Moana Blvd., Kaka'ako. Not only does it carry cute and hip wedding-related items, but staff can also help you plan the whole kit and caboodle—right there in the store.

Whether you just decided to get hitched before heading home or you've been planning a Hawai'i dream wedding since birth, you'll need to get a local marriage license. You must be at least 18 years old, unless you have written proof of approval from guardianship. Proof of age is required—if you're 18, you need your birth certificate. Ages 19 and over can offer state ID or valid driver's licenses. If you were married previously, you'll need paperwork to prove you're no longer married. Blood tests are not required, and we have no waiting period.

Pick up a marriage license packet at the **State of Hawai'i Department of Health, Marriage License Department** (586-4545; hawaii/gov/doh), 1250 Punchbowl St., Room 101, downtown. You can also download the forms from the above Web site and bring them in. Both of you—and we mean both of you, no proxies permitted—must be present. Once the license is issued (have $60 in cash to pay for it), you're free to marry anywhere in Hawai'i for up to 30 days.

The Department of Health can also provide you with information on marriage officiates, including the state justice of the peace. Depending upon the type of wedding you plan to have, a beach wedding may require a permit from the Department of Land and Natural Resources.

RELIGIOUS SERVICES Worshipping and prayer are part of many people's lives in Hawai'i, and its multicultural climate encourages a very healthy and happy mix of viewpoints. O'ahu has hundreds of churches and other houses of worship and meditation ranging from Catholic to Russian Orthodox to Buddhist to Muslim, with selected services offered in English, Hawaiian, Tongan, Mandarin, Tagalog, and more. Ask your hotel or lodging hosts for assistance in locating the closest facility of your choice.

In Waikīkī there are two particularly interesting services open to the public. **St. Augustine By-the-Sea** (923-7024; staugustinebythesea.com), 130 'Ōhua Ave., holds Catholic Mass Mon.–Fri. 7 AM and 5 PM, Saturday 7 AM, and liturgy both Sat. and Sun. The parish has been in existence since 1854, and the striking church, built in 1961, is a landmark.

The **Waikīkī Beach Chaplaincy** (923-3137; waikikibeachchaplaincy.org) hosts a nondenominational Christian service that you can definitely write home about. Called "Church on the Beach," it's exactly that. Different churches come out to minister, sing, and even dance. Beach mats are provided for seating, and the atmosphere is completely casual—you can even show up in your bathing suit! It takes place every Sunday morning at 10:30 in front of the Hilton Hawaiian Village, 2005 Kalia Rd.

For a historic-church experience in the Greater Honolulu area, consider the United Church of Christ **Kawaiaha'o Church** (469-3000; kawaiahao.org), 957 Punchbowl Street, downtown; the United Church of Christ **Central Union Church** (941-0957; centralunionchurch.org), 1660 S. Beretania St., Makiki; the Episcopal **St. Andrew's Cathedral** (524-2822; saintandrewscathedral.net), 229 Queen Emma Square, downtown; or the Catholic **Cathedral of Our Lady of Peace** (536-7076; cathedralofourladyofpeace.com), 1184 Bishop St., downtown. At Kawaiaha'o, one of Hawai'i's most significant and revered historic sites, Ali'i Sunday (check the church's Web site for dates) is a service you won't forget.

ROAD SERVICE If you've experienced a car accident resulting in roadway or vehicular damage, you'll need to report it to the police by calling 911 at the time of the accident, as well as follow up with paperwork afterward. If the accident's relatively minor, move your car out of the way (if it's blocking traffic) and wait for the fuzz.

If your rental car isn't moving, the tire's flat, or you're locked out, first check your rental agreement for an emergency service number. If there isn't one, or you're not driving a rental, members of the **American Automobile Association** (800-222-4357) can still get help 24/7. If you're not an AAA member, try calling **A Roadrunner Towing Service** (957-0236). In business for nearly 20 years, these guys will get you up and running, or drag you somewhere where you can get help. Doesn't matter where you are on the island, what time it is, or what happened. They accept MasterCard and Visa, but it might be cheaper if you pay cash.

TIME ZONES & PHONES Although once you've arrived you may not care what time it is anywhere else in the world, note that you're now in Hawai'i-Aleutian Standard Time—not far enough to cross the International Dateline, but far enough to be irritating when trying to make a business call to New York or check in with Grandma in Cleveland. And since Hawai'i doesn't observe Daylight Saving Time (DST), the time difference between Hawai'i and the Mainland depends on the season.

In November, when clocks are set back on the Mainland, we become two hours behind Pacific Time, three behind Mountain Time, four behind Central Time, and five behind Eastern Time. Once you move your clocks forward for DST in March, however, we remain behind these zones by yet an extra hour. Since most of Arizona doesn't observe DST, either, we're three hours behind them year-round. You can set your watch locally by calling 643-8463 for the exact time.

Hawai'i has only one area code: 808. However, things get tricky when calling another Hawaiian island. Even though we all share the same area code, you will need to dial "1-808" before your number to get through to them. In this book we've left out area codes whenever the numbers are on O'ahu and included them if they're off-island or toll-free. Of course, if you're calling O'ahu from the Mainland, you will still need to add "1-808" to reach us.

For directory assistance, call 411 (there may be a charge for service).

VOLUNTEERING One of the best ways to experience another city or culture from the inside and to feel good about the world is through a bit of volunteering—and "volunteer vacations" have become very popular.

If you'd like to investigate opportunities in Hawai'i that don't require you to pony up dollars for the experience, check out **Volunteer Hawai'i** (volunteerhawaii .org). The organization is linked with the United Way, and through their Web site you can do a search on long- and short-term positions—and even search by the dates you'll be in town. If you find the perfect opportunity, but it's listed as a long-term position, submit a request anyway and let them know your schedule; they often can find a way to use your skills for even just a day or two.

Mālama Hawai'i (malamahawaii.org) is an organization of more than 70 community and environmental groups committed to the care of Hawai'i. Check out their Web site for exciting short- and long-term opportunities.

Another place to look is in the calendar section of papers such as the *Honolulu Weekly*, *MidWeek*, or the *Honolulu Star-Advertiser*, which often post onetime community environmental cleanups and other projects.

SUNRISE IN HONOLULU

INDEX